To Jim & Nancy
Clark with
warm regards!

Shannon
Applegate

LIVING
AMONG
HEADSTONES

Life in a Country Cemetery

Shannon Applegate

THUNDER'S MOUTH PRESS
NEW YORK

Living Among Headstones
Life in a Country Cemetery

Published by
Thunder's Mouth Press
An Imprint of Avalon Publishing Group Inc.
245 West 17th St., 11th Floor
New York, NY 10011

AVALON
publishing group incorporated

Photo on page 151 by Colleen AF Venable. For other photo and art credits, see
acknowledgments section.

Some of the names and specific locations in this book have been changed to protect
the privacy of the individuals involved.

Library of Congress Cataloging-in-Publication Data is available.

ISBN 1-56025-677-X

9 8 7 6 5 4 3 2 1

Book design by Jamie McNeely
Printed in the United States of America
Distributed by Publishers Group West

For a little Grace

Contents

APPLEGATE PIONEER

CEMETERY MAP

Burying My Friends

Make much of your own place.

—Ralph Waldo Emerson, 1836

When I told my father I would take responsibility for the cemetery I did not reckon on having to bury my friends. There is a hollow place in the pit of my stomach. I feel vaguely disoriented and the pull of something, an emotional undertow. I know from past experience these feelings are connected to the loss of a friend.

But there are other feelings, new feelings that add to my discomfort, such as the sense of pretending to be something or someone who I am not. I am dismayed by my ineptitude.

When I agreed to take this all on a few weeks ago I had no idea what I was in for. Ever since, Dad has been bringing more cemetery records, looking relieved as though I have taken quite

KREM'S MARKET
GEORGE & MILDRED KREMKAU
GROCERIES — MEATS — TOYS — GIFTS

Yoncalla, Ore.,_____195__

To _Earl McDaniels_

Address_____

Reg. No.	Clerk	Account Forwarded		
1	2 grave sites			
2				
3	between lot 33932			
4	Blk. 6			
5				
6				
7				
8				
9				
10				
11				
12				
13				
14			$100.00	
15				

Your account stated to date. If error is found return at once
SHEPARD SALES BOOK CO., PORTLAND, OREGON

a bit off his mind. My back room is filling up with shoe-boxes full of scraps of paper—notes written on corners of envelopes, pocket pads, and café napkins in the indecipherable masculine scrawls of various caretakers since the 1950s. Then there are the earlier records: hundred-year-old dog-eared ledgers, and water-stained notebooks from the 1930s and 1940s revealing Aunt Hazel's and her mother, Lucy Samler's, dainty writing describing plot sales, money paid out for maintenance, etc. Yellowing obituary clippings are tucked between the pages. On these are terse notes in inky finality: "Buried here." There are also rolled up plat maps, legal descriptions of the cemetery, and survey notes. The more recent records are in three-ring binders with accompanying recipe boxes filled with alphabetized note cards showing cemetery blocks and individual plots.

As time permits, I have picked my way through the paper wilderness that seems to be my lot in life. Indeed, "lot" and "plot" are the operative words, lately. If this was all there were to my new job as cemetery sexton, things would be fine. I've actually enjoyed lingering over letters that the cemetery has received in envelopes sometimes as simply addressed as: Pioneer Graveyard, Yoncalla, Oregon.

Some of these letters pose practical questions: "To whom it may concern: None of us lives in Oregon anymore and we would like to see if you could sell the unused western half of our family plot (Block X, Lot X) and send us the money." Others pertain to genealogy and family history: "We are looking for the grave of our great-great-grandfather so-and-so who supposedly settled in the Yoncalla area after the Spanish-American War and went into the fruit growing business before his second wife left him."

Until today, in terms of cemetery business, the leisurely putting in order of this paper parade is all I've accomplished—if "business" is the right word for this family enterprise that started over a century ago.

Of course, I've made the most of telling my friends about my new endeavor. My "new job."

"A sextant?"

"No. Those are used on ships to determine longitude and latitude. A sexton. It's sort of Old English. A country sexton. I run a cemetery. Only it's not in a churchyard."

It's a real conversation piece, a place to begin a good story. But today, it is much more ponderous than that.

However, sprinkled lightly, as to be barely discernable, I will give myself a little credit: At least I have risen to this particular occasion, albeit slightly listing, on account of my broken foot. Here I am leaning on my crutches, at the gravesite Lee and Dana Whipple chose not too many years ago. I am waving good-bye to Dana. She is headed back to Whipple Tree Lane with a relative who has come to help her prepare home and, I dare say, heart, for her husband Lee Whipple's memorial gathering: in today's parlance, "A Tribute of Life."

Watching her retreat as she makes her way to the car, I notice her osteoporosis seems more pronounced than it was a few months ago but for all that she still has a get-on-with-it-ness in her steps, especially as compared to her much heavier and younger companion.

The cemetery caretaker before last—who sometimes cared less—sold Lee and Dana these sites at one hundred dollars each. Before the most recent caretaker moved away, he advised me to stick to sales in this relatively empty southeast corner of the cemetery where Lee and Dana have their plots.

"That way," he said in his Louisiana drawl, "you won't get yourself into trouble."

It is the trouble I have come to dread. The trouble I've even dreamed: I am marking a grave in the wrong place. They are digging where someone already is. I awaken imagining I am hearing the thud of backhoe blade against coffin.

The Whipple grave is on a gentle downhill slope that characterizes this portion of the cemetery, which, on a good day, receives the gift of sun. Just beyond the fence, perhaps one hundred yards south from here, broad open fields are cattle-dotted and brushed butter yellow with ash trees that are always first to announce autumn in this country.

It was typical of Lee Whipple to have picked a "resting place"—the way he put it—with contrasting attributes: open space and shelter, sunlight and shadow. It was his reason in the first place for being drawn to this little country graveyard with its immense old trees. He told me this back when I could still sit down with him and Dana under their hospitable roof, sipping tea, talking philosophy, and now and then pouring my heart out.

Before that came the remarkable experience of having this couple of nearly fifty years together in the writing class I taught where they explored their lives on paper. "Come and see us," they said after four years of trying to agree on what happened when. And I did.

I knew so much about all their "whys and wherefores," Dana said later, that they invited me to say a few words at their golden wedding anniversary.

Lee, a retired Church of the Brethren minister, and civil rights leader, was a rosy, dome-browed gnome of a man, who knew about shadows. During the 1960s, Lee, Dana, and their children participated in an experiment in ecumenical living at the York Cooperative in Chicago. The Church of the Brethren conferred on Lee the special title of Minister of Peace when he began working with Martin Luther King and Andrew Young, going into towns where peace marches were planned and attempting to smooth the way with officials in advance.

Lee had seen faces contorted with hate in the Southern towns

he visited. He met people who swore the streets would run with blood if marchers came. Later, alongside the black men who were his friends, quaking in his shoes and sweating profusely as one of the few whites marching, Lee saw the dark side: mild-looking churchgoing mothers and suit-wearing town fathers spitting, cursing, and hurtling brickbats at him.

But light, Lee insisted, always accompanied him, following him to the last days and even after, it seems. When I went to see Dana just after Lee slipped away, I stood at their kitchen window, taking in rows of grapes, gardens, fruit and nut trees flagged scarlet and gold with the season. Beyond was a landscape tiered with rain where the mountain stood—Mount Yoncalla—my mountain. Only it was Lee's, too. He saw its opposite side in the lovely valley where he made his home for some twenty years just four miles or so from the cemetery.

Truly, I've never seen the like: two rainbows. I stood watching them arching high above the summit—one glowing over the other, colors luminous and splendid. Then light flooded over Lee's valley and through the window.

I realized this morning, driving into the cemetery, as mist and sun sifted through high solemn columns of cedar, fir, and madrone, that it is no longer possible to see across the expanse of these five acres. The shaggy, thigh-thick bough of Douglas fir extending over the spot where Dana intends to bring Lee's ashes is an example of a problem that is emerging all over the cemetery. Some black-green lower branches of these giants are drooping low, some in candelabrum curves touching the ground. They sway and break during high winds that sometimes lay siege to Cemetery Ridge as if to say, "You old fellows up here are too proud and tall for your own good."

The tree by Lee's grave, the only large tree in the southeast section, is stout enough that three little girls could not link hands around it. This spot now feels far too sheltered. Besides, the lovely view is compromised. Why are so many of us concerned with the view in a cemetery? Whose view? Our own, I suppose.

When Dana stood here a few moments ago taking in this shaggy gloom, she shivered a little, brushing the tip of this offending bough as though inspecting too-long hair on some youngster she was about to hustle off for a haircut. She said, "Let's just give this a trim, shall we? It's too much. Lee liked it, but it's overgrown now."

"Now Shannon, do I assume correctly that it is up to you what goes on now? I mean you have the say-so, don't you? Or do you have to go through your father?" Then she added something that made me wince, "It's all overgrown, isn't it? A rustic, natural look is one thing, but . . ."

Perhaps she saw my face. Never, ever play cards, people tell me.

She looked me over and sighed, saying, "Well, I'm sure you'll take care of all this as you are able, Shannon. All these trees are beautiful, but they are going to need some care."

Then she asked me which way "the head goes." Grandchildren were looking for a perfect sandstone boulder on the farm to bring to the cemetery to serve as a headstone for their grandpa. But at which end of the plot should it be placed?

In general, how were graves supposed to be oriented? East to west? Because, if that were the case, many people's headstones were placed incorrectly. What about the width of the alleyways between plots? Exactly how large was a double plot, anyway? When she was ready to part with Lee's ashes, could she come up and dig a hole herself? Was it legal? What about putting Lee's ashes in a planter of some kind? And when her ashes were brought up here someday was it all right to mingle them with Lee's? Did they have to have permission? Because that was what they'd discussed. She and Lee would be in there together with lavender or maybe a lily.

Lee and Dana as fertilizer. Bone meal. That made sense. But as to the rest, I had no idea. It's better not to ask a lame sexton too many questions, I wanted to tell her.

Lame in more ways than one. My foot is hurting. I feel sad and awkward. I am a close friend of an elderly woman whose husband, a man I admired and adored, has just died. Suddenly, I am also a sexton—some sort of semi-official. At home I have a sheaf of papers that were sent to Dad when he registered the cemetery as a state corporation. Laws and statutes fatten the thick manual from the Cemetery and Mortuary Commission. Even I, a book woman, an incessant researcher, can't bring myself to read this dry stuff. It scares me. It will tell me what I have to do and what will happen to me if I don't.

A writing woman; not an on-the-ground, hands-on kind of woman. A friend once said to me, "Why, you would rather read about an adventure than have one, wouldn't you.?"

As for getting these trees limbed—how many are there? Fifty? A hundred? Where will the money come from? We're not officially a non-profit but we might as well be. Thank God mowing is not upon us until spring.

Upon "us"?

How many hands will it take to eradicate poison oak whose scarlet triumvirate of leaves blaze against the gray of granite baby lambs and Eastern Stars on old headstones I'm passing, as I limp and pitch up the slope trying to reach my car.

And who will hack her way into the humps of blackberries coiling on the sagging fences I can see as I pause and turn to look below?

"Not if she can help it," I tell myself.

Then there is the matter of the plastic flowers. Is there anything quite so depressing or enduring as that bunch right over there? Those blue plastic roses moldering in a mayonnaise jar wrapped in aluminum foil. But now, close to boot and crutch, a contender appears on the grave of Agnes Peters, 1918–1975. These may well take the prize in the plastic-flower competition: astringent orange daisies poked directly into pale fish tank gravel and strand upon strand of ragged aqua ivy surely chewed by a Rottweiler.

In my mind, I see Dana's piquant face, her large glasses and close-cropped reddish hair that belies the fact she is eighty-something. A few moments ago those blue eyes ignited as she took in the spectacle of a family plot just across the way from Lee's.

She was uncharacteristically adamant saying, "Outlaw plastic flowers altogether. Anything plastic. You need rules, Shannon, and then you have to enforce them." We stood there scanning the low, white plastic picket fence pinioned along the edges of golf green outdoor carpet. Rising out of the center of a profusion of phony peonies was a sign: "Grandma," spelled in reflecting mailbox letters.

"These things just don't fit in here." Dana's lips made an uncompromising line. Shaking her head she said, "No. This is not the five-and-dime. This is *supposed* to be a designated pioneer cemetery."

Red Dirt

This uplifted ridge, shaped like an earthen wave rising from gently tilting valleys, is a perfect spot for a cemetery. It affords the truly long view: From here it is possible to contemplate the distance between this world and the next. Yet, as I wait for the men to arrive who will dig Elsie Patton's grave, I am not moved to consider the possibilities of the Hereafter or even of the here and now. This May morning, I am reading the epochs of the Great Before, trying to decode the ancient signs written in ridge, rock, and sediments rhythmically laid down over the course of millions of years.

The impulse began yesterday when I spoke with a funeral director who told me gravediggers were bringing the vault that Elsie Patton's family had ordered for her burial. The graveside service is scheduled for Saturday, and the gravediggers wanted to install the vault this afternoon. The funeral director said he was aware that things were changing at our cemetery; he wondered whether we would continue to deposit our "spoils" in the same place.

"Our spoils?" Terrible images sprang to mind.

The voice, low and smooth, became faintly patronizing. "That's right, you haven't been at this too long, have you? The spoils: the dirt that is leftover after the grave is dug. A vault displaces quite a bit of dirt and the gravediggers will want to deposit it in the right spot."

"We haven't changed that," I said briskly. "They can put it where they always have."

But the fact is, before yesterday I hadn't thought about how much dirt is leftover after a grave is dug. I've only had the experience of dealing with a few burials, and one of them was not a burial but what, according to the law, is an "inurnment." The family took care of actually burying the ashes in an urn.

Now that I know about "spoils," I understand that the pile of dirt, so surprisingly red, deposited in a low part of the cemetery near the southeast corner, is not merely fill dirt but instead the residue from numerous gravesites over the years.

As for the vault: My sense of what that might be is pretty vague. I came up here to see whether it lives up to my Gothic imagination, and to introduce myself to the gravediggers, who know their way around this cemetery better than I do.

This red dirt: It seems disrespectful, and even profane, to refer to it as "spoils." When wet, it sticks to the shoe, and although it is always red it is distinctly redder after a deep rain. The exposed part of the ridge where I am standing wears red dirt like an old topcoat, or more aptly, like a fireman's dusty windbreaker.

Fire, however, was not a significant part of what shaped this long view I am relishing—unless one counts water-silenced lava extrusions, sending undulant shock waves throughout the warm Eocene seas of some forty million years ago. These extrusions, although volcanic, were not emitted from great lava-spewing cones like Mount Etna, or, much closer to home, Mount St. Helen's, which, even in the 1980s, left ashen pyroclastic footprints over much of Washington. Instead, the volcanism that formed portions of this landscape came from molten basalts oozing through fissures and vents beneath a semi-tropical sea which quickly doused the fire.

As for ice: Cycles of glacial cold missed this place entirely. It is true that, just thousands of years ago, remnants of the ice-hurtling Missoula Floods managed to push broken ice and careening waters all the way into Oregon's Willamette Valley—the southern tip of which is just twenty miles north of here. To say that these floods were vast would be an understatement. It is estimated that at their height they carried icy waters three or four times the present day volume of all the rivers in the world.

Water is the mother of this landscape. An ancient extension of the open ocean once reached as far to the east as today's Cascade Range until it eventually receded, leaving the Pacific Ocean we know today. The seafloor exposed to chastening winds and rains gradually took on the familiar aspect of the hills and valleys spreading before me. The landscape's contours are still changing in ways imperceptible to my short span, but changing nevertheless, subtly altering this comfortably rumpled landscape with its mélange of rough ridges and smooth-sided hills; its creek-coursed wetland swales knuckled with hummocks.

I am picking up a handful of red dirt, ruddy from a smidge of iron and millennia of oxygen. This dirt tells it all. Along with the tinge of minerals, I am holding sea sediments and the pulverized evidence of volcanism at work. And as I let go, feeling it spill through my fingers, this dirt testifies fathoms.

But if this truth concerning primordial waters seems a bit abstract, I can always go back to Fred Applegate's find of a decade ago. Just a few miles from here, he found a fossilized "seashell" atop his sheep hill. Yes, a seashell on top of a sheep hill. How fast can I say it?

When Fred died, the fossil was not among his effects, so we will never know whether the mollusk *Anomia, Acila, Crassastella,* or *Solena* was the decapod that made him shout, "Eureka!"

And now Fred is up here in the cemetery awaiting future geologic epochs, resting in red dirt.

I always bring a little of the cemetery home with me. I've just finished cleaning the rubber hobs of my "graveyard" shoes that are really meant to be gardened in and have wandered sock-footed into the kitchen where I've settled down at the table with a cup of peppermint tea. I'm thinking about the two brothers I just met: Jerry and Terry, the gravediggers.

They arrived driving a pair of gargantuan pickup trucks, emphatically changing the meditative quiet of the cemetery with the slamming of doors and a great deal of yelling as they tried to make themselves heard over engine roar. One truck carried a backhoe, the other a large rectangular object shrouded in black plastic and tied down with ropes.

Who was I expecting? Pockmarked, toothless fellows straight out of a Dickens novel? Or maybe I pictured narrow-faced, liquor-swigging gravediggers from a Bela Lugosi movie? I certainly was surprised to meet these pleasant, robust-looking men, both bearded, very well fed, indeed, but muscular and fit as they surely need to be in their line of work. Considering that they had work to do, they were quite talkative. As they took care of the business of unloading equipment near the site of Elsie Patton's grave, they took turns answering my questions.

A poet named Douglas Jerrold once referred to Jerry and Terry's vocation as ". . . the ugliest of trades . . ." Still, the brothers have apparently been happily digging graves for some eighteen years. Except for slack periods when, I gather, Death, thank God, takes a holiday, and the fact that the brothers must be perpetually "on call," they both claim to like the work.

I didn't ask them if they concurred with something else Jerrold wrote, "Now, if I were a gravedigger . . . there are some people I could work for with a great deal of enjoyment."

The brothers work exclusively in rural locales in cemeteries similar to ours. They are hired by small "mom-and-pop" funeral homes and don't go to big commercial cemeteries, many of which are owned by large corporations. "Those places have their own gravediggers, and they carry markers and headstones, flowers and everything else, right on the premises. They don't have much use for independents like us," Terry volunteered.

The brothers work in three adjacent Oregon counties and claim that they know how to reach each and every cemetery no matter how tucked away amidst hills and fields. Surprisingly, in this geographically large county (Douglas) sprawling over some five thousand square miles where the total population is only slightly more than 105,000, there are more than two hundred known cemeteries, many of which resemble ours. In Oregon, weighing in at only a measly 3.5 million—smaller than the city of Los Angeles—there are at least three thousand cemeteries.

I can only imagine how many tens of thousands of small and medium-sized rural cemeteries are scattered all over the United States. Strictly speaking, many of these cemeteries may no longer be found in rural areas since in much of North America, as in many parts of the world, cities and suburbs have surrounded graveyards of all sizes. What was a rural burying ground as recently as a decade ago may now be next to a Wal-Mart parking lot or even under it.

Because of later urbanization and what seemed an endless availability of open land until the latter part of the eighteenth century, U.S. cemeteries located in burgeoning metropolitan centers did not experience the overcrowding long prevalent in Europe and the British Isles. On both sides of the Atlantic the traditional location of burial grounds adjacent to churches was at the root of overcrowding. It began to occur to city officials, members of the medical community, and more enlightened citizenry in various parts of the world that it was time to remove cemeteries from urban centers, and away from the long arm of ecclesiastical authority.

Ironically, before the advent of Christianity, many societies, including those of the Greeks and Romans, declared it unlawful to bury the dead inside of city walls. It was the Church that brought cemeteries into urban settings, insisting that the dead be buried in churchyards. In England, and various parts of the continent, it was not unusual for a choirboy to find himself gagging as wind brought fumes through the choir loft's clerestory from the decomposing dead buried in an adjacent cemetery. Conditions were even more odious in old cathedrals, where cemeteries had been established literally underfoot. The church granted their most influential and well-to-do members the right to bury their dead in stone vaults located directly beneath the sanctuary floor. In warm weather, churchgoers swooned in their pews.

These unpleasant conditions were not limited to European churches, however, since American parishioners were also seated atop burials in various eighteenth-century churches located in the heart of cities. To have been a passerby, parishioner, or worse, a gravedigger, at New York's Trinity Church in 1822, for example, when officials demanded that the church burial ground immediately be covered with fifty-two huge casks of quicklime because of the offensive odors and danger to public health, is almost too terrible to contemplate.

Perhaps Jerry and Terry would have not answered the call to become buriers of the dead—the result of Terry reading an ad saying "Gravediggers Wanted" a few days after he'd dropped out of high school—if they had been forced to put up with the overcrowded conditions experienced by their historical counterparts.

In 1838, for example, there was a widely publicized English case in which two gravediggers died, "one as if struck by a cannonball." As the pair was working in the paupers' section of London's Aldgate Cemetery (where sometimes as many as eighteen paupers were buried in the same grave) an explosion occurred.

At the inquest, the reasons for the explosion were debated. Some blamed something called a "galvanic derangement," when galvanized energy fields were supposedly destroyed by the proximity of decomposing bodies. Others were certain the explosion was the result of a buildup of "carbonic acid gases" emitting from adjacent burials. It was widely believed that simply inhaling such gases directly could bring instant death.

That all graveyards were full of "miasmas"—toxic mists carrying poisonous effluvia from decaying bodies that supposedly polluted the atmosphere—was a near universal belief for thousands of years. Surely countless cinematic portrayals of mist-shrouded graveyards are vestiges of ancient fears that flourished in times when the nature of contagion was not scientifically understood.

The extent of overcrowding in many graveyards is exemplified by conditions in a nineteenth-century British cemetery of average size—roughly two hundred acres. St. Martin-in-the-Fields held at least sixty thousand bodies. Potential contagion, poisoning of ground water and other health hazards were obviously the result of too many corpses in too small a space.

I asked Jerry if he thought it was true that our cemetery of five acres, currently holding about fifteen hundred graves, had room for at least six hundred more burials—something my father told me that I have doubted.

"Oh yeah, easy!" Jerry told me. He also noted that in Oregon it is legal to bury a husband and wife in the same grave. "You got to plan it out, though," he added. "It means you've got to dig pretty deep when the first one goes so you can have room for another one later."

Despite the obvious overcrowding in European churchyards, church officials were not in favor of moving burial grounds to rural locales. For one thing, many clerics and sextons depended upon the income they received from the sale of plots and associated services on church property.

Church officials were also convinced that the dead would be forgotten if relegated to outlying areas; that corpses might be unsafe in times when grave robbing, on behalf of medical science, was a real problem. Equally distasteful was the fact that "pagan" civilizations such as the Egyptians, Greeks, and Romans had historically located their cemeteries on the outskirts of settlements. The word "cemetery," in fact, from the Greek *koimao* (to put to sleep)—was usually associated with secular burying grounds rather than consecrated religious ones. Clerics were rankled by the ideas of secularism generated during the Enlightenment; the suspect influence of romantic pantheism, and other intellectual explorations that were seen to undermine church authority.

Church objections were eventually eclipsed by health concerns in the late 1700s when various European metropolitan cemeteries were finally removed to outlying districts. Most notable was Père Lachaise Cemetery, established on the outskirts of Paris. With its emphasis on Romantic Nature, and conscious design inspired by the ideas inherent in British "landscape architecture," Père Lachaise would eventually influence American civic leaders who were attempting to address their own overcrowded burial grounds.

Americans put their own stamp on solutions to cemetery overcrowding, however, by beginning what was known as the Rural Cemetery Movement. In 1831, the newly completed Mount

Auburn Cemetery in Boston (now a national landmark) was consecrated by religious leaders as well as hailed by secular supporters, including horticulturists and medical authorities. America's premier Garden Cemetery, soon the principal model for many other nineteenth-century cemeteries in cities across the U.S., sought to emphasize the union of religious and secular concerns: "Eden—the first abode of the living," its founders proclaimed, "Mount Auburn—the last resting place of the dead." The Rural Cemetery Movement was launched; other major cities would soon follow Boston's lead with their own versions of garden cemeteries—among them Brooklyn (Green-Wood Cemetery) and Philadelphia (Laurel Hill).

Superficially, smaller cemeteries like our own would seem to bear little resemblance to places like Mount Auburn and Laurel Hill with their romantic accouterments of bridges and ponds, elaborate funerary statuary, and carefully landscaped "bosky dells." The roads of this little pioneer cemetery are loosely laid out on a geometric grid and do not contain the generous curves, the carefully planned meandering pathways, the deliberate scenic "surprises" designed to delight the eye so abundant in the garden cemeteries established in the mid-nineteenth century.

Still, many of America's graveyards, particularly those established in the first half of the nineteenth century, like this one, share something of the impulse that inspired the Rural Cemetery Movement. They are not located in churchyards and have been deliberately set on the outskirts of towns. Their founders, often fraternal orders that grew out of the forces of the European Enlightenment, have located these burial grounds on hilltops and ridges to make the most of "a beautiful prospect." These burying places are formally called cemeteries as if to define their secular and civic connections as opposed to strictly religious ones. Special trees and other plants, although not chosen by an expert landscaper with a "plan" in mind, have nevertheless been selected with care, often by the families who own plots, and bring heritage roses, lilacs, and special shrubs and trees frequently associated with carefully planned "garden cemeteries."

An early brochure extolling the then suburban comfort of Laurel Hill in Philadelphia promised a place "where the smitten heart might pour out its grief over the grave of a cherished one, secure from the idle gaze of heartless passersby, and where the mourner could rear a flower consecrated to the memory and hope." Similar attributes exist not only in our own cemetery, but in other country cemeteries all over the United States.

But back to Terry and Jerry who likely don't know anything about the Rural Cemetery Movement and probably could care less as they, and their backhoe, ply the back roads in Lane, Douglas, and northern Coos counties where their services are needed.

Jerry and Terry are responsible for digging graves, setting up the paraphernalia associated with today's graveside services, such as canopies, ground covering, and simulated brass railings.

They also sign death certificates after matching them with an identification tag on the coffin, the mate of which is also affixed to the toe of the corpse bearing the same number. This procedure is the result of an Oregon law passed during the 1980s in the aftermath of a nationally covered cemetery scandal. In a mortuary garage in Lincoln City, Oregon, a well-liked local mortician was found to be intermixing human remains that he buried in plastic bags or cardboard boxes and warehoused corpses he had been contracted to cremate.

His crimes against the living and the dead goaded lawmakers in several Western states into changing laws regarding interment. Earlier today, Jerry referred to this scandal as "that Lincoln City mess." Terry added, "It made us all look bad."

I would have difficulty hiring the brothers on my own since they are not listed under "grave digging" in the *Yellow Pages*.

Grave digging is a still a vocation to be concealed. The average person considers not only the task itself, but he who undertakes it, distasteful, if not repugnant. The brothers advertise as a "vault" company. Seeing such a listing, most of us would picture a bank vault not a grave.

I gather that manufacturing vaults and liners provides Jerry and Terry with a nice supplemental income. Liners are concrete slabs several inches thick that are placed on the four sides and bottom of a grave. The casket is then lowered into this boxlike structure and a top is put into place.

Jerry and Terry's vaults are concrete cast in two-piece molds. Also designed to contain the casket, they are heavier and thicker than liners. The vault's principal selling point is the fact that it is so tightly sealed. It also is more expensive. The brothers would probably argue that in addition to taking more time to manufacture, vaults are more aesthetically pleasing. They spray paint their vaults in silver or copper colors.

Why not gold? I should have asked Jerry. Perhaps it would make the vault appear too imperial and ostentatious. Maybe gold spray paint just costs more. When the plastic shroud was removed and I saw that Elsie Patton's vault was copper colored, it just seemed silly—an attempt to make a silk purse out of a sow's ear.

Terry and Jerry asked me if this cemetery requires liners in graves. They pointed out several rectangular depressions where there are older graves.

"Now that's the kind of thing that happens when you don't have liners or vaults. The grave caves in," Terry said in a serious, almost admonishing tone of voice. He added that every grave should have a barrier between the coffin and the dirt.

For a moment I felt defensive then I rallied, saying, "But graves are *in* dirt to begin with. We deliberately bury people in dirt. We expect that they will be surrounded by earth. That's what it's all about."

"Well, you're forgetting the moisture damage to the casket which can be prevented," Terry said.

"For how long?" I asked him, feeling as though he were running a car wash and trying to get me to sign up for the most expensive full-car-wash-deal: the super deluxe, hand-rubbed, anti-moisture-seal-deal.

Terry shrugged. "I guess you could say, longer than it would otherwise. The wet really ruins things. It happens a lot faster without a liner or a vault, you know. And there is other stuff . . ." Terry added, screwing up his face a little as though the topic were distasteful even to a big man like himself.

Childhood's dark ditty came to mind: "The worms crawl in, the worms crawl out, the worms play pinochle on your snout."

"But liners don't stop anything," I wanted to say. "Or vaults either." Not in the long run. Dust to dust. Everything goes, eventually—though in the right conditions the bones themselves outlast other parts of the body.

I stopped myself because I realized there were some economic considerations underlying our discussion. The brothers manufactured liners and vaults, after all, in addition to installing them. Of course *they* thought liners and vaults were a good idea. I did ask them whether the "casket protection" they installed was required by law. They admitted it wasn't. Such things are left to the discretion of the cemetery.

I might have added that there is nothing in Oregon law that states human remains even need to be placed in a casket. If a cemetery wanted to use a biodegradable papier-mâché coffin such as those patented by a pair of Australian women a few years ago, it would be perfectly legal as long as other rules regarding the disposal of the dead were obeyed.

"You should really think about requiring liners," Jerry advised. "People like knowing they are protecting their loved ones. It brings them peace of mind."

It's only been ten years or so since Terry and Jerry began using a backhoe. Grave digging by hand is laborious; they strain the same muscles those assigned to burying the dead have always strained since Neanderthal times. But if a cemetery prohibits use of heavy equipment, digging by hand is what they do.

Watching them, I could see that there is a certain amount of craft involved in the proper digging of a grave. I watched as pieces of plywood were carefully laid down so that the backhoe, and the truck hauling the concrete vault, would not leave tracks over adjacent plots. Jerry told me that when the ground is as hard as concrete they are obliged to use a jackhammer. Jackhammers can collapse liner roofs or vault lids on adjacent graves.

They tamped an iron rod into the earth, prodding until they struck a bordering liner, in order to be sure they were digging in the right place. They proceeded methodically, at an almost leisurely pace. If the prod hit something, Jerry said, they moved far enough away so as not to disturb the neighboring site regardless of what the cemetery sexton's grave markers indicated.

It takes the better part of a day to bury someone in the accustomed way: The site is prepared so that the "opening" of the grave, which is how the funeral industry euphemistically refers to grave digging, typically occurs on the morning of the funeral. "Closing" refers to the burial. Opening and closing: It sounds a bit like buying a home. As I think about it, buying and burying are only one letter apart, and I suppose that buying a grave plot is purchasing a home, in a sense—the final real-estate transaction.

If the weather predictions are good, or something else has come up in their personal lives, Jerry and Terry dig the grave the day before the funeral, as is the case today. It means they will need to make another trip down here tomorrow. Weekend funerals are more expensive, these days, but that is what the Patton family wanted.

I told Jerry and Terry I wanted to charge a fee of thirty dollars for driving to the cemetery, locating, and then flagging, the gravesite—something I do in all kinds of weather and sometimes at very short notice. They looked blank. Then I assured them that I would use the fee for cemetery maintenance.

Earlier on the telephone when I informed the man at the funeral home that from now on we would be charging a location or marking fee, I could hear him sneering. He said coldly, "*Commercial* cemeteries charge for marking graves, of course, but I thought *you* were not-for-profit." Then, he tried to shame me further, saying he would "let the family know that your cemetery has decided to charge a fee in addition to all their other funeral costs." He suggested I should bill the family directly.

I asked the brothers if they thought thirty dollars was unreasonable? After all, I must mark the grave so they can find it. After consulting my records, I drive up to the cemetery and, regardless of the weather, take care of the job.

I also told them the cemetery had recently doubled the price of individual plots from one hundred dollars each to two hundred dollars.

Terry considered his answer for a moment. "Instead of nickel-and-diming folks," he said, "why not raise your plot price to four hundred dollars?"

He added that small- to mid-sized commercial cemeteries in nearby towns charge from six hundred dollars to eight hundred dollars per plot. "And the bigger ones," he named a largish cemetery in the city south of here, "charge closer to one thousand dollars or fourteen hundred dollars if they are perpetual care, endowed cemeteries."

As I was thinking about the "perpetual care"—something I'm going to have to look into—Jerry was blocking out the next day's events like a stage director. "They'll have to bring her in this way," he said, gesturing toward the nearest grassy alleyway with both hands.

Tomorrow, Elsie Patton, lying inside her casket, will arrive at the cemetery in a squeaky-clean, shiny black pickup with a customized canopied bed long enough to serve its special purpose. The truck has a sinister quality heightened by tinted windows that hint gangster more than mortician.

I have seen this conveyance only once or twice and now find myself wondering whether the funeral home has chosen such a vehicle because they think rural people will feel more comfortable seeing a pickup instead of a hearse. Hearses are specialty items and can be extremely expensive. Then, too, I suppose a funeral director could use a black pickup as a second car, if he needed to.

Since the graveside ceremony is typically led by a clergyman or friend of the family, I asked the brothers just what the funeral director's role at the cemetery was supposed to be.

"The funeral director just stands there and looks good," said Jerry, "and raises all the costs by about two hundred percent."

I asked them if they had a list of the services they provided. Terry stopped what he was doing—readjusting a sheet of plywood over the adjacent grave. "We wouldn't want to do that. I mean what we charge might give people the wrong impression. It would *seem* like a lot."

"Just black out the prices then. That's not what's of interest to me. I just want to see exactly who is responsible for what. I had no idea, for example, what you two did," I said.

"Well, maybe we could. Don't want to make no one mad, though." Terry was sweating profusely and stopped to swipe his forehead with his shirtsleeve. His beard was darker than his brother's. A few silver hairs were glinting in it.

"We'll have to talk more about that, brother," said Jerry, who was frowning and standing in the depths of Elsie Patton's grave. He heaved his substantial self over the side and stood slapping the loose dirt from the knees of his overalls. Red dirt. "Man, oh, man," he complained. "This stuff stains."

The sweet spring day of Elsie Patton's funeral is nearly over now. It is almost dusk and the elderly Mason who nightly closes the gate that guards both the Masonic Cemetery and our own Applegate Pioneer Cemetery next door will be up here in a little while.

I am not alone. Memorial Day is coming soon and mowers, mainly middle-aged men, are trying to get their family plots in shape before the weekend is over. When I arrived about a half hour ago, the air was filled with the whine of power weed cutters. Lawnmowers were instigating blizzards of cut grass that stuck to the sides of my car as I passed. Now things are simmering down.

The gravediggers did a good job. I worried about road-ruts since this May has been very wet indeed, and our roads need several loads of gravel we can't yet afford. I am concerned whenever big trucks and heavy equipment enter the cemetery, especially on the alleyways close to graves and older headstones.

I note that Elsie's grave is fairly heaped with fresh flowers. I didn't send her any because I didn't know her very well. Still, her people knew mine. Around here, families are tribes, and our respective tribes tend to know one another. Or, tended to know one another. Times are very different. The faces in this community are newer every day.

Elsie was rather horse-faced, quiet, and kind. As they say, she hadn't been herself for quite some time. Many years ago, in the only extended conversation we ever had, she told me her father had picked up my identical twin great-aunties, Eva and Evea, at the Yoncalla train station during the 1918 influenza epidemic. Her mother begged her father not to go out in public where there might be a possibility of a crowd to expose him to the flu, but he went anyway. She finished the story with, "That's a man for you."

My cousin Susan, who has grown up here, knows more local elders than I do and attends more funerals. She told me that the last service she went to had no hymnal singing, just a cassette tape playing, "Wings of a Dove," sung by Dolly Parton. I hope they did better for Elsie Patton today.

These old hills look splendid now, under this cloud-tossed sky of luminous robin's egg blue. Susan uses exactly this color and a deeper cerulean in many of her paintings. It is part of her Yoncalla palette.

I'm looking southeast, standing by one of our own family plots, close to the Pattons, more or less on the very brow of this long ridge. I don't like to admit it, but the Masonic Cemetery has a slightly better view. Their cemetery is on the ridge's nose-like tip. But the Masons don't have our wonderfully big trees.

Here, by Great-Aunt Eva and Evea's graves the dirt is the color of old ox-blood. Nothing we have planted around these graves excepting the box-wood shrubs, that I see need pruning, grows very well here. As I look around I am struck by the fact that this twelve-person family plot, originally belonging to my great-grandfather George "Buck" Applegate and his wife, Flora, is nearly full. There's still room for my father, of course, when that day arrives, and maybe one or two others. It's amazing how little topsoil is here. Just this packed earth. I like the phrase geologists use: I'm looking at the "parent" material—the real stuff of this place.

Now, the sky is streaked shrimp pink. No. The pink reminds me more of the inside of a large seashell that someone gave me when I was a child of ten or so. I was crazy about collecting natural things, especially rocks. I kept rocks in shallow boxes with labels under each specimen.

But that seashell was a prize possession, too. I suppose it must have been a conch. I would spend long moments with it cupped against my ear, listening to its inside ocean.

I wonder how Eocene oceans sounded? The waters were relatively warm, and the eastern shoreline, less than a hundred miles from here was tucked under the feet of the Cascade Range. Waves must have lapped with a certain placidity, rather than crashed. There were semi-tropical islands here and there, supposedly where avocados grew and three-toed little horses wandered.

If I were standing here during the Eocene, this ridge would surely be many fathoms down. There were at least three species of shark in oceans of the period, thus I might have seen the dark silver flash of fins; hot basalt spewed in black plumes from the ocean floor, its particles fanning out in the shimmering distance, giving up the ghost.

I'll have to settle for be-here-now, however, in this peaceful twentieth-century cemetery dusk. Elsie Patton's largest funeral spray, hanging from its wire stanchion, is pale and shoulder high as I pass; Elsie is now locked up in her vault to keep dirt and water away. The grave is narrow and closed, Mrs. Patton, but time is wide and deep.

> *Rocked in the cradle of the deep*
> *I lay me down in peace to sleep.*
> *Secure I rest upon the wave. . . .*
> —Emma Willard, 1831

God, She Is Thine

D r. Lydia Emery, our beloved town physician, who charged one dollar for house calls, has just died and Susan is making floral arrangements for her memorial service. Dr. Lydia never met a child, a book, or a flower she didn't like. Tucked in a copse of flowering shrubs toward the back of the cemetery, where English bluebells, white violets, and wild Indian camas bloom in spring, a small stone, only slightly lifted from the ground, bears the simple inscription, "Baby Boy Emery." He was Lydia and her husband Jeep's only child who was stillborn.

Susan has incorporated as many wild plants as possible into the two large bouquets that are to sit on either side of the rostrum in the high-school gym—the only town facility large enough to accommodate the expected crowd of mourners of all ages. Cowpea vines, still bearing a few deep pink blossoms, are about all early October offers in the way of field flowers. Cat-tails, sword

31

ferns from the woods, curly dock from the verge of the pasture, Oregon grape sprigs with leaves turning ruddy and faintly orange, and the branches of vine maple just starting to show autumn's brassiness are all natives. Harkening back to her former vocation as a floral designer, Susan has succumbed to purchasing Asian lilies from a local florist because their colors remind her of flicker feathers. Lydia, if she's watching, will approve.

It's easy to conjure up images of Lydia in our minds as the garden shears snip and branches are stuck into florist's Stryofoam that is bound with green tape at the bottom of huge wicker baskets.

Today, some may be visualizing Dr. Lydia teaching Sunday school at the Methodist Church—her religious home despite her Mennonite upbringing—or conducting athletic physicals for high-school students or leading Girl Scouts. Others will remember her hosting Easter egg hunts on the Emery's spacious side lawn—an annual event held for more than forty-five years and anticipated by every local child. Susan and I, however, are thinking about Lydia in our own way.

Lydia was Susan's mother's closest friend. Multiple sclerosis kept Jane Applegate at home in later years, but Lydia saw past the wheelchair and ranged intellectually with Jane, wandering over interior landscapes where poetry grew in groves and the ideas of their favorite writers extended far beyond the fence lines of Yoncalla and nearby Scotts Valley.

One of the bouquets is almost finished. It's huge, almost waist high.

"How will we ever get it into the pickup without having it tip over?" I wonder aloud.

Susan shrugs. "It will be okay." Then she adds, "Remember her handwriting?" In my mind, I see Dr. Lydia's handwriting in all its clarity and excruciating daintiness, surely an anomaly among physicians.

"I remember Lydia's voice," I say, trying, unsuccessfully, to reproduce the sweet, almost unearthly timbre I hear in my inner ear.

"Close, but not quite. There was a lilt. A cadence peculiar to her," Susan says, but her effort to replicate Lydia's voice is no better than mine. "Isn't it odd to think we'll never get to hear her say anything again?" she adds as she clips a branch of vine maple shorter.

We both are quiet for a moment, thinking of Lydia, and Jane, too, whose voice we'll also never hear again. I am remembering all those peanut butter chocolate chip cookies Jane made and left in her freezer; how the whole family ate them for nearly a year after she died, parceling them out as though they were the Sacrament and milk were wine.

"I wonder who the first person was to make a flower arrangement for a funeral?" Susan muses. "Probably, it started with the cave men. Someone picked some flowers and threw them in a hole along with the body, or just stuck them in the dirt on top."

"Even Neanderthals threw flowers into their graves. At least I think I remember reading something to that effect, several years ago," I tell her.

But really my mind is on the impending transportation problem. Susan keeps adding and subtracting elements from the arrangement, standing back and tilting her head as she appraises her work. "The flowers are going to scrape the roof if you keep making things higher and higher," I warn. She ignores me.

At length we manage to wrestle, prop, and wedge both huge bouquets into the covered back of Fred Applegate's old blue pickup that Susan inherited when he died, and that he used to drive like a bat out of hell.

I'm not going with her. She assures me someone will help her unload, perhaps one of the high-school teachers or someone from the funeral home. In my mind I see the kind face of Doug Lund.

I've not found too many favorites in the funeral "industry," thus far, but I admire him. He seems very caring and sincere and owns a family mortuary to the north of us. He was very fond of Dr. Lydia and it was mutual. He or his assistant will surely help Susan.

"See ya' later," Susan calls out the open window. I watch her slowly navigate the rough spots in the driveway. I catch a last golden glimpse of the flower arrangement closest to the back window.

I remember, suddenly, the story Susan is fond of telling about the hapless delivery boy at a florist shop where she worked who was blamed for a truly *monumental* funeral fiasco. Years ago, a family called to request a large, showy casket spray. The head floral designer Susan worked under created an arrangement in a wonderment of beribboned pink and white roses, amidst a high heap of airy drifts of asparagus fern. The family requested that some special sentiment be spelled in gold monogram letters appropriate to the dead woman, but did not want it to specifically designate her as "mother" or "sister" since several family members had chipped in.

The family finally selected the sentiment, "God, She is Thine" and requested that the lettering be large enough to be read clearly from the back of the church. The designer carefully stapled each letter to a long, wide white satin ribbon that was attached deep within the high bosom of flowers. The ribbon dangled picturesquely from the side of the casket facing the pews.

About a half hour before the funeral the delivery boy hastened to the church, and was led to the open casket. After he carefully handed the arrangement to the funeral director, the delivery boy confessed that he briefly glimpsed the head and torso of the dead woman through the opened casket door. He said that as he left the church he saw the funeral director place the spray on the casket's closed lower half and fuss with the ribbon.

The woman had apparently died of cancer, or some other wasting disease—something the boy commented upon when he returned to the shop. The floral designer, who had a macabre interest in such details and when he was not too busy, liked to deliver casket sprays himself so that he could get a look at the corpse, commented that embalmers and cosmeticians could do a lot but weren't magicians.

An hour later the shop owner stormed into the designers' workroom looking for the delivery boy. An angry family member had just called, refusing to pay for the casket spray. It seems no one had noticed until the funeral was in progress that the wide white satin ribbon with its large gold letters said, "God, She Is Thin" instead of "God, She Is Thine." The missing "e" was never located.

I am surprised to learn that flowers have not always played a part in funerals and burials.

"Even Neanderthals . . ." I told Susan, unintentionally displaying my homocentricism. It turns out that what was touted in the 1970s as thrilling evidence that Neanderthals used flowers in their burial rituals now seems questionable. At the time, we flower children liked the idea a lot. We imagined that yarrow, grape hyacinth, and Saint Barnaby's thistle had been woven into garlands some fifty thousand years ago by beings much like ourselves, who were perhaps, our own "primitive" ancestors. Even the Neanderthals believed in "flower power," it seemed.

The archaeologist excavating the Middle Paleolithic hominid remains in Shanidar Cave, Iraq, waxed eloquent at the time, saying that with the finding of flowers . . . "we are brought suddenly to . . . the universality of mankind and the love of beauty that go beyond the boundary of our own species."

Today, archaeologists are more skeptical. They point to the

presence of a cute little burrowing rodent called a Persian jird (*M. persicus*) in the Shanidar Cave. They even wonder whether the hominid remains found there were deliberately buried in the first place. "Intentional mortuary behavior," they say, cannot be proven.

The earliest flower burial, then, is quite possibly an anthropological myth, along the lines that there are two hundred Eskimo words for snow. Flower pollens discovered close to the remains are varieties known to be especially savored, moved, and stashed in tunnels by the busy jirds, whose remains comprise seventy percent of the rodent bones found at the same site.

It is the case, however, that ancient Greeks and Romans and their contemporaries incorporated flowers into funeral rites. In Greece, the deceased was robed in white—the death color for many societies. Floral wreaths, made by loved ones and friends, were placed on and around the corpse. The Roman dead reclined upon flower-strewn couches. Pine and cypress boughs, rather than flowers, were tied to the doorways of their houses to announce the presence of a dead body on the premises.

Flowers have been part of mortuary behavior in places like China, Hawaii, and Japan for millennia. But, aside from customs in Greece and Rome, "saying it with flowers" was a long time coming in terms of funerals in the Western World. As with so many customs we Americans now take for granted (the Christmas tree and teatime, come to mind), the credit or blame for flowers as a part of ceremonial life must be placed upon the sentimental Victorians. That paragon of "virtue," Queen Victoria, was to influence much of the world during her reign (1837–1901). Her personal pattern of mourning impacted generations even following her reign.

Before Victoria's time, however, the only posies that were part of funeral rituals were those fashioned by headstone carvers. In the minds of many Christians, displays of cut flowers, including simple bouquets that were occasionally placed upon graves, were associated with so-called pagan rites deemed more sensual than spiritual.

On cemetery carvings, the flower was used merely as a metaphor for the brevity of human life. From 1825 to 1835, at least thirty-five million British and American religious tracts were published and distributed all over the world that were filled with floral analogies. Certain varieties of flowers became a stock theme of clergy-inspired material referred to as "literature of consolation." These literary efforts—dripping with sentiment—were especially aimed at comforting those who suffered the "untimely loss" of infants and children.

Tombstone makers quickly transformed many of these literally flowery sentiments into popular epitaphs by chiseling them beneath carvings of roses and lilies: "This lovely bud, so young so fair/Called hence by early doom/Just came to show/How sweet a flower/In Paradice would bloom."

The Victorian era was an "age of beautiful death," when grief was pleasure and pain entwined. It was the same theme that earlier

inspired romantic ballads, such as the ballad of "Barbara Allen," when rose and briar mingled atop the graves of two lovers. Love, in the dark romanticism of the time, flowered even in death; sadness was the sister of joy, and vice versa.

Flowers were imbued with symbolism that captured the imaginations of readers and writers wherever Victorianism influenced culture in many parts of the world. The so-called "language of flowers" was deeply inhaled; sentimental books that supposedly revealed attributes and "secret" meanings of various flowers were published in France, England, and America. There is no evidence, however, that people actually communicated in "flower code." The romantic rumor that the popular language of flowers originated in a Persian harem was largely just that.

Two American writers, Susan and Anna Warner, who were much admired by the women in the Applegate family, brought flowers into popular consciousness as symbols of death when they attempted to euphemize the Grim Reaper, with floral analogies. For them, and other writers, Death became "The good Husbandman," who could gather his "lilies" and "roses" at midsummer. Death became synonymous with God, the kindly father, who might choose to harvest the young.

Since flowers, according to Victorian sensibilities, spoke "God's language of love," some British women were inspired to undertake "flower missions." Single flowers or bouquets, intended to lift the spirits, were delivered to the sick and needy all over England. Attached to these floral offerings were appropriate Bible verses. Surely, the urban poor, who were the principal recipients of these floral tributes, would have preferred butter to buttercups. The beauty of flowers, the ladies' mission claimed, demonstrated God's love; mission supporters arranged for flowers to be sent on trains from rural locales to urban centers. Could FTD be far behind?

Connecting flowers to the love of the Creator made them acceptable, even desirable, at funerals. One, and then two vases of flowers sat by the casket during the church service, and later these bouquets accompanied funeral goers to the cemeteries, where they were placed on graves.

Flower giving was soon surrounded by a set of conventions; the need to reciprocate in proscribed ways became a matter of etiquette practiced, sometimes to the point of absurdity, throughout the Victorian world. But it was in America, in the early 1870s, at the beginning of the Gilded Age, that floral ostentation became an art form to be practiced by those who could afford it. The crepe-hung medieval gloom that for some three hundred years had dictated most aspects of mourning and funeral rituals began to lift, as floral tributes opened new and brighter mortuary practices.

During his controversial life, many a virtuous act (and later, an adulterous affair) were laid at the feet of famous Congregational minister, Henry Ward Beecher (1835–1887). It took his death, however, to establish what would become an American tradition: the flower funeral. In order to honor one of the most celebrated figures of the time, Beecher's family broke with a century or more of funerary tradition. Instead of placing black taffeta death badges upon darkly draped doorways, the younger Beechers hung gay baskets of flowers.

Beecher's memorial service may still rank as one of the most extravagant "flower funerals" of all time. In the large church, each of the dozens of gas brackets bore an immense hanging basket brimming with cut roses, azaleas, and other bright or scented flowers. Suspended chains of green smilax obscured the high ceiling along its entire length. Ropes of evergreen and laurel gracefully wound about doorways, pillars, and other architectural surfaces, within and without. A solid bank of flowers, including Calla lilies, rose behind the dais where the casket rested.

The funeral, despite its impressive surroundings had a touch of the personal and quaint: Beecher's old reading desk and chair, brought in to flank the pulpit, were just barely visible beneath masses of asparagus fern, pink and white roses, Eucharist lilies, and white carnations.

Three white doves were cloistered in a thicket of sword ferns upon the Bible stand. A huge floral cross bore gold monogram letters that spelled, "Our Chaplain." The initial "B," formed in blush-colored roses, occupied the center of a gigantic pillow sculpted in white roses.

As the extravagance and cost of such floral displays—and the funerals with which they were associated—grew, many mourners in the 1890s attempted to cut costs. Some companies that sold caskets and other funerary accessories began offering dried and silk flowers. These "immortelles" as they were advertised (the predecessors of today's plastic creations that I have come to so detest) were about fifty percent cheaper than real flowers and could be purchased already arranged. Set floral pieces included the familiar motifs already associated with tombstone designs of the period: the anchor, heart and hand, lamb, and shield and sickle. Especially popular were emblems associated with America's burgeoning fraternal societies.

When the twentieth century began, many culture-watchers foretold a shift in popular taste as far as floral tributes were concerned. Certainly, funeral styles changed, but "saying it with flowers" became culturally engrained—a theme constantly reinterpreted by enterprising florists who eventually formed their own industry.

Now, in another century, set pieces such as "Gates Ajar," "The Broken Column," and the "Unstrung Harp," whose

symbolism rests in the sentimental era of the Victorians, are still available in today's floral-shop catalogs.

"Where will Dr. Lydia be buried?" I asked Susan later. She has spent the afternoon with Lydia's niece who is up from California. It is certainly not a question I would have put to our old friend Jeep.

According to her niece, Lydia, who served as one of the navy's few women doctors during World War II, had a love of the sea I never knew about. Jeep was in the marine corps in the South Pacific, and Lydia was stationed in various locations stateside. Their letters sailed like paper boats back and forth across the Pacific during the last years of the war.

"It is really quite romantic," Susan tells me. "Lydia was cremated, and when Jeep goes, his ashes are to be mingled with hers and both of them will be thrown into the Pacific. At least, that was what Lydia always wanted."

It's hard to think of Jeep alone in their house—a turn-of-the-century Queen Anne cottage originally built by Mr. Wamsley, who is buried in our cemetery. Jeep, who worked in the plywood mill after he got out of the marine corps, brought Lydia out West. He did his best as he remodeled the cottage; still, it has always felt too dark to me, with warren-like windowless rooms and storage closets that he built large enough to sleep in. These closets are all lined with deep plywood shelves.

They needed shelves. Lydia and Jeep were both born with an accumulation gene. They collected rocks, sea shells, pottery, coins, stamps, fishing floats, old magazines, and books, books, books. A floor-to-ceiling bookshelf occupied the longest wall of their living room. The front portion of their kitchen—converted into an informal waiting room where the children of Yoncalla sat fretfully on their tired mothers' knees waiting to see Dr. Lydia—was lined with bookshelves, too, which contained children's books and an extraordinary number of volumes concerning the natural world. The waiting room also held portions of the Emery's rock collections and most of Lydia's potted plants.

Jeep once told me that they had an entire closet stacked with canisters of wildflower slides, and I believe it. Both Lydia and Jeep were experts on wildflowers, and when the opportunity presented itself they took adult classes on volcanism, geology, and local history.

Jeep and Lydia had the form of wanderlust that must find its satisfaction on a limited budget during weekends and holidays. Lydia never learned to drive, so Jeep was always behind the wheel. He drove Lydia when she made house calls, as well as when they made nature trips. They had favorite spots all over the Northwest, but they seemed to like best those places that they could visit often and watch over time. Noting natural changes, even minute ones, gave them great joy.

Years ago they gave me a wildflower book I still treasure. In it I found some of Lydia's notes concerning the Wolf Creek watershed. She was always making notes on things: on subjects ranging from Persian poets to hex signs on Pennsylvanian barns.

She probably didn't realize that she left notes tucked into this wildflower book: "Six miles—Violet adunca grows near the six-mile post. Seven miles—Pull off the road on the right past the covered bridge. On your left, on the rocky hillside, grow wild strawberries. See also Orchids (Calypso bulbosa), Lambs' tongues, Grouse flowers, and Dwarf Oregon grape."

Now, this is what I'd like to say if asked: The Pacific Ocean is mighty big. Doesn't it make more sense to comfort those of us left behind? That's what cemeteries are about, after all. Lydia was certain she was going somewhere else where she would abide forever. What's left of her might as well stay home in Yoncalla. I'd like her to be up in the cemetery; close to the Johnny-jump-ups, the dog-toothed violets, and Baby Boy Emery.

Grave Goods

"**W**hy does everyone assume someone else will clean up their messes and then become furious when they do?"

I'm complaining to Kathy, the city administrator, who is shaking her head and looking sympathetic while standing behind the business counter in Yoncalla's City Hall—a flat-topped brick building that also houses the library.

Kathy, an attractive, spunky woman in her forties, raises her eyebrows and remarks with a touch of chide, "Well, like I said last week . . . I told you if you tried to make cemetery rules . . ."

"Guidelines," I interrupt.

She shrugs. "Rules . . . guidelines . . . whatever you want to call them . . . if people around here think you are trying to tell them what to do they're not going to be happy. What does your dad think about it?" she asks and then answers her own question with a quick laugh. "The Colonel probably thinks you should just shoot the s.o.b. and be done with it. I don't imagine he is any too pleased with all this."

But perhaps because I am not laughing, she looks serious again. It is not that I mind when people make quips about my dad. I myself have been known to joke about The Colonel—as he is almost universally referred to—but not today. The Colonel is away, and I'm here. The cemetery, in all its glory, is mine to manage. We have other family members on the committee, but I'm the official sexton, the one who gets the calls.

"Did you talk directly to the sheriff's office?" Kathy asks, meaning the office that is located in the county seat, some thirty miles from Yoncalla.

I nod. "Fat lot of good that did. I told the dispatcher that I wanted to talk to somebody else besides the local deputy, and she *still* tried to transfer me to him."

The phone rings and Kathy, alone in the office, deals with an inquiry about a water bill. I scan the wall as I wait, noting various plaques awarded to Yoncalla for winning pie-eating contests at the North Douglas County Fair. The glass case to my right is filled with a dozen or so unframed historic photographs with curling edges. All of them are pictures taken by Uncle Gus sometime in the 1920s. In one photo, Alta Daugherty—who is buried in our cemetery—is about eight years old. She is posing, holding a Brownie camera, her bobbed hair angling prettily against her cheek, as she pretends that she is snapping a picture of ten-year-old "cowboy" George Roberts. Whirling a lasso over his head, George is wearing an oversized, obviously borrowed pair of boots.

Uncle Gus kept various outfits on hand so that people could dress appropriately, and with whimsy. I have a photo of my sophisticated mother, Edie, for example, that he took in the 1940s in which she looks like Annie Oakley, toting a gun belt and sidearm.

I peer into the case to scrutinize the little cowboy's outfit more closely and recognize Aunt Hazel's cowboy boots—the pair with the stitched white tulip designs. We still have them at the Old Place, along with her saddle.

"Sorry," the administrator says finally. "Now, why was it you didn't want to talk to the same deputy again? I'm not clear on that."

I'm feeling a little exasperated. Using an expression current among high-school writing students that I teach as an artist-in-residence, I answer, "Because the deputy blew me off."

I try to clarify, saying, "He was rude." I describe the conversation. I tell about my frustration as the deputy kept interrupting me; how even when I explained that I was the cemetery sexton in Yoncalla, and that I had just received a threatening phone call from a local man who left an obscene message on my answering

machine, the deputy grunted. He said that he already knew about the situation, that he had received complaints about *me*, that same morning, from various members of the Kelly clan.

"The Kelly family is up in arms . . ." I tell Kathy who says, "That sounds about right. There are a few hotheads in that bunch."

I go on. "They claim that 'valuable articles' were stolen from the top of one of their family graves. They want to lodge a formal complaint, the deputy said. I tried to explain our side of things and what we are trying to accomplish in the cemetery but he cut me off, claiming he had to hang up. I called him right back. I asked him what he would do if his wife had received a phone call like that? What if some guy was threatening to come after her?"

"What did he say to that?" Kathy asks, indignation making her voice rise.

"He said he had a pretty good idea who the fellow was. He was one of the Kellys who had talked to him earlier. But the deputy wouldn't give me the guy's name, or promise to do anything about the fact that he had threatened me. He's obviously taken the part of the Kelly family. He kept asking, 'What in the heck are you people doing up there at the cemetery? Why would anyone take stuff off a little baby's grave?' "

Kathy's eyes widen as she grimaces. "This is about a baby's grave? Whose baby is it? Or I guess I should say whose baby *was* it. Can't be old Mrs. Kelly's. Well, I guess her name isn't Kelly any more. I don't think her son has the name Kelly either. Kelly, a wild guy, if I remember rightly, was the second or third husband. The baby is maybe one of her grandkids."

"I don't know the baby's name. All I could get out of the deputy was Mrs. Kelly's, or whatever her name is now, phone number; that, and the fact that the woman was the baby's grandmother. When I finally talked to her, I forgot to ask the baby's name, so I can't look it up in the cemetery records. There aren't any Kellys listed in any of my books. I have no idea where the grave is located."

Kathy suggests, "Why don't you look under 'Bayman,' I think that might be the name of the-husband-before-last. I know he's buried up there. They brought a cemetery quit claim in here for me to notarize, before you took over the cemetery."

Just talking to Kathy is upsetting me all over again. I confide, "Even if I can figure out something from the records, I'm not ready to go up to the cemetery yet. Not alone. Maybe when my husband gets home from work. Daniel won't mind. I'm sure he'll go with me especially when he hears what is going on."

"The guy on the telephone really got to you, didn't he?" Kathy says.

I nod, then say, "I'm sure that is exactly what he intended to do. The trouble is I don't know what else he is capable of." As I say this, I feel my heart begin to beat faster. The man's rage was terrible: "I know where you live—you cunt . . . you fucking bitch. Pick up the phone you whore! I know you're up there. I can get up there in three minutes, you cock-sucking whore." Etc. etc.

Who says only sticks and stones can hurt? These words still ring in my ears, exactly as he spat them out. I gather my wits, look at Kathy and give what must be wan smile. "I guess it takes nerves of steel to be a cemetery sexton, all right, and I just may not be up to it."

"I'm really sorry this happened, Shannon." She rummages around her desk, finds what she wants, and writes down the name of a deputy who is on a different shift. "I think he'll be on after five o'clock. You might get further with this guy." She sighs, adding, "Well, now you know why the city didn't want the responsibility for the cemetery. Between dealing with the public and insurance liability stuff . . ." She trails off and glances at her watch, then folds her arms and grins. "But I've got to give it to your Dad. He kept on trying. I know it made The Colonel mad when the council kept turning him down. I'm not sure he's even speaking to the mayor these days."

According to letters in the cemetery files, the effort to carry out Aunt Hazel's will by formally conveying the cemetery to the city of Yoncalla, went on for at least ten years.

I name several of the towns around here whose city governments have taken the responsibility for various cemeteries. I do a little more venting. "Even when cousin Albert was the mayor, Dad couldn't get the city to take over the cemetery," I say, remembering how angry my father still gets every time the subject arises. At one point my father even threatened to sell the cemetery to anyone who would buy it. "Hell, let someone make it a pet cemetery . . . see how people like that!"

A few months ago, fed up, he told me that he was considering clear-cutting it, claiming that a timber cruiser had estimated the cemetery's trees at a value of forty thousand dollars. I'm still not sure whether Dad would ever have followed through with clear-cutting; it was a tactical maneuver. He wanted to ensure that his tree-hugging daughter would step up to the job of sexton. The Colonel has his ways.

In the meanwhile, he kept paying for the liability insurance and such maintenance as there was. In my opinion, he got on the wrong side of the city council right after Aunt Hazel died, and they never forgot it. Disgusted after the first two rejections, Dad contacted the Office of State Corporations and had the cemetery's name officially changed from Yoncalla Pioneer Cemetery to Applegate Pioneer Cemetery—an action that offended any number of local people.

"I think this town has got a thing against Applegates," I say, tucking the note with the other deputy's cell phone number on it into my pocket. It's Kathy's lunch hour now.

She pats my hand and says, "When they start up on you, just tell them what I tell them, 'Sit down and take a number!' "

I'm not really ready to go back to my house any more than I'm ready to go up to the cemetery. I can see our place in the distance as I swing onto Old Highway 99. Our big green barn has a look of feudal fastness, as though one could hole up in it, fending off the forces of darkness. The shoulder of the hill rises protectively behind the barn—backup, like a buddy in a tavern fight. But at the moment, the old bungalow, so in need of repair that we have dubbed it the "Tumblelow," seems insubstantial and not very comforting. It is merely a pale wink of white, with a red roof vulnerable at the lonesome end of a driveway off a dead-end road. I think, *He knows where I live.*

I turn around and decide to go see my cousin Rob Applegate who participated in the cleanup day. I want to tell him what has happened, and ask him whether he thinks I should register a complaint about the way the deputy I've spoken with is handling the situation.

On the way to Rob's I review things: In my favor, I immediately called the woman whose family grave was disturbed and apologized profusely. I explained that we had announced the "cleanup day" in the local paper, and that our new guidelines were published in the same issue. People were advised that we were going to be cleaning graves, and that if they didn't want us to, they could call us.

I also told her that we were trying to improve things in general. We intended to have some of the larger trees limbed, to fix potholes in the road and parking lot, and to spray blackberries and poison oak.

"Our intention was just to remove old plastic flowers and other grave decorations that looked as though they had been there a long while. We tried to be selective."

"You shouldn't have moved nothing!" the woman said angrily.

I remember telling her that most cemeteries have rules. The Masonic Cemetery has theirs posted on their cemetery gate, for example. I asked her if she would like me to send her the little brochure we've printed that describes the handful of guidelines we would like people to follow.

She ignored me; stuck instead to the subject of what had been "stolen from the grave."

"They was valuable articles—statues and things like that. A little blue horse, for one thing. And a bunny. They belong on my grandson's grave and we want them returned."

"If someone removed statues of any kind, I'm not aware of it," I said to her and apologized again.

Not for the first time, I mentally sort through the piles of junk we took to the refuse site: dozens of broken glass jars, all manner of trash, and plastic flowers so old that scientific experiments searching for miracle molds could have been conducted on them.

The last thing I said to the woman was, "Someone . . . I think it might have been your son . . . called me on the telephone a while ago. He screamed filthy things into my answering machine."

"Well, that's on account of . . . it was his boy. His baby. We buried him at the foot his grandfather's grave. We got permission," she said but couldn't remember from whom.

I told her that if I personally had seen the objects she described I would have left them where they were. But apparently, someone in our group picked them up.

I added, "We are all volunteers, including me. We are doing the best we can."

"Tell them to leave things on people's graves alone," she said refusing to be mollified.

"Tell your son not to call me again. Ever."

"Grave goods . . ." a friend, Mirra Meyer, who was an anthropology major in what she describes as "the mists of long ago," says later. "Look at the incident from that perspective."

A blue plastic horse from the toy department at Rite Aid or Wal-Mart? It's hard to think of a mass-produced My Little Pony toys in the same context as a ninth-century Viking ship, say, or an exquisitely carved and painted Northwest native canoe—both of which were buried, according to an article I've found, fully provisioned, so that their dead owners should want for nothing in the afterworld.

Superficially, a stuffed toy bunny seems light years away from the lapis lazuli inlaid chests and jewel-encrusted headdresses buried with noble Egyptians. More obscure, and more interesting to me, are the grave goods of the Scythians. These Indo-Iranian people had women warriors who were apparently encoffined in entire tree trunks and buried with lavish grave goods of gold and silver jewelry. Food-stuffs were not only buried beside them but even horses who sometimes wore their own felt headdresses that were made to resemble stag antlers. Armor, various weapons, eating utensils, ritual paraphernalia, and, occasionally, pounds of marijuana, apparently intended for smoking in the afterlife, were included in some Scythian graves.

Grave goods are universal. Cultures all over the world, and at all times, it seems, deposited various goods in their burials— usually things the dead person used while alive: shears and sickles, spindle whorls and needle cases, mortars and pestles, such as farmers have uncovered around here when plowing their fields. It seems local Kalapuya people deliberately broke a corner of the mortar bowl if it belonged to someone who had died. We have one of these in the Old Place my great-grandpa supposedly found in the oat field.

The nature of grave goods is a reflection of the social status of the buried individual as well as a window into the values of his or her culture. For example, during the four years when the

Spanish explorer Cabeza de Vaca, was held captive on the Gulf Coast of present-day Texas, he was impressed with the status accorded to children by their native parents. He wrote later that the Indians on Isla de Malhado "love their offspring more than anything in the world and treat them very mildly." He also recounted that when a child died, the whole settlement mourned, "the lament lasting a full year, day after day."

Childrens' and infants' graves excavated by twentieth-century archaeologists would seem to confirm de Vaca's impressions. Bone and stone tools, shell ornaments, whooping-crane bone whistles, and other grave goods were almost as plentiful in the graves of the young as they were in those of adult males, who, de Vaca observed, were the most important members of their society. The graves of married women, however, revealed a paucity of grave goods, suggesting that female status decreased dramatically after childhood.

And then there is the story of the grave goods found with an aboriginal Jaara infant, near Charlton, Australia. Wrapped in a possum-skin cloak, the dead infant was shaken from his resting place in a hollow tree trunk by an ax-wielding road builder in 1904. Following a well-publicized coroner's inquest, the bundle was sent to the Melbourne Museum where it was neatly catalogued before being placed in a specimen drawer. There it lay, untouched until 1994.

The bundle was remarkably preserved, and filled with an astonishing array of one hundred and thirty objects sprinkled with ochre-colored powder. These objects included an emu feather apron, necklaces, and even a tiny leather boot. The boot helped establish the fact that the baby had died during the period of white contact.

Because it is within the context of my own culture, I can imagine that leather boot, such a little thing, surely, but large in meaning. An emu apron, seems a more exotic artifact. Even so, I can easily understand how the small bundle that held the remains of the Jarra Baby came to symbolize the terrible, attenuated friction between Australian blacks and whites about what is sacred.

After long years of negotiations and changes in law, the museum finally agreed to return the baby's bones to the Djadja Wurrung people; but the museum wanted to retain the baby's grave goods because of their historical significance. For many years, grave goods have been the booty of museums all over the globe. It has finally been decided that Jarra Baby and its precious grave goods will eventually be returned to the Djadja Wurrung people, who, when that great day arrives, plan to play their didgeridoos, dance, and perform a traditional cleansing ceremony.

"The idea that you can separate the remains from the grave goods is repugnant and totally inappropriate," said the chairperson of the Aboriginal Heritage Board.

In my capacity as captain of the cemetery's Aesthetic Police Force, I am conducting an inspection tour this morning. I can see I have some more thinking to do: Are grave decorations and grave goods one in the same, or are they different?

In the United States, flowers and flags have long been the staples of grave decoration ever since 1868, the year when Decoration Day, now known as Memorial Day, was officially declared for veterans wanting to commemorate Civil War dead. In many cemeteries, including ours, groups such as the American Legion, or Veterans of Foreign Wars, sponsor the placement of American flags on the graves of all deceased servicemen. Correction: men and *women*. An elderly local man, Tip Wexler, brings small flags to our cemetery and places them on graves, including those of my identical twin aunties, Eva and Evea, who were army nurses in World War I. Tip also is responsible for removing the flags before the weather turns bad, although lately he hasn't been feeling well enough. This morning I notice a fair amount of flag fade. I hope Tip manages to get up here in advance of that other old man named Winter.

Plastic flowers, particularly our new age "immortelles" molded in industrial-strength colors, have been part of this cemetery's landscape for at least two decades. Nowadays, many people live far from relatives and may even be unaware of their great-grandparents', or even grandparents' burial sites. On the rare occasions when family members visit a cemetery, they want to feel they have left something enduring behind that shows somebody still cares. This is one rationale for buying fake flowers. Here is another: Fresh flowers cost too much.

I've got to face it. I'm never going to like plastic flowers. But I now realize that fact doesn't give me the right to forbid them; I am responsible for this cemetery but it is not "my" cemetery; it belongs to the people of the town of Yoncalla even if the city refuses to take care of it.

The guideline thing is obviously not working. "No temporary fences," we asked. "No outdoor carpets." I note that as we improve the cemetery, people seem to be a little more attentive to their plots. The downside is that by cleaning up things, we seem to have attracted even more plastic flowers and temporary fencing.

I guess this will be the standard: When things visibly deteriorate—as when last Christmas's fire-red plastic poinsettias turn pink—off with their heads. If people bring additional plastic flowers, wreaths, etc. for the holidays, when the next one comes around, decorations from the previous holiday will disappear into this sexton's large, also plastic, lawn bag. So much for grave decorations. Grave goods are a more complex issue I'm thinking, as I make my way over to the Masonic Cemetery that is on the other side of the parking lot.

At the Masonic, I find that grave goods are as plentiful as flat markers. This cemetery is now fairly close to what I think of as a "lawn" cemetery, but on a more modest scale. The Mason's have obviously expended considerable effort to make it this way. The flat markers make it easier for them to mow. Everything in this cemetery speaks to a more modern age. Here, wind chimes are ringing, and shiny Mylar pinwheels are whirring. Bright metallic and glass objects of almost every description are placed over many graves, along with garden statuary, framed photographs protected by Saran Wrap, and "country" cut-outs of swans, geese, angels, and puppy dogs all painted on plywood.

Friends tell me that cemeteries all over America are beginning to fill up with these latest incarnations of grave goods. Yesterday, I found a pack of football cards in a sandwich bag on a grave in our cemetery. Last month, I saw a five feet high plastic basketball hoop straddling a teenager's grave in a lovely old country churchyard outside of Portland. If I knew more cemetarians, I would doubtless hear even more stories.

In aggregate, I detest the tacky look of these things, the mishmash, the jumble. As far as I am concerned, what such modernday grave goods reveal is this culture's unabashed, indiscriminate materialism; its fixation with fads and obsession with sports.

Still, in a culture where values constantly shift, we do seem to have something in common with the sixteenth-century Indians of Isla de Malhado whom Cabeza de Vaca observed. Like those natives who once lived in today's Texas, we place a high value on children's lives, especially children who are our own. On the other hand, given the failure of school budgets, the dearth of children's medical care, and our societal hesitancy to invest in remedies for child neglect and abuse, our "love of children" does seem to have limits.

Here in the Masonic Cemetery as I move from grave to grave,

pausing at each one, what strikes me is the preponderance of grave goods left for children and infants.

Once, cemeteries were filled with infants, and even had sections referred to as "babies' corners." Today, there are far fewer infant graves. Perhaps because of this, they have a special poignancy in this culture, where we like to keep death distant from daily life.

Now I am looking down at the grave of a ten-year-old boy, who died just a little over a year ago; I find myself peculiarly moved by the things I see upon his grave. I realize suddenly I'm reminded of Edane, one of my grown daughters, who is still a devotee of the cartoon dog Scooby Doo—a love affair that began when she was ten years old. Little Ronnie must have liked him too, since there are a half dozen "Scoobies" here. There are two Scooby Doo's with bobbing heads. A flashy, highly-glazed ceramic Scooby, nearly a foot high, extends his forelegs around what used to be called a Dagwood sandwich (in honor of a cartoon figure from my own childhood.)

In contrast to these Scoobies, the others look worse for wear, as

though they have been through at least one wet winter. It appears that someone, maybe one of Ronnie's brothers or sisters—who may also have hand-painted several heart-shaped rocks, arranged across the grave—returns now and then, bringing new additions to refresh Ronnie's Scooby collection. Smaller, unpainted, heart-shaped rocks are heaped around the largest rock of all—the one that serves as Ronnie's headstone. Its blood-red writing with decorative gold squiggles says, in simple present tense, "You are loved."

What if I had a child who died, and all my resources had been sucked into a sinkhole of hospital expenses? What if I didn't have the two or three hundred dollars it costs these days to buy an average-sized headstone? As I examine this grave, with its glow-in-the-dark rubber snakes, and its sealed package of a rub-on tattoo of a cross and crown (the only "religious" symbols I see here), I can't escape the sense that something fundamental has changed in the manner in which many of us mourn our dead.

Our traditional ceremonies, especially our funerals, have failed us; Bible verses and platitudes spoken by some member of the clergy who may not have met the person we are grieving just doesn't cut it anymore. Hence, the tendency these days for memorial services with an informal feeling, rather than the somber funerals where the dead are enshrined before us in expensive caskets.

Lately I have been to several Celebrations of Life, where participation is appreciated and even expected. Get up and show your grief. Get up and tell us something about the dead that can make us cry or cheer us up. It is a memorial, and we want our memories tugged.

Culture is dynamic, ever collecting and discarding. We seem to be learning a thing or two from the Latino population these days. They are increasingly part of our culture showing us "gringos" a great deal about grieving. American cemeteries are reflecting Latino influence—love of family, passion, playfulness and color, bittersweet celebrations, such as *Día de los Muertos* (Day of the Dead), and an abiding love for "the departed ones," which includes leaving gifts on graves.

This is a perspective that helps me view these grave-top expressions of caring a little differently—with more respect and less judgment. Maybe I can train myself to watch the deterioration of these touchingly ephemeral grave goods with detachment. After all, the metaphor is clear: Over time, everything disintegrates, gradually disappears. Memories and memorabilia fade, and so do we.

Tenderness

Coyote said, "Oh it would be better . . . if people did come back, if they awakened on the fifth day." Cougar said, "No . . . when a person dies (from now on) he will . . . be dead for all time . . ." Coyote went back, he wept.

—Kalapuya Texts, Part III

I telephone Esther. I breathe in the spicy fragrance of incense cedar and fir needles from the gallon plastic bag I have just unzipped as I wait for her to answer. Through the Tumblelow's tall dining-room windows I watch silver streamers of rain flowing from over-full gutters.

It is potpourri-making time again. The air is filled with the heady redolence that announces the approach of the winter holidays, usually my favorite time of year, a season to make gifts for friends and family.

This morning, I walked down the hill to the Old Place and brought back several large hand-turned wooden bowls from one of the pie-safes. Great-Granddaddy Buck or Grandpa Paul, made these bowls. I also found a venerable oblong maple wood trencher that Great-Great-Grandfather Charley carved, the signs of the knife that carefully shaved its surface still visible. From my own pantry, there is a set of deep stainless steel bowls. A cat could sleep in the largest one.

Bowls both wooden and metal almost cover the top of our dining table; some are already brimming with blends of dried plant materials gathered by Esther and me throughout the year. The biggest bowl is heaped with lemon verbena leaves, tangy and sweet. Orange and yellow calendula petals collected from the herb garden down at the Old Place add color along with slivers of lemon peel. Ovular deep green leaves from the boxwood hedges bordering the front walk bring a bitter, but strangely pleasant smell to the mixture. Like so much in life, a contrasting note adds zest.

Esther's oldest granddaughter lisps, "This is Salista," into the telephone after several rings. "Just wait," she advises. "I'll go get my Nana." I follow her instructions, waiting and wondering just how many years Esther and I have been doing this. Three, no four now—before her Salista was born. We choose plants known to be useful to either Esther's ancestors or mine. A few, such as resin-laden Douglas fir needles, and heart-shaped leaves from the dainty, throat-soothing Yerba Buena vine were treasured by Indians and pioneers alike. Esther and I delight in knowing that her great-great grandmother Dunifo, and mine, Melinda Applegate, shared their knowledge of curative plants with each other. The potpourri we make each year has become a symbol of the connection between our peoples that we continue to foster and pass on to our own children, and now grandchildren.

One of the reasons I'm calling Esther is to ask whether or not

she has any more dried rose hips, since I have run out. Their cheerful flash of red enlivens the earthy range of greens, grays, and browns in the forest blend of Yerba Buena, moss, lichen, and conifer needles we call Green Feather.

In past years, just after the first hard frost, when rose hips are their ruddiest and highest in vitamin C content, we have clipped enough branches from naturalized sweet briers and native Nootka roses to see us into the next potpourri season. We hang these upside down and forget about them until the following year. The rose hips maintain their rich crimson color because they have dried slowly.

But last year was not a good rose hip season. Attempting to do in the ubiquitous blackberries along the road and on fence lines, the highway department also sprayed many wild roses with herbicides. This year I am resorting to sticking rose branches cut only a month or so ago into containers that I have placed close to the woodstove to hasten drying. Some hips are shriveling past beauty and others are turning dark as old blood.

I'm feeling a bit dark as I force myself to do all the things that go along with this particular season. I may want rose hips, but what I need is a long talk with an old friend. Esther's perspective is always valuable. Perhaps, she will burn some sage and say a blessing for my brother, Rex.

I'm breathing in and breathing out, feeling the gift of it. In a few moments I will doff rain gear and go to the shed to bring back a load of firewood in my blue wheelbarrow. I could make numerous trips back and forth—three or four in row with my wheelbarrow loaded to the proverbial gills, if I wanted to. Without getting winded I could run up and down the hill between the Tumblelow and the Old Place several times—a distance of 300 yards or so—and still sing a song.

Inhale, exhale. I feel my own vigor guiltily, as I imagine Rexito, six-feet one, twelve years younger than I, full of charm, intelligence and hustle, breathing oxygen through nose tubes and lying on a hospital bed in the M.D. Anderson Cancer Center in Houston, Texas.

Until yesterday, we all thought it was pneumonia and exhaustion. I've received and placed umpteen phone calls in the past twenty-four hours, all concerning Rex and his condition. I imagine these exchanges as black threads crisscrossing the usual borders of our family map, reaching from Oregon, to Arizona, to Texas, and back again, always converging in a dark, sticky web of relationships in Houston. I have spoken with a whole cast of characters, each shocked and worried: my mother and my father, who are long divorced; each of Daniel's and my six grown children; two stepmothers; not to mention several talks with my sister; and even Rexito's fiancée, whom I have never net.

I last spoke with my brother on Thanksgiving. Now he can barely speak at all; now, we all know he has lung cancer. Death is literally breathing down Rexito's neck.

Yet here I am on the telephone again, when part of me wishes I could just disconnect from everyone. But the other part hates to be alone today. Talking is better than just waiting for the results of more tests to be relayed. Yet talk is also distressing. My discussion with Dad, for example, is extremely difficult. He keeps downplaying the condition of his only son and namesake, saying things like, "Rex can beat this. They have probably caught it early. Rex is only forty."

"Rex is forty-one," I told him, two or three hours ago.

"Well, whatever he is," Dad said, "I intend to sit tight right here. I'll go to Houston only when it's absolutely necessary—*if* it's necessary. I won't be pushed into anything by a bunch of hysterical women."

But for some reason, at least at this moment, I'm feeling calm. A bit depressed, a bit distracted, disjointed, but calm. I notice there is ringing, a chiming almost, in my ears, a kind of inner-space sound that happens when I'm tense. Esther finally comes to the phone. I hear her murmuring to Salista as she picks up the receiver.

Over the long years of our friendship, Esther's and my personal lives have centered upon our families, especially our children. We have also cared for our elders in myriad ways but have only lately absorbed the fact that some younger people now consider Esther and I elders. "Elder": two letters more to "elderly."

"Hey, can you believe how old we're getting?" is my greeting to Esther. She laughs and tells me, "Like I always say, I'm happy about it. For one thing, being an elder means you are at the front of the food line at pow-wows." At social gatherings at her house, the same rule applies. When Indian friends are around, no one is coy about age if he or she wants first crack at what is best on the table.

Before I can ask her about rose hips, Esther says, "I can only talk for a minute, dear. I'm up to my neck in papers from my files, trying to get ready to testify at the meeting in Cottage Grove tonight. We're talkin' *burials*," by which she means Indian burials.

Developers are ready to heave-ho a significant part of Mount David in Cottage Grove and Esther is speaking out against a proposed housing division on the Kalapuya people's behalf. Historically, the Yoncalla/Kommena group was the southernmost branch of the twelve bands of the Kalapuya tribe, and Esther has come to be recognized as one of the top leaders of the Kalapuya people.

Indian graves are believed to exist in the general vicinity of Mount David, and although all Native burials are now federally protected under the Native American Graves Protection and Repatriation Act (NAGPRA), activists in Cottage Grove want to avoid the accidental disturbance of graves and to officially underscore the importance of Mount David as a sacred site. Lately, Esther has been spending a lot of time researching and testifying before the planning commission, city council, and other groups.

"It's pretty strange when you think about it, Stutz," I say, using the nickname I've had for her for more than twenty-five years. "How does it happen that we both find ourselves dealing with burials, these days? It certainly isn't everyone's lot in life. How the hell did we get here?"

"You mean tending?" she asks in that quiet, firm voice of hers. "This part of the cycle is all about tending, you know that." She sighs and adds more softly, "When you think about it, this has always been the way for us women. We are tenders of the young and old."

"And now, the dead as well," I add before I say good-bye.

"I'll call you back in an hour or so," she promises. "I want to hear about how your brother's doing. Maybe I can even come over later before I head north for the meeting. I have some more lavender for the potpourri I forgot to give you yesterday."

"What about rose hips?"

"Nope," she answers. "Sorry."

I hang up and shiver, not only from cold. I am thinking about the word "tender." I let it roll around, first as an adjective, then, a verb. Gradually "tender" takes on nuances unconsidered until now. I can't bring myself to go outside to the woodshed, yet. To be a "tender" of someone or something requires attention, and commitment. Patience and tenacity are often necessary. And time, time, time. "Not enough of . . ." an inner voice says. "Is running out. . . ." I say aloud.

I rummage through the drawer of the telephone stand where I keep odds and ends and candles of various sizes. I choose one that is wine red and light it for my brother Rex, placing it on top of the bookcase in the living room. I am standing still for a moment, my arms folded over my breasts, still thinking about the word "tender" and watching the wavering candle flame that answers the invisible chill slipping under the front door of our crooked little house.

I try to rouse myself. I need some firewood. But I don't go. Instead, I pull my thick volume of *Partridge's Etymological Dictionary* from the bookcase. "Tender: From Latin, *tendere*, 'to stretch'; thin, finely drawn, hence weak, vulnerable as in a tender shoot." My even heftier *Oxford's* adds, "easily touched or wounded; susceptible to grief."

Finally, I tug on my rain boots, put on my hooded jacket. I pass the dining-room table and find myself stopping again, stalling out, in front of one of the smaller bowls, absently sifting star anise, cloves, and slivers of orange peel through my fingers. Maybe there is something to this aromatherapy stuff I decide, inhaling fragrances that evoke the season's essence. I feel a little lift as I pluck up crinkled crescents of orange and deliberately crush them between my fingers. Bits of color glow now in the warm browns of anise stars, nubbly cloves, and broken sticks of cinnamon. I blend all these with the contents in the largest bowl on the table; a bowl half full of bluish balsam tips and inch-long snips of branches from last year's Christmas tree, a fragrant Noble fir that keeps on giving.

It comes to me: Yuletide begins right now, at this very instant. I am making merry, or trying to. Letting it spill through my fingers.

Already this season is a mixture of mystery and terrible knowing. I have to live it moment to moment. But there is this I can count upon: Deep tenderness there will be.

Esther Stutzman has been involved with burials and cemeteries much longer than I have. I remember seeing a picture of her in a local newspaper when we were both living on the Oregon coast in the mid-1970s. She had braids to her waist and back then was truly raven-haired. Today, we call her Skunk Woman because of the stunning contrast between white hair and black.

Did she actually have on a flak jacket in that newspaper picture or was it simply that her stance conveyed militancy? I remember thinking that she was someone formidable as I looked at the picture of her glowering, standing hip high in a ditch, a backhoe visible in the background. A sewer line was being cut through an ancient Native burial ground near Charleston, Oregon, and she and other Indians (the term she prefers) were watching the construction and protesting.

At that time, state laws concerning the disturbance of graves and theft of burial objects were weaker than they are today, and largely untested. Federal laws protecting archaeological sites on public lands weren't passed until 1979.

It was still possible in the early 1970s to walk into a certain museum on the Oregon coast and see an Indian skull on "display"—

as the old ladies running the museum referred to it. The badly typed exhibit caption explained that the perforation in the right temple was the work of a settler's gun pressed into service during a "massacre." The Indians, of course, were at fault.

Laden with symbolism, the human skull has often served in emblematic ways. The skull's appearance is easily generalized. Looking pretty much the same, it has appeared on flags, rings, crests, countless other objects sacred and profane, and in countless works of art beginning with cave drawings. Perhaps this is one reason why it is easy for some people to think about a skull as an artifact rather than as an individual. Still, just as each face is one of a kind, so is each skull. For example, the series of lines that resemble rivers on a topographical map, and trace the places where cranial sections connect, are slightly different in every human being.

After Esther and I became friends, she told me about her feelings concerning the skull "on display" at the museum—a frequent "field-trip" choice throughout her school years. As a woman, empowered by Indian activism, she revisited the museum, asking the curator for the skull so that she and other tribal members in the region could give it a proper burial.

"I was always aware that that skull could have been one of my relatives," she said. The museum refused to release any local Indian artifacts in its collection, including the skull, regardless of the fact that it was widely known that many objects had been plundered from graves.

Even when Esther wrote a series of letters to the Board of Directors and returned to the museum accompanied by a university archaeologist with impressive credentials the answer was the same. When she next visited the museum the skull was no longer exhibited, but the elderly woman whom Esther privately called "Blue Hair," claimed the skull had been misplaced. Since it could not be located it was impossible to return it to the tribe.

"I still wonder what that old lady did with it," Esther said recently. "Now, that the law is in our favor (the Native American Graves Protection and Repatriation Act passed in 1990) Blue Hair could find herself in trouble. She's dead by now, and I hope her relatives are treating her better than she treated mine. Or maybe I don't."

Since Esther and I were both directors of small museums about forty miles apart during the 1970s it was probably inevitable that our paths would cross. Her father was a Coos Indian from what is known today as the Coos Bay region. She ran a newly established museum in a tribal hall and I was the first curator, then director, of a small museum in Bandon, a resort town further down the coast.

Our fate was intertwined long before the 1970s, however, without our realizing it: When we had already been good friends for a decade or more we discovered that Esther's mother's people were part of the Yoncalla band of the Kalapuya. Her great-great-grandfather, Chief Halo (as he was known by settlers), welcomed the three Applegate families into the valleys where Esther and I now make our homes some one hundred and fifty years later.

When I fume over cemetery litter, worry about how historic headstones will be repaired that young vandals toppled and cracked in the 1980s, I despair over the lack of respect some people have for our cemetery and cemeteries in general. Then I think about the condition of Esther's ancestral burying ground that is unmarked, and only a few miles from here.

Halo, or more properly, Kamafeema, which is his Kalapuyan name, is buried beside some of his relatives on an oak-clad hill on a large acreage currently "caretaken" by a toothless crazy whom we suspect of making methamphetamines in his dilapidated trailer. Despite him, and others who have lived near the burial site over the years, nothing indicates graves have ever been disturbed. Esther and others watch the property carefully. If it were financially possible she would buy the whole valley; once beautiful, now subdivided, and clear-cut within an inch of its life.

Years ago, I heard a story about the family who were the second or third owners of the property. They knew the location of Halo's cemetery and deliberately placed their chicken coops over it. I have never understood whether this was a sign of their disrespect or whether they imagined they were somehow protecting the graves. Probably, it was the former.

Kalapuyans, according to Esther, like many other Native people, traditionally did not visit their cemeteries except when they needed to bury someone. The most important factor was to leave the body undisturbed and on its original site.

As Esther put it to me once, "We know Halo's bones are there; should his spirit wish to visit, as long as no one bothers the bones, the spirit has a home to return to. Other people will not be bothered."

Many Native people, she went on to say, believe that in order for the spirit of a dead person to enter the next world, his human remains must stay intact. To have a body without a skull, or any other part is a terrible thing. "That is why what happened at Sand

Creek in Colorado and Little Big Horn in South Dakota and in other places during battles with the whites is so hard to put behind us," she explained.

In the aftermath of those bloody confrontations, when Indians returned to gather their dead, they found insult had been added to injury: White soldiers, well aware of Native beliefs concerning entry into the next world, mutilated and dismembered corpses, deliberately intermingling and scattering body parts.

But didn't Esther think it was important to place a monument on her ancestors' graves, I wondered, envisioning some sort of interpretative marker that might be placed in the future.

"If we mark the burials, what's going to happen?" She shook her head emphatically as she answered her own question, "A bunch of white people, who think its cool to collect arrowheads, beads, or other things will just start digging around."

Indian people know that despite new laws, artifact hunters are still brazen and willing to take risks. In the mid-1980s, an Oregon man plundered two ancient basket burials of Paiute children which had been secreted with a cache of grave goods in a Nevada desert cave for at least a thousand years. Later, after scrubbing the rare burial baskets with a household cleaner, he placed them in his living room—a veritable gallery of Indian artifacts illicitly obtained by years of looting. He buried the children's remains, minus skulls, in a corner of his Grants Pass, Oregon garden. Later, he told his associates that what made his sunflowers grow so well was his special "Indian fertilizer."

When these matters were finally revealed in the 1990s and charges were brought against him, he was found guilty. Recently, this conviction was overturned by the appeals court.

The man has announced plans to link his Web page to eBay so that he can continue to sell arrowheads and other artifacts. The skulls are still missing, and some speculate that they have already been sold on one of the many Internet sites supported by a thriving global market trading in illegal Native American antiquities.

A number of U.S. artifact dealers specialize in bones; among them, an Oklahoma vender who calls his company "Skulls Unlimited." It is not illegal to buy, possess, or sell human bones, other than those of Native Americans. In the last few years there has been a brisk business selling the remains of third world people. Human skulls are still the most sought after item among collectors.

Collecting human remains in the United States is nothing new, of course. It has been an official, and unofficial pastime at least since the 1850s. As late as 1897, the Field Museum in Chicago was still sending expeditions to plunder the graves of Native Oregonians.

Years ago, when working on a research project, I heard the story that when Kintpuash—a famous Modoc chieftain known as Captain Jack—was hanged by officials in 1873, his corpse was decapitated by an army surgeon. Kintpuash's head, swimming in preservatives in a lead-lidded jar, was supposedly shipped off to Washington, D.C., where it remained for many years until it "disappeared" from the collection of an unnamed museum, perhaps the Smithsonian, formerly known for its stores of human remains.

Recently, I learned from an acquaintance in the parks' service that the body of the highly respected Nez Perce leader, Chief Joseph, originally buried in the late nineteenth century, is sans skull. The story goes that well into the 1940s an Idaho dentist used the skull as an ashtray in his office and bragged about it.

These stories are both appalling and unprovable, still what can be proven is that when Native peoples and others were lobbying for the passage of NAGPRA the skeletal remains of more than a half-million Aboriginal people from various parts of the world were still held in public and private collections. At least twenty thousand of these remains in the Smithsonian's collections were identified as Native Americans eligible for repatriation to appropriate tribes under NAGPRA.

As Native people are permitted to reclaim their dead and treat them as their custom dictates, some scientists, including any number of bio-archaelogists, decry the loss of research materials. Some archaeologists I have spoken with argue that the study of human bones can help reconstruct demographic populations of prehistoric peoples. Aboriginal health and nutritional issues can be better understood. For example, cavities in teeth indicate dietary changes.

But an old friend of Esther's and mine, an archaeologist employed by the U.S. Bureau of Land Management, puts the issue of who owns the bones of the past succinctly enough. "What are you gonna' do?" Isaac Barner says. "The remains are always someone's relatives." For the most part, he comes down on the side of the Native people. He understands their concerns as well as the depredations of the past.

Still, he admits that the study of some remains have the potential to address broader issues, such as entry into the new world. "Where did people come from?"

He feels a certain amount of ambivalence concerning scientific access to perhaps the most famous set of bones uncovered in America in recent times: those of the more than nine thousand year old Kennewick Man, whose partial skeleton was found by a pair of college boys in the muddy shallows of the Columbia River in 1996, and whose fate has been the focus of numerous court fights between Native Americans and members of the scientific community ever since.

In the course of one of our presentations, when Esther and I visited Umatilla elders on their reservation last year, in whose traditional lands the Kennewick Man was discovered, we learned firsthand how the Confederated Tribes in the region felt about things: The "Ancient One" was not an archaeological resource, but a human being. As one of their leaders said, "When a body goes into the ground, that is where it's to remain until the end of time."

It is now the third day of this terrible waiting, and I am getting ready to leave for Portland in honor of Julian's second birthday. No grandmother in her right mind would miss that, and I can worry just as well about Rexito in Portland as I can here.

I have packed several small baskets filled with various pot-pourri mixtures to deliver to kindred up north. Loading up the car, I realize I have enough gear for a trip to Tasmania. On my way out of town I plan to take Esther's share of the potpourri to her house.

First I will need to head to the cemetery though, I remind myself, since I need to see if the grave was dug for the old fellow who died a few days ago, and to make sure our recent storm hasn't landed huge tree limbs across the access to the grave where people, probably some of them elderly, will be walking when they attend his graveside service tomorrow.

I call Daniel at the office to say good-bye. Then I call Dad to tell him I'm leaving and to give him the number of a friend's apartment where I can be reached at night.

The phone rings just once. "Yes . . . Colonel Applegate," Dad's voice seems strained, muffled even. Clearly, he is sitting next to the telephone. Perhaps, he is expecting a call from someone else.

My message is brief and so is his, though his is charged with pain. He tries to sound matter-of-fact. "I'm going to Houston," he says. "Rex has indicated he doesn't want to do the chemotherapy bit. It's pretty bad, I guess. They tell me now is the time to see him. The Cat Woman is going with me," he finishes, referring to my friend and stepmother, Carole.

"I'm sorry," I say, feeling my stomach constrict. I'm feeling sorry about everything but especially for him, at this moment; for the choked up sound in his voice that he cannot hide.

"Sorry doesn't do anything, does it?" he says without heat, as though plucking at the first thing that has come to mind. It sounds like something he heard as a kid, an automatic reference that fills in conversational space where there is room enough to drown.

He mutters, "Just a minute," and comes back with his travel itinerary that he reads aloud and wants me to write down.

His voice is close to normal, full of imperative. "Did you ever do anything about that cemetery plot I set aside for your cousin Roger and Rexito, like I told you to? Is it on your books?"

"Yes," I answer.

"Well, as soon as the weather is better I want that cement curbing done. I've contacted a fellow down here." His usual practicality is kicking in and is soon followed by fierceness. "I'll tell you one thing. I am not going to argue with people in Texas about this. It's simple. Rexito is coming back here, and that's the end of it."

There is a long pause. I hear his ragged breathing. He clears his throat. I imagine the tears in his eyes. "I'm waiting for another call," he finishes. "I'll keep in touch."

"I love you, Daddy." There's silence on the other end.

Breathing in Bosnia

*. . . [T]hese are the lessons of Bosnia that have stayed with
me and perhaps, have altered me. The wild beast is out there
and the ground no longer feels steady under my feet.*

—Peter Maas

I have always thought of my father as larger than life, but I see
now he is not larger than death. This thought comes to me as
I am driving back from his house on the Umpqua River, as
images of our shared afternoon reel like frames of old silver-
nitrate film stock, the kind that catches fire when improperly
handled.

It was partly the setting of our conversation—the room, a
building actually—that left me feeling uneasy: Dad's "annex" filled
with riot control gear, bomb baskets he'd patented, shelves filled
with fighting knives, drawers in wall-to-wall cabinets holding

handguns, Wild West fancy shooter posters, Masai shields, sev-
ered animal heads hanging on walls with African skins. "Lions,
tigers, and bears," I want to chant these dangers, like Dorothy
going into the woods in Oz on my way to see the wizard behind the
curtain, my father behind his vast desk, restless in his swivel chair.

This is the same room where I taped the interviews I have
been working on for the past few years—my father's life of
more than eighty years on six cassettes. Or at least, the part of
his life that has to do with his experiences as a boy and young
man. Others, and even he, himself, have chronicled his military
career during WW II and his experiences during the late 1960s
when he first came into prominence as a nationally recognized
expert on riot control. But he tells me things that transcend the
"official" version: how he spiked the punch at the Women's
Temperance Union meeting in the basement of the Yoncalla
Methodist Church when he was a teenager; how working on
the road crew with his father, Paul, in the 1930s to earn college
money he witnessed a den of baby rattlesnakes being blown
clear to smithereens—the air wriggling with them in dark wavy

lines, falling on hats and car hoods, as a huge boulder was blasted to build Highway 38 clear to the coast.

Showing a mixture of irony and mild contempt for the interviewing process, Dad used to ask rhetorically, "Well, are we going to work on 'posterity' again today?" That was six months ago, before his only son died; back when he still seemed to be enjoying reviewing the highlights of his early life.

"Better get the stuff while he's still sharp," his publisher said to me several years ago on the occasion of Dad's seventy-fifth birthday. "You'll need it when you write his biography." Not I. It's not for me to do. I am too close. Still I am doing my part to preserve an historic record that I would willingly share with others. And I have felt closer to my father in the process, the hours slipping by in a kind of rare absorption, just the two of us.

But today was all business, the two of us sitting surrounded by weaponry in the big room where the windows are covered and barred, where heads of elands and moose hang on wood-paneled walls, looking down gravely with unseeing brown glass eyes. Phone calls kept interrupting our conversation. He had changed his will, he said. There were practical matters to discuss. And after that, just as I was about to leave, he shot one last question. "Have you ordered the stone yet?" He meant Rexito's headstone. He may not have remembered that he asked the same question when I arrived. Rexito: the headstone and footstone of our conversation, of my father's and my relationship, in fact, these past months. It was as close as we got to his grief.

I wanted to speak with Carole privately, so I asked her to show me her new kittens; after we walked the runs and discussed her cat-breeding business, I asked her about Dad. I am so grateful she is my friend, as well as stepmother—that she is always forthright.

"I think he's a little better," she said. "I don't catch him sitting and staring into space like he did the first month or two. But he's busy. Too busy! It drives me wild. The fax machine starts ringing sometimes before four A.M. He gets calls *all day long!* People ordering the new knife, or one of his videos, or wanting him to write an article on point shooting, show up at some gun show or other, or make a speech. Honestly, I don't know how he can keep this up. It just doesn't quit. And of course there's a lot of back and forth about Rexito's affairs. He's still arguing about the funeral expenses that outfit in Houston charged. As you can imagine, it's taken quite a bit just to get the ashes sent." I knew that Rexito's fiancée originally intended to bring them to Oregon herself, and then her plans changed.

Then Carole described how, a week ago, she and Dad made the two-hour drive north to Eugene and went to the airport Federal Express office to pick up the box containing half of Rexito's cremated remains. "Of course, someone had to sign for them—Rex Applegate signing for Rex Applegate II."

She continued: "Rexito always signed his letters to us Rex II, you know. I was driving, while Rex just sat there, holding Rexito on his lap in a box. I thought he might want to talk to me about it but he didn't. I asked him if he wanted to stop for lunch, he said he wasn't hungry. He just sat there . . . all the way home. I felt so sorry for him. But you know your father . . ."

Suddenly, I want to cry. I think of my own grown children, Jessica, Colin, Ione, Max, Edane, and Katherine. I think of my new grandson, wiggly baby Julian who regularly warms my lap and never got to meet his great-uncle, Rexito. Still, Julian went with Jessica to both the Houston funeral and then, a month or so later, to Tucson, for a memorial gathering given by Adela, Rexito's heartbroken mama. There, a mariachi band played the song Rexito once strummed for me on a borrowed

guitar when he was fourteen years old: "Cielito Lindo"—
beautiful heaven.

We are all exhausted by death. But Dad wants a memorial
service here, now that Rexito's ashes have finally arrived. Now
that Rexito is on Oregon soil, so that he can become Oregon soil.

This is a reality still hard for me to take: Part of Rex will be in
Oregon; the rest of him will be placed in the crypt of his mother's
people in a Mexico City cemetery.

"Lisha," I asked my sister when I heard of this arrangement,
reached after attenuated family negotiations, "how do you feel
about all this?"

"Well, Rexito and I both come from these two cultural streams,
you know, Sister. Each of them needs to be acknowledged. But
I'll probably end up being the one who takes the rest of Rex to
Mexico. Mother won't be able to handle it. I don't think she will
ever get over this."

What a tangle American families are these days: multiple mar-
riages and divorces; whose child is it, most? To whom does all
that remains of that child belong? Which parent, which side of
the family? Which cemetery?

Lisha and I try to be a bridge. Being close is not a matter of
genetics to us, but a matter of choice. Sometimes it takes work
to be "whole" sisters instead of half sisters. Rexito, Lisha, and I
didn't meet until both of them were teenagers and I was in my
late twenties. Lisha and I had an immediate affinity. Rexito was
harder for me to know. Perhaps I was jealous. Dad finally had
the son he had always wanted back in his life after years of
estrangement.

For her part, Lisha once told me that there was always "a
Shannon" in her life. "Your picture was on our living room wall
when I was little; I knew you were out there, Big Sister. I knew
your name from the time I was beginning to talk."

I have just realized I have been participating in the preparation of my own gravesite. A few moments ago, I spoke to a company about delivering dirt to the new extension of our main family plot. The cement border is finally finished surrounding a dozen potential gravesites intended for our generation. We need at least two more truckloads of dirt to level off the site. When we bury Rex's ashes—the "cremains" as people in the funeral industry call them—he will be all alone; the first in our generation to die. He will wait for the rest of us to join him.

I was surprised by the texture, weight, and color of the first cremains I ever experienced directly: My friend Penny Anderson's partner, Les Simon, blew into my hair on the day we scattered him from the top of Mount Scott. I think I even tasted the neutral grayish grit of Les. Drolly comedic, Les would have enjoyed my consternation and laughed as we all tried to give him the "brush off" after the wind picked up.

Yesterday, I called a local monument company to ask when Rex's stone would be ready. I forgot to take a copy of the order with me to the river to show Dad. Therefore, he insisted I call him and read it to him over the telephone, which I did earlier this morning. In matters like this, and lately there are a veritable slew of them, he addresses me as if I were his secretary. When I was twenty-six, newly divorced with two small children and a doubtful future, he wanted me to go to secretarial school. That, he said, would solve my problems. Get a skill. Everyone needs a secretary.

Today, I feel secretarial. Something of my father's organizational style has, over the years, rubbed off on me. My life, like his, is arranged in various manila folders. The fat file in front of me on the dining table, containing copies of all of Rexito's faxes sent over recent years, is one Dad gave me. He wrote "Rex II" on the front of the folder with a red indelible marker. Beside it are other folders upon which I've written things like "Revised Will and Testament," "Headstone Info," etc.

There are but two pieces of paper in the slim file marked Headstone Info. One, torn from a tablet, contains notes I jotted down while investigating varieties of stones handled by a local company as I spoke with a company representative on the telephone, last week. The other is smaller—a yellow duplicate of the order form for Rexito's headstone: "Carnelian 12'' x 24'' x 4'' Rock Pitch Sides: no design. Letters and numbers are polished. Sandblast around them in panel line. $384.00 plus installation."

Dad is adamant. He says he wants everyone to match. He told me to be sure to order *exactly* the same type of granite that has been used for other headstones in our family plot which contains all of the descendents of Great-Grandfather George (Buck) Applegate. The woman at the monument company told me that just asking for a red granite headstone wasn't sufficient: there were several types of red granite available. She would need to visit the cemetery with her sample book and make comparisons.

When we met at the cemetery she commented on the fact that all of our graves were oriented in the traditional Christian manner and noted that some cemeteries were moving away from the practice. She said she hoped we were not considering changing orientation in our newer section.

Beginning in Christian times heads were oriented to the west, and feet to the east, which is why, she explained, in places like Wales, the east wind is sometimes described as the "the wind at the dead man's feet." On Judgment Day, as Christ appears at dawn in the east, Christians are supposed to rise from their positions on their backs and stand facing Him.

I later found myself wondering about cremated remains. How

would anyone know where the head and feet were exactly? I realized also I didn't know anything about Rexito's spiritual beliefs but suspected he wouldn't care which way his own or any other grave was placed, or what parts of him we were burying in Oregon.

The woman's sample book contained numerous examples of tiles made from slim squares of granite and must have weighed twenty-five pounds. We took turns carrying it. Still, I was glad we decided to walk rather than drive to our uppermost family plot because the woman was friendly and very informative. She explained that wives, for example, were usually buried on the left side of their husbands—"the heart side," she said.

When we finally arrived at our destination, we admired the view and then spent ten minutes or so walking among the family headstones. Finally, after comparing shades of granite we settled on what her sample book called Carnelian from a South Dakota quarry, although a sample named Red Wassau from Wisconsin was quite similar.

When my father insisted that all of our stones be fashioned as alike as possible and that the shades of granite match, I concluded that he was applying his military sense of precision; things in his eyes are better, somehow, when uniform or part of a predictable pattern. For example, he called his first dog Kim. Several dogs thereafter, of different breeds and temperaments, bore the same name.

Why shouldn't Rex's stone be unique and an expression of his taste and personality, I wondered. In other parts of the cemetery there are many Applegate headstones in diverse sizes and shapes. Some are marble, others are granite, and one family stone is a tall, irregularly shaped local rock that maintains its natural contours. Anyone buying a cemetery plot up here does not have to think exclusively in terms of monuments flush to the ground, as is the case with many modern cemeteries that put easy maintenance before personal expression. Here, we don't have restrictions on shape or height. Dad is imposing unnecessary limitations.

But there is another way to look at this: Perhaps Dad's desire for similarity springs, at least partially, from other motives. As a family, we have a special corporality—a "body" from the same Latin root as the word "corpse." The "body"—the family itself— is the whole of which we all are parts. We are literally *members* of this body, representing portions or limbs of the family corpus. In our choice of headstones, Dad wants to *re*-member—to emphasize that each person in our family group is part of a whole.

The fact that all along Dad has felt so passionately that Rexito's remains belong in Oregon is surely part of this urge to re-member, to put back what has been torn asunder by circumstance. Rexito never lived in Oregon as he *should* have, but he'll be here now. His burial here is a kind of a symbolic return to ancestral soil.

"For Christ's sake," I can hear my father muttering in my mind. "Where do you come up with these ideas?"

Even so, I think I'm right. I think I probably know more than my father does on this subject. Many people, gone for years, want to be "returned" to a family cemetery for burial. Recently, a man who had traveled most of his adult life, had never lived in Oregon, but learned that distant relatives were buried in our cemetery, was thrilled to buy a plot here. He had tears in his eyes when he gave me the check. He evidently felt connected with a family he hadn't known in his life but would rest beside in death.

My friend Kit Sibert, who recently visited Cuba where she lived until she was a teenager, told me that the only private property Cubans in exile are permitted to own are family cemetery plots. Is this someone's idea of dark humor, or an acknowledgment that

Death's dominion is inviolable despite revolutions? Perhaps in Cuba it is understood that even exiles have a right to be buried next to their kin despite political differences and years away from one's native land.

Historically, many cultures have given special rights to the owners of burial plots. The ancient Romans, for example, whose laws typically favored property owners, nevertheless underscored the sacrosanctity of cemeteries. If land where a cemetery was located was purchased, the new owner was legally obligated to give access to descendents of the dead buried there even as generations passed. More than two thousand years ago Roman laws were more enlightened on the subject of people's sense of connection to their dead than laws in most states today.

Both the Greeks and Romans believed that the bodies of their dead belonged in the family cemetery regardless of where the dead had fallen. Greeks required that their slain warriors be cremated on the battlefields where funeral pyres were erected as soon as the fighting stopped. It was so important that a Greek soldier be buried in his home soil with appropriate ceremony that even though a military campaign might last for years, the charred bones of the dead soldier would eventually be brought back to Athens literally or metaphorically "upon his shield." Once, when a victorious Greek general succeeded in protecting Athens from "despoilers" but failed to burn bodies of fallen warriors on the battlefield and instead hurried back to collect his laurels, angry Athenians banded together and succeeded in having him executed.

Maybe my father thinks of bringing Rexito's remains to Oregon in the same way. Dad, a lover of military history, surely knows the protocol of ancient armies. He has never said so but I'm certain he thinks of his only son as a fallen warrior—an exhausted and disillusioned corporation patriot who saw too much of the world, especially the third world, for his own good.

Initially though, Dad reveled in Rexito's "tours of duty" for Brown & Root Services Corporation—a construction-and-engineering subsidiary of Halliburton, the world's largest oil-and-gas services company. In five years, Rex wrote, he served in "as many military theaters." He worked in Kuwait, Somalia, Rwanda, Haiti, and Bosnia-Herzegovina.

In the front of the Rex II folder I pluck up my brother's most recent résumé. As "deputy project manager" for various Brown and Root assignments, it states that he frequently distributed as much as three million dollars cash per week to pay for services in countries where banks and other infrastructures were nonexistent in the wake of war.

I feel worn out from today but also restless and irritable, as though the night in front of me won't offer much respite. I've shooed the cat from my lap and am about to close the folder and head for bed when I see a Telefax message Rexito sent from the Sheraton Hotel in Frankfurt, Germany, a few years ago. It is the Sheraton logo that catches my eye. The message reads, "Col. Rex Applegate from Rex II: Dad, I am off for more fun in the African sun. Rwanda/Zaire/Uganda. Do not know where I will be exactly, yet, or when I'll be back . . ."

But it is a remark my brother once made that rings in my ears as I make my way to bed. "Sis, it's like this—I work for the biggest undertaker in the world."

What I have is a case of survivor's guilt, I realize, as I pull myself from the night currents, where things swim after me. I get up and put on my robe, chilled from a dream in which Dad was standing on the shore of the Umpqua River near his house calling out Rexito's name. I know the full depth of what I am about to say: Dad could have more easily lost Lisha or me.

I don't want to be left with this terrible feeling of distance from my brother, my grief so mixed with other emotions that when I cry there is a tightness in my chest, a choked feeling. How can I get closer to this man who should not have died so young, whom I should have known better, should have written to, should have, should have. . . .

"Yeah, Sis, it's a helluva way to see how the other half lives. I have a front row seat." He said this the last time we ever talked at any length: on the night before Jessica's wedding, as we sat on the front porch steps of the Old Place. He had a cigarette in one hand and a beer in the other and we were alone in the twilight, looking out upon family fields ranched for almost 150 years.

I remember thinking that my little brother was looking older, every bit of his forty years. He went on: "I've got all these stories, and no one wants to hear them. Really, I'm not kidding. None of my friends want to hear them for Christ sakes. *No one wants to hear them, not even me.*"

What was going on in my mind as he said this? I surely knew that immediately following the wedding, Rex was returning to Bosnia. I remember that I was tired, exhausted nearly, with wedding preparations. Maybe I was wondering if I should get all of the bread cut for the brushchetta that evening or wait until the following day. Or perhaps I was worrying whether there would be enough champagne to go around for two hundred people when the time came for my brother to make the corny west Texas congratulatory toast he was planning for the bride and groom.

Here is the sore place: I didn't say "Rex, tell me. Talk to me." I wasn't listening either.

Less than a year after that evening on the porch in the place we both loved, Rexito and thousands of other Brown and Root employees were laid off as management of the parent company, Halliburton, changed under a new "streamlining" CEO—

ex-secretary of defense, Dick Cheney. Just months after being laid off, Rex started to get sick, then sicker.

Perhaps, he was already getting sick the winter he was working in Bosnia. All sorts of possibilities about the origins of our brother's illness have occurred to Lisha and me since his death. Rexito worked in a half-dozen countries where exposure to environmental pollutants was, and continues to be, a fact of life. Recently, I learned that depleted uranium, used in many types of modern weaponry, is still detectable in Bosnian soil and will remain there for years to come. The depleted uranium (called DUs) there is a side effect of the series of unrelenting air strikes that ended only a few months before Rex arrived to do his part in repairing Bosnia's infrastructure.

DUs can be ingested through water or breathed in through dust. Even at relatively low levels they have been linked to various forms of cancer. It may have been more than smoking cigarettes that contributed to my brother's ill health and the eventual diagnosis of lung cancer. How much depleted uranium had his system absorbed even before his arrival in Bosnia?

I am drawn, once again, to the folder filled with faxes that still rests on the dining-room table. "Laying in wait," I almost said. Like a land mine. I turn on the lamp, sit down again, and begin to read: "I guess the best way to explain my job," Rex advises Dad in this fax I'm looking at, "is to say that your son is a Combat Accountant." He explains, "I just bring the money (usually very large amounts of it) because there is usually none and that makes me a pretty choice target. This is really not how I ever envisioned using my masters degree in international financing . . . but I would not trade it for any other type of job I could think of."

Dad brought copies of Rex's faxes to share with family members from time to time, but this folder contains the originals. As I run my fingers over the pages they feel slippery and insubstantial, too flimsy to bear the weight of what they have to convey. Here is the five-page, single spaced transmission Rex sent from Bosnia in March 1996 that I have read and reread several times; poring over it for clues about the nature of Rex's last assignment, about the nature of Rex himself.

Earlier today, I found a map of Bosnia in our atlas. The big page is still open on top of the flowered tablecloth beside the folder. My fingers slide over place names—Zvornik, Mostar, Zepa. I travel down rivers like the Drina with my magnifying glass, looking, in vain, for the Save River that Rex writes about where the pontoon bridge was built.

I remember reading a copy of this particular fax soon after Dad received it. At the time I felt critical and uncharitable, though of course I didn't make comments to my proud father. It seemed to me there was a lot of posturing for Dad's sake, as Rex described ducking for cover on his way to a job site as he and an ex-soldier of fortune "took a little road trip down to Slavonski Brod and the pontoon bridge" and reached ". . . shelled and burned out villages that were completely abandoned . . . Suddenly I heard this whisssh, whisssh go right by me followed by a kraaaack, kraaaack and I knew immediately what that sound was . . ."

Please, I wanted to ask, does every male in this family suffer from testosterone poisoning? *Whisssh whisssh. Kraaaack.* The sounds were reminiscent of a video combat game and not a real war in which desperate people were still shooting at each other in ruined cities regardless of peace accords. Rex wrote: "Well, getting shot at was so much fun that I took a trip down what is known as Camp Harmon (named after a WWII Medal of Honor winner) . . ."

But there is a subtext deeper than bravado that I have discovered. Toward the midpoint of this same fax I find that Rex's tone has changed. He writes, "It is odd how we find our own prejudices blinding us to the realities of life,"—or death, I want to add now, as I try to see Rex as he truly was. Tonight, I understand how I've always looked at Rex, and his role in our lives, through Daddy's glasses. I see them now in my mind: the yellow plastic lenses that clip-on to prescription bifocals, that are supposed to make objects appear more clearly in the fog. Only, while they may have worked for Dad, they didn't do a thing for me. The truth is, it was my bias that was coloring things.

I felt closest to my brother when he was a teenager. In those days, it was hard for him to hide his tender heart. He was especially kind to women and older people. He loved animals and responded to the beauty of the land. It was so clear that being reunited with his father, with his Oregon family, was important to him. And it is this part of Rex I remember as I read on, as his words convey the heaviness of his days as he was breathing in Bosnia each smog-choked day. The lung-searing thickness of atmospheric pollution, partially a result of coal-produced heat, depressed him. His spirits were low, and lower, weighted down in the hip-high Bosnian mud where "humvees and hemmets are stuck up to their doors."

"It was so cold," he wrote in January 1996, reflecting upon the recent Bosnian winter, just three months after NATO forces bombed rebel Serb positions near Tuzla, ". . . that the diesel fuel froze . . . we had to keep four trucks running all night long." It infuriated him, he wrote, to see where a MASH unit had been placed. The "guy" who had decided to place it in a swamp, Rexito opined, "should be cashiered out of the military for pure incompetence."

Rex estimated that Brown and Root stood to earn somewhere ". . . between $40 to $70 million in *profit* for this event alone. . . ." Even so, Rex was upset by what he saw as waste and mismanagement. He confided his fury to one of his supervisors, who, before hiring on as the Balkan war theater manager had been an auditor for Arthur Andersen. Although he was supposedly in charge of all support services in the Balkan theater, Rex fumed, "I can't believe the guy! He has merely sequestered himself in his comfortable office in Hungary and refuses to come out." Rex believed that the man valued his own personal safety over that of his numerous employees despite that his oversight was badly needed in the field.

There were landmines and snipers virtually everywhere in Bosnia. Regardless of the Dayton accord, Rex was certain new mines were still being placed, adding to ". . . the six million land minds unaccounted for in theater." His first trip to Tuzla, Bosnia's second largest city, ". . . a mere thirty-seven miles away" had taken four hours or more because of mine fields and snipers.

"In theater . . ." that military turn of phrase that seems to describe war as a production rather than as an engine of destruction where campaigns are "staged." Rex, a late twentieth-century man who visited forty countries in five years, used metaphors that while not precisely theatrical did originate in the screen and video culture of his own generation. Three years before he got to

Bosnia while working in Mogadishu, Somalia, he wrote to Dad that "Club Mog" was someplace between *MASH, Catch-22,* and *Apocalypse Now.* "Truth," he wrote without much originality but surely with feeling, "really is stranger than fiction."

Perhaps it was at "Club Mog," that Rex first learned how cheap life was in some of the countries where he found himself. In one of the few conversations he had with Lisha about his experiences working for Brown and Root he told her that some of the traffic accidents he was required to settle with cash payments while in Mogadishu were most certainly staged. Children died after being pushed in front of cars by their parents, so that claims could be collected.

After Somalia, if I read my brother's letters right, his cynicism deepened perceptibly and an even deeper world weariness took hold. In one fax, he listed the official names of various "operations": Haiti "Operation Uphold Democracy," Saudi & Kuwait "Operation Vigilant Warrior," and Bosnia "Operation Joint Endeavor." When he noted U.S. government sobriquets for "actions" in Somalia, Rwanda, and Uganda—"Restore Hope," "Continue Hope," and "Support Hope," his doubts, edged with disgust, shone through: ". . . and all those HOPES—I am beginning to think they are all without hope."

God knows what Rex learned in Rwanda in the aftermath of the horrors of the Tutsi against their Hutu neighbors. Was this where Brown and Root earned its reputation as "undertaker" in the aftermath of the 1994 slaughter in Africa's most densely populated country? What took place in Rwanda in a harrowing three-month period as 800,000 people were killed in an "ethnic cleansing" even outstripped the horrors of Bosnia. It was the displaced Bosnians, however, who came to haunt my brother.

Writing of Tuzla, my brother said, "This was singularly the most depressing atmosphere I have ever experienced." This is quite a statement, coming from a man who had seen "up close and personal" so many hellholes of contemporary conflict.

I am trying to imagine Rex during that bitter Bosnian winter in January 1996 when he was setting up an office in a little town that was formerly an industrial center located six kilometers from Tuzla. He reported that he was working on the second floor of a former power plant that was "the size of Chernobyl, although non-nuclear." The plant was no longer producing power, perhaps because it had been badly damaged during the NATO bombings. His office was cold.

In the last page of my brother's fax from Bosnia he mentioned that it was snowing most of every day in January; that he was watching the people of Tuzla trudge doggedly through the dirty snow, "as if it did not exist with an almost mindless determination." He went on to observe, "There is no mirth in their expressions and it is as if the very act of breathing is a matter of reflex that would not otherwise be undertaken."

Rex may not have known exactly what had happened to the people of Tuzla before he got there, but he obviously sensed their distress. He most certainly had been briefed on the massacre at Srebrenica. In the wake of that devastating "ethnic cleansing" in a town that was supposed to be a UN "safe zone" survivors began streaming into towns like Tuzla where at least 60,000 refugees stretched the resources of the already battered city. Even before Srebrenica's tide of survivors spilled onto city streets, Tuzlans experienced terrible deprivations. Among other things, they had the Bosnian Serb army's daily shelling for much of the war. It is no wonder Rex was struck by the countenance of the Bosnians he came in contact with, many of whom were still grieving the loss of friends and family members who had disappeared from their lives only months before.

I remember hearing about Srebrenica on my local FM station

as I was washing dishes. It caught my attention because there was a report concerning, among other things, burials. In the wake of the Dayton accords, Serbs were hurriedly removing "evidence" from the sites of their killing fields near Srebrenica and other Bosnian communities. They were trucking corpses to remote locations in east Bosnian forests where they piled bodies into mass graves. As the corpses were uncovered by investigators, desperate relatives arrived at these sites hoping to locate the bodies of their loved ones by identifying such things as scraps of homemade plaid shirts, still clinging to otherwise unrecognizable human remains.

Sometimes people insisted on guiding officials to these makeshift graveyards despite the fact that fighting had not stopped entirely and they were risking their own lives. Individuals who chanced to witness such clandestine burials became obsessed with their responsibility to reveal their location, leading UN soldiers or any other person who would listen to the sites the Serbs had hurriedly bulldozed. One man stood over the killing field he'd led authorities to and said that the mass grave had, in effect, become his village. He told a journalist that God had permitted him the privilege of coming back to his "village" so that he could give his loved ones "decent burial"—an important tenet of his Islamic faith. Other survivors never located their dead at all.

Rex wrote that calling some of the people that he saw in trudging through the snow in Tuzla ". . . survivors is being unfair to the rest of the living because merely existing is not in and of itself being alive." He was chilled by the faces of these passersby and observed, "I have seen other wars with casualties that have been scarred by their experiences but never people (like these) who appear to be devoid of their souls to the point where they are merely walking cadavers."

Rex witnessed the legacy of conflict, felt it piercing through him like the cold. "There is still a hatred that burns within the core of the people here like a demon caged merely awaiting the opportunity to escape and unleash its fury."

My brother's obituary said: "Rex Allen Applegate was a joyful, caring human being—a mentor to his many friends." At two memorial services his friends rallied, speaking about Rex's sense of humor, his deep sense of loyalty to his country and those he cared about. But who was Rex's mentor while he was in Bosnia? Did he have anyone he really talked to?

"While my friends have often asked what it is like it seems that they are only asking out of duty and do not really want to know," he went on to say. "I have found that if in any way I endanger their perceptions of reality in their orderly and structured world back in their comfortable homes in the U.S. they become dismayed. It is as if they want to believe that their problems are the only ones they are capable of understanding and dealing with which I used to think was only natural. Now, I am not so sure anymore . . ."

"This is the only form of venting I have at my disposal," he admitted near the end of his fax. "It also has the benefit of allowing myself the opportunity to reflect upon not only what is happening in my life but to those around me. I will admit these places have had an effect on me. . . . I find it easier to keep these mental masturbations to myself. It is safer for everyone that way."

What I would say to my brother if he were here beside me is that I'm not sure there is any safety in *not* saying things. They have a way of welling up, of poisoning the well, in fact.

I wonder if Rex thought the whole notion of post-traumatic stress disorder was unmanly and unprofessional? He told me once how he resented "psycho babble and labeling." Still, there were many veteran journalists who reeled from bearing witness to Bosnia's horrors. Peter Maas, shaken to his core by what he was forced to report, confessed that he could recall the precise day when he "finally . . . fell spiritually sick."

I read now the last words of my brother's fax: "A wise man once said, 'never pass on an opportunity to keep your mouth shut.' That is sage advice that I am trying to learn and perhaps in another forty years I may even accomplish it."

And you didn't get another forty years, Rex. And I don't know why.

I close the manila folder, stand up, pull my warm robe more tightly around my shoulders, and walk to the night windows. Across the valley, the cemetery rises on the ridge above the town; it is invisible at this moment, bathed in night, but I can feel it. It is a dark safe place just southeast of yard lights and streetlamps whose halos seem to shoot sparks, as I cry.

All of the people in the town know where their dead are. They are named, resting alone or in pairs, bearing the numerals of their life spans. Their stones are marble or granite; gray or red. Red carnelian. Like Rex's. Like mine, someday.

If we choose, we can all go up to visit and stand undisturbed, talking to our undisturbed dead. We can mow and clip and leave flowers. We can wait a week, a year, or even a century, before standing over them and reading their names, taking comfort in the fact that while everything else changes, they are still there where we left them.

In small Bosnian towns, where nothing was sacred or safe, Serbs were not merely killing but deliberately, even zealously, desecrating old cemeteries, pushing over and pulverizing headstones beneath the heavy treads of their bulldozers. They defiled old graves with the same machines that they used to shove new corpses into ditches deep in the woods.

Brother, tonight this is where my impure grief leads me; pulling me inexorably toward the dark of the old trees, ticking, ticking like a Geiger counter, finding you, at last, near the vast trembling grave of the world.

The Dead End of Elm Street

Six months ago, worrying about potential vandalism on Halloween—the night when headstones topple or worse in cemeteries all over America—I decided to talk to the woman who lives closest to the cemetery. I asked her whether trick-or-treaters made it as far as her place.

"Oh, no," she said, giggling. "We're left pretty much alone up here. I don't even buy candy anymore. I haven't seen kids in the cemetery on Halloween, either. They must have all seen that horror movie." I was puzzled. She went on, "You know, *Nightmare on Elm Street.*"

I still didn't get it though I later found out it was a film directed by Wes Craven in 1984—a classic in its genre.

She looked at me as though I were unbelievably slow. "Well, all the kids in the movie lived on Elm Street. That's where all the trouble was. Here," she gestured toward the cemetery road, "on *top* of this being Elm Street, we have two graveyards on it," she said. I must have looked blank. "On the *dead end* of Elm Street, get it?"

I smiled, but what I was actually feeling was embarrassment. I didn't want to tell her, or admit to myself, that until that moment I hadn't any idea the street had a name. I referred to it as Cemetery Road, if I called it anything.

To that point in time, there had been no occasion upon which I was obliged to provide a physical address. Even now, knowing the name of the street, I still say something like this, "Just go to the top of Applegate Street and turn left on Douglas Street. There you'll see a little white sign shaped like an old tombstone pointing left. Follow Douglas a ways, and take the first road on the right, a sharp right. That's Cemetery Road—it's a bit narrow—it dead-ends at the parking lot. The Masonic Cemetery is on the left, the Pioneer is on the right." I usually hear myself add, "Where all the big trees are." It's a point of pride that we still have our big trees. Sometime ago, the Masons cut down most of their large conifers to make mowing and upkeep easier.

But six months ago, after talking to my trick-or-treat advisor on the day before Halloween, when I left the cemetery, I made it a point to stop at the corner where the road to the cemetery meets Douglas Street. Sure enough, there was a sign on the corner that read "Elm St."

Why was I so dense? True, it is a short sign on a tall pole. "Elm" is just three letters long, and "street" is abbreviated. Painted green with white lettering, the standard style for signs around here, the sign is neither showy nor excessive—which surely makes local people happy, since everyone is against government waste of any kind and, as far as that goes, against government, period.

It would be nice to say that trees in leaf, or some other visual obstruction, interfered with my mentally registering the sign. The sign *does* sit on a little embankment and "Elm"—written on a stubby little board—sits at a perpendicular angle atop the significantly longer "Douglas," making "Elm" a bit hard to see.

But, all these rationalizations aside, the fact of the matter is that the sexton who prides herself on her powers of observation did not know the name of the street her cemetery was located upon.

The only thing that can really be said in my defense is that I have gone back-and-forth to the cemetery since childhood and didn't need a sign to get there. But honesty dictates remembering something else from childhood: Many grown-ups pointed out that I was inclined to miss the obvious. "If it were a snake . . ." they said, it surely would have bitten me.

For the past year, every time I come to the cemetery I try to make it a point to look up and read the signs. "Douglas" and "Elm" they say again. Two trees: Douglas refers to Douglas fir and not to Stephen A. Douglas, the Civil War-era politician after whom our county is named.

Douglas fir, elm, and a third tree species, cedar, are why I'm coming to the cemetery this nippy spring morning, so far from Halloween. I'm hoping I'll arrive before the cutters from the tree service I've contracted. When I make the turn I will be able to see the parking lot.

I wave to Tip Wexler as I drive past his hurricane-fenced compound that encloses two modular homes, outbuildings, and an immaculately kept and expansive yard.

Just before the Wexler's place on the north side of the road there is a proliferation of manufactured homes that I still think of as trailers. These places feel as though they have appeared overnight, but in reality they are part of a trend on this end of Yoncalla. A local man has been selling these lots near the cemetery. Fortunately, there is still a nice stand of approximately forty-year-old Douglas fir, owned by the same man that provides a green space between the "mobile homes" (a compromise in terms) and the cemetery's western border.

It's taken almost two years for me to face the fact that our big trees must be limbed. The cemetery fund could not have covered the payment of a tree service were it not for donations made by two families who live out of town but have dead buried up here. Despite this, in order to reduce costs, volunteers, including Daniel, me, and our children—who, in fact, are no longer children—will be dealing with all the cut limbs and what is bound to be a general disarray of woody debris. Larger pieces of wood will be bucked into lengths suitable for the fireplaces in the Old Place; the rest will be burned or ground into sawdust by a stump grinder. We will fill potholes with the results.

On one level, I loathe the idea that I am about to witness a distinct change of appearance in trees that are between one hundred and fifty and two hundred years old. Still, I know safety requires this cleanup. Since taking responsibility for the cemetery I have read headlines in my mind: "Elderly Woman Visiting Her Husband's Grave Skewered by Falling Limb." "Child Pinned Under Branch Suffers Injuries."

Aside from the danger to life *from* limb, which potentially is beyond the scope of our liability insurance—insurance Dad now wants me to pay from the dwindling cemetery fund—there is also the problem of cleaning up after storms each year when branches large and small are scattered over the cemetery.

A few days ago, when I told Tip Wexler that we were going to have some work done on the cemetery trees, he said, "You ought to just cut them down and be done with it." I told him we'd *never* cut them down if we could help it and that his profession was showing.

Tip has been associated with the logging industry most of his life; he was one of several members from the local Masonic lodge who decided that trees in their cemetery had to go. A wonderful old fellow with a huge heart, Tip opens and closes the road gate each day and keeps an eye on things.

But we disagree when it comes to trees. The other day he wagged his finger at me and said as a parting shot, "Shannon, dog-gone it, you *know* trees have no business being in a cemetery!"

This morning I could rebut his objections very nicely since I have been reading about cemetery trees for several days now as I have been researching for just the right tree to plant by my brother Rex's headstone in the new family plot.

In the process, I have learned a great deal about trees and now know that the elm tree has always been associated with cemeteries. In fact, naming this particular street "Elm" which dead-ends at the community's only cemeteries may signify much more than the inclinations of nineteenth-century town-founders across America to name streets after trees.

Yoncalla has streets that follow this pattern: Alder, Birch, Cedar, Douglas, and Elm—a combination of native and introduced trees, arranged in alphabetical order. A sheep rancher friend commented recently that he "always figured the street is called Elm just because they needed an 'E.'" Was he right? Could it be that simple?

My first thought was to consider which of the five trees named in these streets still had a connection to the town's visible landscape. Today, there are many cedars and Douglas firs of prodigious size on their namesake streets, as well as in other parts of town. Alders are still found around here, on lower, wetter ground, and the birch, an introduced tree, may have been present in years gone by. Settlers frequently planted trees that were native to the places they had left behind: birch, elm, locust, catalpa, English, and black walnut are just a few examples.

Beginning in the 1930s, the American elm, a shade tree much beloved in towns all over the U.S., began to die as a result of the ravages of Dutch elm disease that gradually swept across the country. It is not surprising, then, that the elm, admired for its dense, broad crown of spreading and nearly upright branches, is no longer evident in the yards of today's Yoncalla.

But were there elms on Elm Street before the 1930s? As far back as community memory reaches, no one recalls any noteworthy elms, and certainly, people agree, none along Cemetery Road, as most elders refer to Elm Street.

It was 1856 when the first horse-drawn buckboard creaked up to the spot that Aunt Hazel's grandfather, George Arthur Burt, had decided to set aside for family and then community burials, on the southwest corner of his property awarded him under the Donation Land Claim Act. Sitting in that buckboard were my thrice-great-uncle Lindsay Applegate and his bereft and stricken wife, Betsy. They were not following a road in those days, but, instead, a meager wagon track that eventually reached the low ridge where George Burt told them they could bury their youngest child. The homemade box of fir, or white oak, was perhaps small enough for Betsy to hold securely beside her as she sat on the buckboard bench while Lindsay drove. Or perhaps, farther back in the wagon, one of "poor little Jerome's" older siblings sat rocking with the motion of the wagon, steadying the little coffin, and watching over baby brother for the last time.

One hundred and fifty or so years ago, the only trees the Lindsay Applegates or anyone else would have seen along the cemetery route were few and far between and trees that Mother Nature planted. The most prominent and beautiful tree in this locality—as is still the case in other parts of Oregon—was white oak (*Quercus garryana;* called "Garry oak" as well as "Oregon oak"). Growing in open places, individually or in scattered stands on grasslands and sunny slopes, pioneers discovered that these remarkable trees were often three hundred to five hundred years old.

White oaks supplied Native people with an important food in the form of acorns; their thick, gray, fissured bark helped them withstand annual baptisms by fire set by local tribes who used burning to harvest wild sunflower seeds and improve hunting grounds. Along with a few ash trees and a half-dozen other deciduous varieties, oaks dominated the landscape and were quickly cut down by settlers who found that their hard, heavy, finely-grained wood "split clean" and was excellent for fence posts.

By the 1880s, a few young Douglas fir trees, seeded naturally, were part of the landscape along Cemetery Road (perhaps called Elm Street by then, though the record is sketchy.) More abundant were the apple trees, a mere fifteen or twenty years old; favorites in early orchards around here included Gloria Mundi, Spitzenberg, Winter Pearmain, and Baldwin.

Even the lilac-haunted yard of the turn-of-the-century Queen Anne cottage, still occupying the corner of Douglas and Elm, did

not boast an elm tree, according to old pictures. No elm, then, bore witness to high-hatted Masons, who, wearing sashes of their degree, shown in sepia-tinted photos, walking three deep as they solemnly make their way up the cemetery road in order to "funeralize" at the graveside of a brethren. There, the Masonic farewell ceremony required the incorporation of yet another tree into their ritual: Willow branches, representing the Resurrection, were supposed to be carried by each mourner present.

Members of the Masonic orders, as well as other fraternalists, (especially the Order of Oddfellows) established cemeteries throughout the country so that they could observe their special burial rites and provide their members and families with inexpensive and secular burial places.

Many of Yoncalla's town fathers were Masons, including George Burt, who, during the California gold rush, arrived on a sailing ship he had leased in partnership with a number of Connecticut lodge brothers. A few years passed in the goldfields before he made his way north to Oregon, married Ellen Applegate, and eventually founded the town of Yoncalla. In the decade following the burial of tiny Jerome Applegate, George Burt was to bury his wife, Ellen, and several of his children.

Whoever named the cemetery route Elm Street, whether George Burt or someone else, lived during the Victorian era—a time that percolated with secret fraternal practices and was saturated with symbolism of all kinds. Many people associated the elm with death. Since ancient times, elms were used for coffins: The rot-resistant merit of its pale wood made the elm perfect material. What better name for a street with two cemeteries on it?

In the British Isles, where many American customs originated, elm was death's consort. Well before the sixth century, when the lozenge-shaped wooden box we think of as a coffin began to be customary, the elm had already been pressed into service. Crudely hollowed-out elm logs—bark still clinging to them—often cradled human skeletons or charred bones. Some of these burial logs were riveted with small brass strips that decorated the exterior bark—a harbinger of more elaborate coffins that in future eras would be scrolled, inlaid, imbricated, monogrammed, and otherwise ornamented with metals of all kinds.

Elms, however, are not the only trees connected with dying and death customs in Great Britain and elsewhere. Over millennia, and in many parts of the world, trees have always been perceived as sentinels guarding death's gateway—the cemetery.

Underscoring emblematic and actual connections, trees have been part of cemetery landscapes all over America for centuries. Famous cemeteries carry names such as Forest Lawn (Glendale, Ca.), Spring Forest (Binghamton, N.Y.), Greenwood (Brooklyn, N.Y.), Evergreen (Rutland, Vt.), among others. Names of specific trees are celebrated in cemeteries called Cedar Hill (Hartford, Conn.), Laurel Hill (Philadelphia, Pa.), Elmwood (Detroit, Mich.), Oak Hills (Washington, D.C.), Pine Grove (Waterville, Maine). Across the U.S., in the literally thousands of small cemeteries like our own, the pattern of naming burial grounds after trees still holds.

Strongly associated with death, and planted in our own and countless other cemeteries, are laurel, boxwood, myrtle, holly, and other broadleaf species that do not shed their leaves. Trees, and shrubs that grew as tall as trees, were especially significant in ancient European and British Isles burial grounds because of their symbolic connection to the idea of everlasting life, as conceived by both Christians and "pagan" Celts. Many of the plants strongly associated with tree-worshiping Druidism would eventually find their way into churchyards, with the possible exception of mistletoe, which had too strong a connection to the magical rites that remained anathema to European Christians.

But it is the yew tree, the tree that Tennyson immortalized when he wrote, "Old yew, which graspest at the stones/That name the underlying dead . . ." that is most associated with cemeteries. This is the European yew, of genus *Taxus* still valued for its use in hedges and topiaries. In ancient times, it was the sacred yew of the Celts, associated with the crone aspect of the goddess Hecate in whose honor its greenery was woven into funeral wreaths. Later, is became a churchyard tree, often mammoth and solitary, occasionally surviving as long as three thousand years.

It is a smaller New World cousin of this yew, the Pacific yew, that I have chosen to plant near my brother Rex's headstone. The bark of this tree might be considered sacred in a modern sense, at least to me: It is used in the treatment of cancer and has saved more than one friend of mine.

Prolific in cemeteries all over the Christian world, the holly tree, like the yew, was also originally connected with the Celts and considered highly poisonous, though sacred. Like many customs whose pagan roots have been deliberately disguised, the use of holly and its symbolism was eventually altered and incorporated into sanctioned church customs; its leaves became a reminder of Christ's crown of thorns and the red berries symbolized the color of His blood.

The symbolic connection between evergreens of all kinds and eternal life is obvious. Thus spruce, cedar, pine, fir, and yew, etc. were present in graveyards of both polytheistic and monotheistic peoples in different parts of the world.

The cypress tree, an evergreen of special significance, figured prominently in ancient Greek and Roman death customs. In Asia, cypress, valued throughout ages as coffin wood, is still favored by the Chinese.

Port Orford cedar, a member of the cypress family and an

Oregon native, is a prominent tree in our cemetery and a popular ornamental in many public spaces throughout America. Several Port Orford cedars still stand that were planted near Albert Applegate's grave in 1867 by his young widow, Nancy Applegate. Heartbroken by her husband's death, the story goes, Nancy wanted to live long enough to look up and see the handsome spires and drooping bluish branches of the Port Orford cedars when she rode horseback in the valley below. The indomitable "Nan" got her wish, and was still riding horseback well into her nineties.

I'm glad to see that there are no tree cutters in utility trucks, waiting for me in the parking lot. It is blessedly quiet up here, for a while longer anyway. I don't like to have these big trees limbed, but their branches, sidling down the huge girth of their trunks,

frequently reach the ground and even cover headstones. Some foresters call Douglas fir like these "wolf trees" because they have grown in the open, often without companions, and have had room to "wolf" the space around them by spreading out. I like the term a logger friend of mine, Charlie Schnell, uses better: "grouse ladders." There are still grouse around, but all the wolves—the sacred animal of the Kalapuya tribes—are long gone from our part of the world.

As I stand here, it is impossible to see clear across the expanse of the cemetery on account of the plethora of lower branches on firs and cedars. Like the Port Orford cedar, the Incense cedar (*Calocedrus decurrens*) is not a cedar at all but a member of the cypress family. As far as that goes, the Douglas fir tree (*Pseudotsuga menziesii*) is not really a fir, but a pine. As I look around, walking under the chill canopy of these huge trees, I wonder whether the cutters can finish all their work in a single day. I set eleven o'clock as our meeting time, since they will be driving from the coastal part of our county—a domain the size of the state of Connecticut. If they have to come back tomorrow, it will be more money. Will their equipment get them into the hard places deep within the rows of headstones?

This is the nightmare vision I have imagined since my father told me he was thinking of clear-cutting the cemetery: Men in yellow hard hats revving up their chain saws. While chain saws scream, trees crash to the ground in a scented rushing hurtle that inevitably ends in sounds of cracking granite and splitting marble. And there I am, in this vision, standing by, helplessly watching the obliteration; the smashing of obelisks, the crosses, the hearts, and columns, and the hand-carved names and numerals. The sum of lives. Born. Died.

It is ironic that I am the one who has invited this potential carnage into the cemetery. I actually called these guys up and said,

"Hey! Come and bring your chain saws." They will need them since many of these limbs are as stout as the thirty-year-old trees that are in such profusion on the backs of logging trucks these days. As I crane my neck, looking up into the crowns of these shaggy monsters, these colossally green, upended squid, with feelers dipping and gently swaying, I see how many dangerous limbs there really are.

And so, having shifted myself into overwhelm, mildly depressed now, and very sorry that I did not wear a warmer jacket, I will do what any sensible sexton should on a rather fitful spring day: Time to get out from under the weather and the frankly oppressive shade of these big trees of which I am so fond. I can worry about money, and stew over the dwindling cemetery fund in the relative warmth of my car as I wait for the tree-service guys.

History is much more entertaining: Here at the cemetery's edge, near the parking lot for instance, is a particularly large Douglas fir that Finns of yore would have put to good purpose. It comes to mind now because Finns lopped off the lower limbs of such trees on one side in order to transform them into memorials called Cross pines. In some parts of rural Finland, until fairly recent times, Cross pines stood on the verge of burial grounds where, in effect, they became an organic form of headstone. Some theorize, in fact, that even the idea of upright headstones was originally inspired by such memorial trees.

Before Finnish mourners incised the initials and dates of the dead into an ovular space that was, judging from the photograph I saw, carved into the cadmium layer of the selected pine tree, they buoyed up their spirits by tippling spirits of a liquid kind—perhaps potato vodka or some other regional drink. After delivering the coffin to the grave, before burying it, mourners made sure the corpse had its own bottle of liquor tucked away for future use—a variety of grave good that warmed Death's cold clutch.

The gift of liquor seems more propitiation toward the dead than generosity, however. Upon leaving the cemetery, the funeral entourage would stop for a moment and, after saluting the Cross pine, would begin whisking and lightly beating each other on the back with twigs of silver fir and juniper. Meanwhile, a communal chant would commence. The chant was supposed to ensure that the dead man's ghost would not follow them home.

Although I am not a drinking woman, a little jolt of some form of warming liquid would suit me just fine about now, as the wind picks up. Alas, there will be no waiting in the car with the heater on for the likes of me. I see two utility trucks, slowly coming up the hill, one complete with a crane and bucket large enough to hold two men. The day ahead will be long and chill, and from the look of the clouds, a bit wet as well.

Fear of Trees

T he cemetery sounds like a battle zone. The two young men working for the tree service ride in a bucket attached to a huge, hinged arm that they shift and swivel artfully until they are within safe range of the limb they are attacking with their respective chain saws. The steel arm reaches up about fifty feet at maximum. What makes this dangerous is the fact that the "widow makers"—tree limbs hanging up on other branches, or dangling precariously—are well above this level. Eric seems about my son Colin's age, in his mid-twenties. How I would hate to have a son of mine swinging around in trees like this. The other cutter looks like some of the high school boys I teach, but he is probably as old as Max, my youngest son.

I say to Eric, "It's a good thing you're not afraid of heights!" He lifts his silver-colored hard hat, swipes his sleeve across his forehead, and grins, "But I *am* afraid of heights." He pauses, and adds as though surprised to hear himself say it, "I guess I hate this, and I love this, all at the same time. Still, it really pumps me, every time." His shoulders are broad but his legs are thin, slightly bowed, under his "high-waters"—pants without cuffs which just clear the tops of his work boots so they won't get caught in anything as he's working.

As his partner takes his turn in the "bucket," Eric takes a break and strolls over to our oldest family plot, where I am working. He takes out a little round tin of Copenhagen, tucks a pinch of tobacco into his cheek, and peers at the headstones for a moment as I continue dragging cut boughs outside of the cement borders surrounding my great-great-grandparents' family plot. By following behind the cutters, thus far, I have managed to make at least a dozen piles of limbs like this one in various parts of the cemetery.

Eric hunkers down, apparently computing dates since he says, "Gee, she was only sixteen when she died." He gently touches the moss-furred numbers and letters. "Who was Harriet Applegate?" he asks. "Is she your relative?"

I tell him she was my great-great-auntie; an aspiring artist, poet, and novelist, who died from complications due to pneumonia during the Civil War. "She was a real fan of Abe Lincoln's," I tell him. Seeing his eyes widen with interest—important when talking with any young person before going on—I add, "When she painted her pictures, she used the blank side of school atlas maps because paper was so hard to come by. She also made her own pigments and tints."

He stands up, still looking down at the stone. "What are pignents?" He is unconscious of mispronouncing the word. Such a bright young man, but he shows the deficiency of so many who drop out of high school to work in the woods or a sawmill. This pattern has persisted for many decades in the Pacific Northwest.

Good hourly wages and benefits were once the inducement. Now, jobs in the woods and sawmills are drying up. Eric is lucky to have a part-time job at a tree service.

I continue, "You know, pigments . . . substances that give color." He nods, and says, "Yeah, I knew that."

"Harriet used red from the pokeberry bush. They brought seeds with them in the family's covered wagons all the way from Missouri. She made yellow and yellow-green from Oregon grape root; her browns and blacks came from black walnut husks."

"Way cool," he says.

Seconds later, after his partner's chain saw revs up, a limb crashes. We both run to the headstone that has come within inches of being struck by a thigh-sized branch; Mr. Shangles's obelisk juts like a dark accusing finger from its unexpected nest of green boughs. Almost miraculously, not a single headstone has been harmed thus far.

Eric takes his leave and strides toward the truck, shouting something I can't hear to his partner. There is something to admire in his and his partner's nimbleness: a swift and sure union of man and machine. I am surprised how quickly the work gets done; and yet there doesn't seem to be anything careless about it. Suddenly, I remember how fast the forest behind the Old Place went down on green knees after a timber company bought it; now you see it, now you don't.

Things are changing, although not quickly enough from my perspective. Throughout the controversies surrounding logging in federal forests, those who call themselves supporters of "The Industry" frequently portray one another as the *real* lovers of nature—not like those white-wine-drinking urban, imported environmentalists who don't know where their toilet paper comes from.

From a conservationist's viewpoint, this love affair with nature on the part of The Industry is difficult to square with the all too obvious depredations affecting streamside health and loss of wildlife habitat. The stark plenitude of denuded hillsides, and the compromised watersheds speak for themselves. And, still, The Industry wants more; complains bitterly about "locked up" public forestlands.

I watch Eric, imagine him breathing in the invigorating fragrance of fir resin and freshly cut cedar. He stops for a moment, looking up almost reverently into a Port Orford cedar's blue-tipped crown, and then, from his rare perch, glances toward southeast valleys where mists rise and roil. An almost imperceptible rain spangles his silver hat. I am watching someone who is happy, who clearly loves the outdoors. A while ago, Eric noticed and knew the name of the pileated woodpecker, whose scarlet crest and striking black-and-white body lifted in swift indignation at the first choking sound of the chain saw.

And what do I know about the swell of pride pouring over the psyche of a one-hundred-and-sixty pound boy, or man, for that matter, as he and his little machine topple two-ton giants?

Susan's father, Fred Applegate, whose headstone is under one of the Port Orford cedars Eric now hovers near, worked in the woods for years as a timber faller. Fred's hard hat and McCullough chain saw were prominent elements in the floral arrangement Susan made for his funeral.

I wrote and delivered Fred's eulogy at the Methodist Church, repeating something he told his family: Once, up on Smith River, just as he was about to fell a huge old-growth fir, he claimed he heard it sigh, "with the sound of a thousand summers."

He grew furious at environmentalists who scoffed at a logger's love for the woods, but was not unaware of the paradox: killing the thing one loves. *But it does not mean there is no love.*

This congregation of light and shadow, this fellowship of roots and stones: These lines come as I stand here surveying the cemetery's length and breadth. I had become accustomed to the cemetery as it was, with its shaggy nooks, dim lots, and plots—a collection of parts. It is a sum, now, and more than that: One green thing, one place, dark at the center but illuminated on every edge. Now it echoes the internal landscape that lives in my psyche.

Six weeks of backaching work is what it costs to see this landscape whole. Daniel, Susan, Cousins Rob, Marilyn, and others, including several of the children helped. I don't know when I have worked harder physically. I feel new strength in my arms from pulling heavy limbs and heaving countless chunks of wood into the back of the pickup. It was the rhythm of *ka-thud, ka-thunk*. As they say, I shall be warmed twice with this firewood. And there is symmetry: By tending the dead, the living are comforted.

I can now see our grandfather trees as the individuals that they are. But I have reason to reconsider this metaphor inspired by what I formerly thought of as the trees' old age. It turns out that the big Douglas firs up here are hardly grandfathers. Instead, they are in their prime, still virile, still growing taller.

With the side limbs, so porcupine sharp, sheared away, it has finally been possible to run a tape measure around the base of each big tree. Cousin Everett Johnston, who majored in forestry, helped Daniel and me inventory the trees. In the right conditions, he said, Douglas fir can live for up to one thousand years. By that measure, the largest tree in the cemetery—such as this approximately two-hundred-year-old behemoth I am now passing with its deeply furrowed trunk that is nearly twenty feet in circumference—could last hundreds of years more.

Here, on the Pacific slope, at least a dozen species of conifers can reach two hundred feet in height; only the Eastern white pine once compared. Because Douglas fir is the most valuable tree in world timber commerce, it is probably understandable that the Industry thinks of it almost exclusively in terms of its usefulness as lumber. At the prime of life, while still producing height, trees like these big fellows are nevertheless referred to as "decadent, over-mature, or senescent."

If, in years to come, our cemetery trees are permitted to keep growing as the landscape surrounding them fills up with more people and God-knows-what, what a community treasure they will be! By our count, there are more than fifty conifers of significant size along with thirty broadleaf trees, including madrone, oak, big-leafed maple, and other species. A few hundred years hence, even deeply incised granite headstones may prove unreadable, but trees and wildlife habitat, if undisturbed, will still remain.

Because these firs and cedars grew in the open, with plenty of surrounding space in which to develop their "wolf tree" characteristics, they withstood weather and wind far better than their "managed-for-timber" counterparts. Even though they have now been trimmed, the protection they afford each other, and the strength of their well-established roots, should continue to permit them to survive healthily in this protected setting.

Without large intervening limbs to disguise their contours, many of these trees reveal a peculiar and mutual characteristic: Their double, and (occasionally) triple tops, rise candle-like from a single trunk, testifying eloquently to winter ferocities that shaped them about one hundred and thirty years ago, when historically low temperatures raked this region where it rarely even freezes. It's difficult to believe, given the exceptionally mild winters of recent years that during the winter of 1861–1862 snowdrifts in this part of Oregon were more than three feet deep. Brutal ice storms, family letters say, cycled throughout that miserable winter. The tender leader branches of young fir trees on Cemetery Ridge must have survived these conditions. These trees were forced to develop two or more lateral branches. Eventually these branches rose to crown each tree with twin or triple tops.

In the valleys below, during that bitter season after snow and ice, came inundations of rain and river. Flooding was followed by freezing, exhausting the local populace of settlers who had reason to question their impression of Oregon as a mild land of milk and honey. My ancestors and other ranchers were so short on feed that winter that they sent boys and girls out to collect a tree-hanging lichen (*Usnea*) known locally as Old Man's Beard to help sustain sheep and cattle.

Today, walking down the cemetery's middle lane I look up into

the canopies of these splendid trees, grateful to be privy to the story they tell, and comforted by the knowledge of their health.

"Now, we'll just leave you alone." I want to reassure them, if, as they are looking down on me, they are wondering why I have come here today armed with stout clippers and a long-handled orchardist's saw.

What I have on my cemetery agenda this afternoon is really more a sprucing up than a serious pruning. It's too late in the season to prune anything dramatically. Spring is upon this place, as testified by the abundance of choirs of robins. Green, self-sown grasses cover some old graves I am passing that are dotted with grape hyacinths, white violets, and naturalized paper-whites just beginning to bloom. Even in the cemetery's shady center, fragile spikes of dazzling green emerge through the drab blanket of duff, composed of fir needles and dead oak and madrone leaves.

My goal today is to repair, or at least hide, some unsightly accidental damage from last month's tree-limbing marathon when crashing branches damaged several boxwood hedges and a variety of shrubs and bushes, including the fifteen-foot-high snowball bush I am heading toward near the cemetery's center. A week ago, it looked more dead than alive; it is a historic planting, probably as venerable as the snowball bush in the Old Place yard, and I want to take care of it.

Not much has changed; all I can do is leave it alone and hope it comes back. But I have to tackle one of its largest branches that is hanging by a proverbial thread, from my vantage point, at least twelve feet above sloping ground—far too close to the Westenheiser plot's wrought-iron Victorian fence in a loose footing of ancient concrete.

For the millionth time in my life, I find myself wishing I were six inches taller. Even with my long-handled saw I can't seem to manage cutting the offending limb. "Damn it," I say aloud. I lunge ineffectively, stretching to the point of hurting. "Damn it to hell," says the sexton in her uncemetery-like voice. Still, there is no one, at least among the living, to hear this unattractive outburst.

A voice at my elbow says suddenly, "Mrs. Applegate?" To say I am startled would be an understatement.

"I'm so sorry, Mrs. Applegate," says a woman who introduces herself as Opal Carson, from our neighboring town of Oakland. "I surely didn't mean to scare you."

Caught off guard and being caught swearing are bad enough, but I detest being called Mrs. Applegate. I am married, but I am not anyone's "Missus," and although I am perfectly delighted to be Daniel Robertson's wife, I continue to use the name I was born with.

Mrs. Carson's pleasantly round face looks serious. Perhaps I am glowering at her. I pull myself together. She is still apologizing. "I walked in . . . you must not have noticed my car. It's by the Masonic. We have people buried there, too."

"Please call me Shannon," I smile, trying to remember my manners.

"I've been over by my husband's people," she says pointing in the direction of the northwest corner. She grins suddenly, adding, "I guess you just never know exactly *who* might be talking to you in a cemetery, do you? Could be someone's dead relative."

In a better humor now, I allow this is true. I judge her to be about seventy. She's wearing a bill cap that makes her look slightly jaunty, and one of those powder blue, grandma-style, teddy-bear sweatshirts—a quaint local costume.

"I just wanted to tell you how nice the cemetery is looking," she continues. "Someone in Oakland told me there was finally a lot of work going on up here, and I decided I'd take a peek since I had to make a run to the Feed and Seed in Yoncalla anyway."

I give her my cemetery spiel: how we're hoping to raise money for a gate, our plan for an historic inventory, and would she like to participate, etc.

She takes it all in and then says, "I've been coming up here off and on for thirty-six years now. It has looked so overgrown these past ten years or so. Really, it was just too depressing to see all these blackberries, broken headstones, and poison oak. We've kept up with our own graves and come on Memorial Day. But I always leave feeling guilty. I do quite a bit at our Oakland cemetery. But a person just has so much time . . ."

I examine her shoes. They seem thick of sole and stout enough for work. She is probably seven inches taller than I despite the fact she seems to be developing a little osteoporosis. Moments later, it is obvious she knows how to handle an orchardist's saw a lot better than I do. She has the branch from the snowball bush on the ground in no time flat.

We chat about the Douglas fir and cedars and what it took to get them limbed. She looks up into the canopy of firs and tells me, "I've always loved these trees, but my mother-in-law cannot abide them." Then she seems ready to add something but instead purses her lips.

"Really?" I say with obvious interest, hoping she will elaborate.

Opal Carson shakes her head. "Some people have got strange ideas . . ." I can see she wants to "dis" her mother-in-law after all. She gives in to the impulse. "There is room for both her and the father-in-law in that plot over there. All her own people are buried there—including her mother and grandmother but, no, she doesn't want to be in this cemetery."

"Maybe you should bring her up here and show her that things are improved. It's been several years since there has been any serious vandalism . . ."

But Opal Carson is still shaking her head. "None of that would matter a whit, I assure you. It's just that . . . well, she's afraid of the trees." She points at an especially large incense cedar for emphasis, and then makes a claw-like, "gotcha!" gesture with her hands. "They're gonna get her when she's in the ground, she figures."

I'm speechless. Opal Carson, though, is ready to take her leave and go on about her business.

"Well, keep up the good work," she says, with a friendly wave, as she heads in the direction of the parking lot.

I could have told her about the apple tree I read about—the one that grew near the grave of Roger Williams (1603–1683), Rhode Island's founder—but it is probably just as well that I restrained myself.

It is a curious tale: As Providence, Rhode Island was expanding in the mid-nineteenth century, a group of townspeople, trying to develop what had formerly been outlying districts, decided to move Roger Williams's grave from his formerly private burying ground where he had rested some one hundred and seventy years.

Of course, Providence's developers rationalized the relocation of Williams's grave by planning an impressive downtown monument where his exhumed remains would be placed. Both the situation and the solution have been repeated over millennia in every part of the world. Dead people always seem to occupy spaces that are eventually coveted by living people. In the United States alone, many cemeteries have been removed to other locations, often, none too carefully. Some cemeteries have been relocated more than once.

As those exhuming Roger Williams's body gathered for their task, it was noted that a stout old apple tree grew near his grave. As the digging began, the shape of the coffin could gradually be traced from a black line of organic matter. It was soon discovered that the apple tree had sent down two main roots and had obviously developed its root structure so that it might benefit from useable nutrients produced by Williams's decomposing corpse. The largest root had pushed its way to the precise spot originally occupied by Williams's skull, made a turn as if passing around it, and followed the direction of the backbone to the hips. Here the root divided into two branches, sending one along each leg to the heel. Then both turned upward to the toes. One of these roots, it was reported, formed a slight crook at the knee. Not a single bone remained, yet there did Roger Williams still abide, the living roots forming an uncanny outline of his body. Roger Williams had become an apple tree; had bloomed; had born fruit; had, quite literally, been eaten.

This story does take the idea of tree-hugging to previously unimagined lengths. Still, I have several friends who tell me they want a "green" funeral, who find this image of Roger Williams's apple tree quite transporting.

I have one friend, a naturalist and environmentalist, Wendell Wood, who insists he doesn't want to be buried at all; instead, he wants to be left at some county disposal site where he can wait for everyone to bring him offerings.

But I suspect he is pulling my leg (again) and that his real sentiments come closer to those of other friends who insist they want to be buried in biodegradable containers; the sooner decomposed, the better. Some people I know claim they are leaving instructions to have themselves unceremoniously "composted" in their flower gardens.

All over the world, especially in Great Britain and Australia, the "green" burial movement is gaining momentum, as awareness about the polluting side effects of cremation and other problems become more widely known. For many, a papier-mâché coffin, or even a just a wrapping of natural fiber cloth around an unembalmed body seems more in keeping with their worldview and values.

As I consider these things and watch the retreating form of Opal Carson, however, who now disappears from view behind the huge columnar trunks of these giants we both admire, I cannot help but wonder: If I had shared the story of Roger Williams's apple tree with her, would she, like her mother-in-law, develop her own fear of trees?

Three Owls

DIED 21st JUNE 1850

I am a brother to dragons and a companion to owls.

—Job XXX:29

I awaken in the middle of the night to cricket murmur, summer
heat, and sweat clinging to my skin, thinking, as I have each
time I have awakened since July 14: "Dad has died . . . My
father is dead now." This knowledge is like a heavy stone heaved
into a bottomless well.

No. The stone isn't moving, I find, short of breath. It is sitting
obdurately upon my chest. I have to rise. I can't just lie here in
this bedroom in the bungalow where my father was born; where
I know my grandmother, Meda, labored and cried out. That first
morning of his life, she must have awakened with newborn little
Rex bundled in the crook of her arm. Propped up on pillows, to
take him to breast, she surely saw the light coming through this

narrow window, the same window I now see at the foot of my bed, slightly illumined by moonlight.

Since this cycle of sleeplessness has rolled over me, on cooler nights I have migrated toward my favorite end of the couch in the living room, where the cat comes to me. We sit and comfort each other in the dark. But tonight—or is it morning?—I move to the front porch swing and hear it sing as I give a little push. The moon shines down above the eastern hills, and my feet feel cool as they graze the floorboards.

The furrowed trunk and drooping limbs of the incense cedar, Dad's birth-tree that was planted by his father the day he was born, rises in the yard before me, perhaps forty feet from where I am sitting. Until three weeks ago, Dad, eighty-four, was alive and seemingly well. Now his tree grows on without him.

The evening after we learned that Dad had suffered a stroke, three feathered messengers appeared in his birth-tree; quite literally, it seemed to me, bringing a message home to roost. Dad had been about to lead a seminar in San Diego when he had a stroke. He was taken to a hospital where it was discovered he had also experienced a small heart attack. A C.A.T. scan revealed there had been at least one previous heart attack. Soon after, he was diagnosed with "the old people's killer"—pneumonia.

At first, his condition was downplayed: Nothing to worry about. Despite this, the moment those three owls settled themselves upon the cedar tree's lower branches, I was filled with foreboding.

The owls appeared while we were sitting on the front porch with houseguests a bit after dusk. Daniel was especially fascinated. They were a novelty; during all the years we've lived here we have only seen a few owls on our one hundred ten acres, and never at such close range. Once, Daniel saw a pigmy-owl in the plum thicket behind the woodshed. Last year, a great horned owl perched briefly on an oak tree by the creek. At least one resident barn owl has lived nearby, whose droppings appeared in the hayloft for one or two seasons, and whose ghostly white whoosh of wings startled us one evening as it hurtled up from the shadows of the barn gable.

The three visitors to the cedar tree, however, were definitely Western screech-owls—a species we have never seen before. They were easy to identify because of their unusual call—a series of short chortling whistles that accelerated in tempo exactly as described in our *NGS Field Guide*. After spotting them from the porch with binoculars, we spent some time watching them and then decided to risk edging our way under the cedar tree with a flashlight. We took turns looking up into the tree, clearly seeing their markings, their rounded heads, ear tufts, brownish-gray plumage, and remarkable topaz-colored eyes gazing down at us.

At any moment, we expected to see the trio lift from the branches, but they did not. Strangely, they appeared unruffled as we observed them. I peered into the cedar boughs and saw the light in their eyes shining back at me. Finally, one houseguest took her camera with a flash attachment to see if she could get a picture. Surely the owls wouldn't tolerate that, we all said, but it was getting late, we had been owl-watching for some time, and were ready to go inside. Why not try?

Even the camera flash accompanied by our excited murmurs from the porch as we watched, did not disturb the owls. It was clear to me: Those owls wanted to be seen.

The owl, especially the screech owl, even in this day and age is still considered a harbinger of death in many parts of the world. So potent is the owl that most American Indians will not touch owl feathers, much less use them as part of their regalia.

But the visit of these owls kindled my apprehension for other reasons: The Applegate family crest has three owls emblazoned

upon it, and the owls, despite the close proximity of other large trees in the yard, had chosen Dad's birth-tree to roost upon. Even Daniel, without a superstitious bone in his body, was impressed by the symbolism. After I left for San Diego to see Dad at the hospital, the owls continued to appear. They stopped coming after Dad died. We have not heard them since, even in the distance, although tonight I half-expected it.

Since childhood, I have felt compelled to "read the signs." I have always tried to see what was disguised, tried to decipher an encrypted world. The process began when I was three or four years old during the years when my father and mother and I were still a family, living in Mexico. It was a culture rich with symbolism which I could not escape; where housemaids dragged me to cathedrals; where beautiful blue-robed women wore starry crowns and answered your prayers; where skulls were made out of sugar; where scapulars and strange charms could produce miracles; where the not-good could be warded off.

As years have passed, I have sometimes wished I could just float comfortably upon the surface called face value, but it is in me to dive, and this is a night for diving.

I am thinking about dreaming and the act of dreaming as I sit here rocking. I do not mean the ordinary dreams that arise from the turmoil of daily life. Tonight, for example, the dream I left abruptly was a series of disjointed vignettes, nevertheless understandable, given yesterday's frustrations, which included the failure to reach the bagpiper we want at the memorial service; the revelation that insurance for the Old Place has been cancelled; the phone calls, one after another, to various insurance companies; the phone calls from dozens of Dad's acquaintances; and having to repeat myself until I feel like screaming or bawling out loud.

When I awakened a little while ago I was perspiring. In my dreams, hoards of people—dangerous people—were thronging to the memorial service because they had read about it in the newspaper. I saw their faces pressed against the windows down at the Old Place, their features distorted behind the wavy surface of the windowpanes. I could not keep them away; they pushed their way into the house. These are real fears projected into dreaming. The article about Dad reprinted in several newspapers made this memorial service sound as though it were "come one, come all."

But the dream I am thinking of now is another sort of dream; the kind of dream that some psychologists refer to as a "marker" dream. It comes from a much deeper place and recurred throughout my childhood. It began when we lived in Mexico City and continued even after Mother and I left Daddy to go our way alone. Once, as a young mother, I had the same dream again, but never after that.

The dream began with pure motion, the sensation of being lowered, so that I was swaying or swinging a bit so that I could see without actually seeing richly colored fabric strips that held me like a sling or cloth cradle, while above me people I seemed to know were standing in a ring and singing or chanting. What is below me? Where am I going? It is the darkest dark, yet, oddly, I am calm. As a child, I remember clearly that I did not consider this dream a nightmare.

Connected to this particular dream is a peculiar method to which I resorted in order to go to sleep as a young child. I would lie alone in bed, in a small bedroom that opened to a hall bounded on one side by a Spanish-style wrought-iron balcony. To awaken mother, who was two rooms away, my cry had to be distinct, and I did not always succeed.

Eventually, I learned to comfort myself by entering what I now know is a hypnagogic state where I experienced the "twilight zone" of consciousness that exists between wakefulness and sleep. If I succeeded in reaching this state, my anxiety about being alone disappeared.

I invoked this state by turning an imaginary coin in my mouth; eventually, after I was certain I was feeling the slight pressure of the coin resting upon my tongue, I would lift the coin to the roof of my mouth and turn it over. I always knew whether the coin was heads or tails. I wanted to be able to trace the familiar heads-side with my tongue. This was the ritual's conclusion.

The heads-side of the coin was literally a head—that is, the profile of a helmeted warrior. I have always wanted to draw this profile and the precise contour of the helmet, but I cannot seem to get it right. I want to say exactly who this figure was but his name always eludes me. Perhaps he was Etruscan or Greek, but as the years have passed I know I have contaminated my initial impression by looking at too many images of old coins, hoping to jog my memory.

Still, there may be something to my connecting it with Greece. Some months ago, I learned that over millennia coins have played important parts in the world's death customs. Not only were coins placed upon the eyes of the dead in order to keep them shut, but relatives—almost always family women whose job it was to clean the corpse—often placed a single coin in the mouth of their loved one. The coin was intended to pay Charon, the ferryman, who waited to take the dead across the River Styx. Woe betide the unfortunate shade without a fare, for lost and alone he or she would wander for a hundred years. Similar beliefs are still held by some Buddhist sects and, with but few variations, were part of ancient Scandinavian lore.

What does this mean, I wonder? What is the nature of the coin I carry in my psyche? As life floats me closer to regions of the netherworld whom am I supposed to pay? On a night like this, so warm and sad, I drift. Looking past the moonlit branches of my father's tree I see the sheared summer-gold of our front pasture that is as pale as sand and smell the faintest trace of field pennyroyal—"horse mint" Great-Uncle Vince always called it—wafting up from the ditches.

Far across the valley, the town's street and yard lights glimmer in jewel-like clusters. To the southeast, the dark begins again; I can just make out the black crown of fir trees resting on Cemetery Ridge.

Ever since the cemetery has become part of my daily life, people I care about keep dying. Of course, people die, regardless. And my exaggerated sense of responsibility is just that—liberally laced with "magical thinking," especially at this late hour. My taking over the cemetery does not *make* people die even if it sometimes feels that way; feelings are not facts.

Still, I can't escape another question that runs deep. Was I somehow "born" to all this? The wind stirs, touching me lightly on my cheek. I want to ask, "Daddy, is that you?"

It is morning now and the day already promises to be hot. Walking down from the Tumblelow to the Old Place I see signs that the deer have been in the yard again. They have been nibbling at the limbs of the apple trees and one old rose. Fortunately, the gate to the big garden was closed. I think of Dad. He loved the strawberries we grew. Last summer, after Dad finished his usual inspection tour around the Old Place, he grinned and said to Daniel and me, as we passed the fenced garden, "Well, how are those strawberries of yours getting along?" Of course, we picked him some. It was fun to watch him pop them into his mouth. I don't how many strawberries he managed to get home to Carole. Colonel Superhawk loved his fresh strawberries.

Colonel Superhawk: The nickname never bothered him; he liked it, and used it for his own purposes. He actually introduced himself as Colonel Superhawk at some national conference years ago. He told me he put it this way, "My bleeding heart liberal daughter calls me Colonel Superhawk, and that's good enough for me." He got a big laugh.

I unlock the back door, hurry to disarm the house alarm, and head for the small room that Dad had been converting into his "shrine" over the past few years. "I'm going to get my 'shrine' all ready," he said to me only a few weeks ago. "When you give your historic tours and get going on all the ladies in the family and so forth, you can send the *men* in here."

Some months ago he put the finishing touches on his shrine: The various knives he designed are neatly arranged in a small glass case hanging on the wall over the mirrored sideboard. On the walls are framed documents and awards, such as the "Outstanding American Handgunner" award he received in 1996; a certificate stating that he was member of the National Rifle Association's Board of Directors, and another one announcing his admittance into the Cutlery Hall of Fame. He also had a framed photocopy, already fading, of a document issued by the War Department certifying that he had served in the Military Intelligence Division from 1942–1945. Dad also selected a few photographs for the shrine wall, including a picture of the two of us taken in the 1980s by a photographer for *National Geographic* magazine who was doing a story on Oregon Trail descendants.

High on the wall, hanging over the sidebroad like a star shining down, is a homemade plaque that either Grandpa Paul or Great-Uncle Vince made in shop class way back when. Its principle feature is a painting of a gate with an apple sitting in front of it. The apple is studded with red and green chips of glass. Under this image is what is supposedly our family motto, although I've never seen it except on this darkly varnished plaque. Carefully lettered are these words in Latin: *Vincit Qui Patitur* (He Conquers Who Endures.)

When Dad began working on his shrine a few years ago and began to bring in boxes of things, I was frankly uneasy. He once told me that as a high-school kid, coming to visit his grandparents, Buck and Flora, at the Old Place, he had witnessed his grandfather "get ready to go." In 1931, shortly before Buck died, but before anyone had been aware of his illness, his great-grandfather began gathering up all of his tools and papers and putting them into a chest.

"I just had the feeling," Dad said, "that he wasn't going to use any of those things again and that the old boy knew his days were numbered. I was very impressed by the way my grandfather handled things." The same big wooden chest is still in the east front room that has traditionally been called "the men's side."

A few months ago, during one of the visits he made to the Old Place after Rexito's death, Dad arrived with several boxes of additional papers, magazines, photographs, and keepsakes. All of these items were destined for the sideboard's lower compartments. This particular batch of memorabilia included dozens of magazine articles written about him, many with catchy titles such as: "Colonel Applegate—Connoisseur of Close Combat" and "He's Sort of a Thinking Man's Rambo."

Dad was no slouch in the catchy title department. He brought a copy of an article he had written sometime in the 1980s that examined the internal situation in Mexico; a situation he was convinced could lead to a Communist takeover. He titled it "The Evil Empire Eyes the Big Enchilada." His most recent title for a book he co-authored, *Bull's-Eyes Don't Shoot Back*, is quintessential Colonel Rex. I didn't give these latest additions to his shrine much thought as I helped him consolidate space to make room for the boxes.

Now, as I stand here looking at the pictures atop the sideboard—a recent portrait of Dad and one of Rexito dressed in his Texas best on Jessica's wedding day—I realize that just a few months ago, whether consciously or unconsciously, Dad was putting away his life. Perhaps it was just after the heart attack—the one that he didn't tell any of us about.

It is all I can do today, tired again from not sleeping, and feeling weepy, to make myself go through this damned sideboard so full of my father. But I will do it because I am trying to find some photographs of Dad, and anything else that I might incorporate in the display I'm preparing for his memorial gathering, which Carole has decided to call "A Celebration of Life." "That's more the kind of thing Rex would have wanted, I think, don't you?" she asked me.

As I open the right top drawer, it occurs to me that this sideboard, apart from my father's connection to it, has its own history. It once sat in Aunt Hazel's house on Douglas Street in the room that had originally been the dining room. In the early 1970s, when Susan and I alternated overnight care for Hazel, she was still conducting various business affairs from this sideboard. Because she was increasingly immobile, she was spending more and more time in a levered bed that had been moved into the dining room and placed close to the oil stove.

Aunt Hazel kept her postage stamps, checkbook and grocery receipts in this small right-hand upper drawer I have just opened. I can see that it must have originally been intended for silverware since it is divided into various sized compartments that are lined with green felt.

Hazel used the left-hand drawer for cemetery matters. In it, she stored a receipt book as well as notes and letters received about the cemetery. Kept in a plastic recipe box were cards listing blocks, lots, and plots. Two binders and assorted older records were located in the large lower portion of the sideboard behind a pair of doors where Dad's boxes of magazines are now. Aunt Hazel stashed the cemetery plat-map which she had specially mounted on a stout wooden board, under her bed.

Dad used to say that when Aunt Hazel was younger she virtually ran the town of Yoncalla out of her sideboard. She owned not only the cemetery and a section of prime timber, but the community telephone office, a sporting goods establishment that Gus ran, a gas station, and several other downtown buildings.

When I helped take care of her, she was still a handsome woman; it was not difficult to recognize her as the model for many of Gus's photographs. However, envisioning the nearly ninety-year-old Aunt Hazel I knew toting her own gun and fancy shooting at the exhibitions that she and Gus put on in various parts of the West was more difficult.

Hazel probably didn't much like the fact that I knew so much about her life as a young woman but Dad couldn't resist "telling on her." He loved her like a son, of course, and was her principle heir, yet he had the kind of bantering relationship with her that she must have once had with Gus. Just like Gus, Dad, enjoyed "getting a rise" out of Hazel.

Childless, Gus and Hazel were devoted to many young boys of their acquaintance. Because Dad lost his mother and was

Hazel's much younger Applegate cousin, he became a stand-in son. Dad lived most of the time with his mother's sister, Verlie Tracy. Still, Gus had a powerful influence upon my father, who became exactly the kind of rough-and-ready boy both Gus and Hazel craved. Whenever possible, and much to the annoyance of other members of his family, Dad preferred Gus and Hazel and visited them as often as he could.

I was instructed to call Hazel "aunt," and I thought of her that way. Of the many stories my father shared with me about Hazel, my favorite was about the time Gus wanted her to clamp a cigarette between her teeth so he could shoot the tip off, and she refused. It was not that she didn't trust his shooting, she was just death on tobacco. Undeterred, Gus continued to smoke Chesterfield's until he died. But back when both of them were still giving shooting exhibitions for Peters Ammunition Company, Hazel succeeded in getting Gus to let her put a piece of chalk in her mouth instead of the dreaded cigarette. It worked to great effect—as the chalk shattered with the impact of the bullet a little puff of chalk dust added flourish.

Hazel inherited the cemetery from the Applegate side of her family. Her grandfather, George Burt, married Ellen Applegate. Hazel's mother, Lucy Burt Samler, kept up the cemetery for years before passing it on to her only daughter. At least once a month, while I took care of Aunt Hazel, someone arrived at her front door, usually unannounced, making inquiries about buying a cemetery plot from her or trying to verify that there was still space available in a parent's or grandparent's or even great-grandparent's family lot that had been purchased untold years before.

Like her mother before her, Hazel rarely questioned lineage or demanded proof of ownership. Often, there was nothing save the word of the inquirer to validate that the person was entitled to a place in the cemetery. She might be an inveterate "penny-pincher"—

something Dad accused her of all the time, only partly in jest—but Hazel was not about to deprive a person of a burial place even if that person were stretching a family connection or deliberately lying.

I remember an argument Dad had with Aunt Hazel. I can still hear the rumble in his voice. He thought she should raise the price on an individual plot from fifty to seventy-five dollars. After all, there was liability insurance to pay, mowing charges, etc.

With the help of her best friend, Marione Lasswell, Aunt Hazel used to mow the whole five acres herself—the push mower clacking for however long it took to finish the job. But by 1970, she had grown frail, and she let Dad engage various men whom she paid a modest amount to take care of the cemetery. Still, she continued to regulate the sale of plots and keep up the records in her office—the sideboard.

Thinking of her now, I realize that while Aunt Hazel lived, there were no downed tree limbs or trash on the grounds to mar the cemetery's vistas, and there was plenty of gravel on the roads. When she finally reached ninety, she had someone drive her up to the cemetery so she could make an inspection tour. The condition of the cemetery was a source of pride—a responsibility she took seriously.

It strikes me, as I think of these things, that I did receive some training for my job as cemetery sexton; I just didn't know it at the time. There is so much I didn't know at the time.

The top of the sideboard holds a row of books, including multiple copies of Dad's best-known work, *Kill or Get Killed.* My mother, Edie, typed the manuscript from his handwritten version in 1943, a year before I was born, when they lived in Blue Ridge Summit, Pennsylvania. Dad was chief instructor in the art of hand-to-hand combat at Camp Ritchie, Maryland, at the time. A few years ago, this book went into its twenty-eighth printing—a fact Dad rubbed in by saying, "Shannon, when you get to this point, *then* we can have a conversation about writing books."

Next to the copies of *Kill or Get Killed* are several rare editions of *Riot Control Materiel and Techniques,* a book still considered the primer on crowd management and counter-terrorism—subjects for which Dad's expertise was internationally recognized. As I look at these books, I realize how easy it would be for a "souvenir" hunter to tuck one of them into a jacket pocket. For that matter, there are plenty of mementos all over the house that the light fingered could easily filch.

Crowd control: How ironic. Now it is up to me to think in these terms. If Dad can still laugh, wherever he is, I bet he's doing it. Maybe I should take one of his books up to the Tumblelow with me so I can read it tonight when I am awake again at 3 A.M.

My stomach is beginning to hurt, and every muscle feels tired even though I haven't been doing much except talking on the phone and worrying. I feel as if I were walking in glue or underwater. It is hard to think straight.

Dad's shrine room leads to the little side porch where speakers at the memorial service will stand addressing guests seated at chairs and picnic tables in the yard. Inevitably, even if I decide that the house will remain closed, there may be people who try to come into the Old Place through this side porch door I have just opened. Even the breeze feels hot today but there is plenty of shade under the horse chestnut tree and big myrtle trees where people will gather. I'll make sure I stand behind the speakers in the porch doorway instead of sitting in the family row. That way, I can be a better hostess, make sure the order of service is followed, and guard the door at the same time without seeming obvious.

Yesterday, I called some police officers in the county sheriff's department who knew and admired Dad. They have agreed to attend the gathering wearing their uniforms. They won't be on duty but they "will keep an eye out."

Still, even if most of the house is closed, I would like visitors to see Dad's shrine. But I don't know how to manage that. Along with dignitaries, professional associates, and friends of all kinds— many who have called Carole to offer condolences and tell her that Dad's obituary has appeared in several national newspapers, including the *Chicago Tribune* and the *New York Times*—there are scores of acquaintances.

Carole and I, as well as other family members, have fielded dozens of calls from people who say they "know" Dad from gun and knife shows. They feel entitled to attend his memorial. Many are surely well-meaning people but there are bound to be some "types" that Dad always referred to as the "Walter Mittys"—

wannabe soldiers of fortune and misguided gun nuts, with a few paranoid militia members sprinkled into the mixture.

It seems crazy to have to worry about the safety of the house when we family members will have so many other responsibilities. It's my decision to make and I've got to decide soon. Open or closed? I think of the poem General Patton wrote that hangs by Dad's fireplace down at the river: "On the fields of indecision lie the bones of countless thousands . . ."

Okay: Closed. The potential size of this gathering scares me to death. No, not death.

It is 2 A.M. How long will these bouts of sleeplessness last? Will they be over after the memorial gathering? Will they ever be over? This has been going on for many months; before Dad died, in fact. Six months. It started when Rexito died and has only got worse.

Lying alongside me on the couch are all these photographs: Dad as a handsome second lieutenant; Dad standing with his friend and fraternity brother John Wayne when they met in later years in an Acapulco nightspot; Dad looking dapper in a tux at a 1930s Sigma-Chi party at the University of Oregon. In this photograph, wearing his military policeman uniform he is practically leering at the beautiful all-American blonde movie actress, Carole Landis, as he is shepherding her around some official installation. He told me once that he had dated her a few times.

I'm astonished at another photo, one at the bottom of the pile that I must have fished out of the sideboard yesterday. I can't remember ever seeing it before. I could have used it to threaten Dad. It isn't exactly the kind of picture that he would have wanted sent to *National Rifleman* or *Soldier of Fortune*. Dad is wearing an evening dress and blonde wig at a Mexico City costume party. Perhaps, it was in our house there on Monteblanco. I recognize the tile on the fireplace.

More manly are several shots of him playing tennis, looking slim and fit. "Sexy Rexy" the co-eds at the University of Oregon called him. In another picture, this one sepia-toned that Gus may have taken, Dad looks like an illustration in a sentimental children's book. He's an adorable toddler standing in the midst of blooming dahlias taller than he is that were planted in the Old Place yard by his Grandfather Buck.

This, too, looks like a "Gus" picture. Dad, perhaps ten or twelve, is holding a rifle in one hand and a dead digger squirrel in the other, and appears to be climbing over a field fence. In another snapshot, this one obviously from the 1950s, he looks beefy and bearded in front of a rack of huge sea bass on some Baja beach. This must have been after Mother and I left to go back to the United States.

And speaking of Mother, here she is, looking lovely but slightly shy in her 1940s hat and smart suit standing beside Dad. He looks especially tall and impeccable in his uniform, hat in hand. This is their wedding day in Frederick, Maryland, in 1941, and they are on the steps of the church where Stonewall Jackson fired his revolver into the ceiling after arguing with Barbara Fritchie. " 'Shoot if you must/this old gray head/but spare our country's flag,' she said . . ." How many times have I heard those lines? If you're a daughter of a pair of patriots, you have heard this poem.

In the stillness of this summer evening, I feel a serenity I have not experienced in weeks. Seeing him like this, all around me in these photos representing each period of his life, I feel comforted. I carry him in pictures. I carry him in blood and bone. I have passed him on to my children. I think I can sleep. At least, tonight.

Goodnight, Colonel Superhawk. *Vincit Qui Patitur.*

The Naturalist's Cat

Deciding to leave home for so long a period wasn't easy for me, but in the end I surrendered: Two whole months—December and January—to write, draw, paint, hike, and explore this part of the Oregon Coast, and be accountable only to myself. In the whole of my adult life, I have never had so much time to call my own.

Daniel and Susan are watching over the cemetery and the Old Place while I am here for my writer's residency at Sitka Center for Art and Ecology. At home, in the wake of deaths and changes, I was reeling from increased pragmatic responsibilities and unexpected financial revelations. Limited family resources have been compounded by the fact that Daniel still has two more years of law school. Susan, living upstairs in the Tumblelow, is helping with expenses until her own house is finished, but daily life in a small space with three busy people has been complicated,

145

to say the least. Traveling back and forth as an artist-in-residence several times a week to schools scattered over a county that is as large as the state of Connecticut left me physically depleted.

But more to the point, during this year that I have come to call *Año del Muerto* (Year of the Dead), I have suffered from a case of emotional and even spiritual exhaustion. There have been so many adjustments of various kinds that I haven't had time to really contemplate, much less accept them. For months, I have felt that I have been walking through a dark and buffeting storm with my head lowered, my eyes struggling to focus upon the shifting ground directly in front of me. I have needed shelter; time to look up and assess the damage.

It all began with Rex's death from lung cancer last December that was followed by the sickness of my writer friend Jody

Procter who was to die in June from the same form of cancer that took my brother. Just three weeks later, my father's unexpected passing shocked us all. What should I say killed Dad—a broken heart?

Being here has been a gift, but now my time is nearly over. I find my mind drifting toward home—away from the writer's life I have been relishing on this coastal slope where I am surrounded by huge Sitka spruce with the luminous blue line of the ocean just visible through my studio window. I don't want to think about the cemetery in the rain. I'm guessing road repairs will be needed because of the severity of the winter. I don't want to worry about how I am going to pay for things when I get home. Nor do I miss the phone ringing or the renewal of my scurrying around that I will need to do for many months ahead to help keep us solvent. Nevertheless, I feel an inexorable tug toward home. The tide is changing.

The other day, after a long walk along the beach at low tide, I climbed a huge rock, carefully finding footing on slippery lower ledges that were weeping seaweed the color of old bottle glass. Finally, I sat down in a basin-shaped depression that was too high to have been pooled with seawater. There, for some moments, tired from my climb, I sat watching revelations visible only when the tide is ebbing: Bulbous-tipped whips of kelp, amber and fleshy, lay stranded on dark glistening sand along with orange fragments of crab shells macerated in the great maw that is the remarkably un-Pacific Ocean. The setting felt remote; the end of the world. But the world was there, represented by empty Clorox bottles, snake heaps of bright blue plastic rope, rusted oil cans with corporate names dented and shortened to "Ex" and "Tex," and a large, barnacle-encrusted metal barrel containing God-knows-what that the waves had wedged into a driftwood thicket. And everywhere, of course, easily seen from high on my rock, were jagged flecks of white Styrofoam that winked enticingly at flying gulls and oyster-catchers; hors d'oeuvres for seabirds to choke on laid out upon a smooth tablecloth of sand.

High and dry on my own perch, even though I knew that danger would soon come crashing all around me, my vigilance broke. I let myself cry uncontrollably. Death is a big wave.

It is nine o'clock on this January night and wind is howling through stout branches of Sitka spruce as I listen to the last movements of Brahm's *Requiem*—a storm of desolation and consolation if ever there was one. I have just put away my watercolors and have finally finished the painting of a Mexican candelabrum that I have been working on ever since I arrived at Sitka.

My sister, Lisha, sent this wonderfully garish and certainly macabre artifact to me for Christmas. Its principle feature is the same feminine grinning death's head known as *La Flaca* (The Skinny One) that is found on many objects associated with the partly pagan, partly religious holiday *Día de los Muertos* cele-brated in many Latin countries, especially Mexico. On the can-delabrum's coiling rim, just above the shoulders of the colorfully long-skirted *La Flaca*, sit two small plaster owls. Lisha wrote that she had never before seen owls on *Día de los Muertos* mementos. They reminded her of the Western screech owls that flew onto the branches of Dad's birth tree shortly before he died.

The candelabrum holds places for three candles—I have chosen white ones—all of them burning now, and flickering at me, casting moving shadows on the wall. The candles represent Rexito, Dad, and Jody. I especially think about Jody here at Sitka as I enjoy my writer's life. Why do I get to keep on writing when he no longer can? And I remember, as the flame of his pale candle flares in unearthly bluish brightness, how despite the cancer's inroads, Jody kept on working on his book *Toil* until the very end. Toil, indeed.

Tonight after finishing the watercolor I add the words "Año del Muerto 1998" at the bottom in lettering black and gold. With a soft breath, I blow each candle out, watching three faint smoke trails rising, disappearing.

An evening alone with my thoughts as spruce branches rap on windows stretches ahead of me. I can't seem to fall asleep before 2 A.M. despite my long walks and much reduced ingestion of caffeinated beverages. And so I write. Of course I do.

Last night, in the midst of physical isolation, when everyone else at Sitka Center had gone home for the evening, I thought I was left completely alone up here save for the passing elk herds that sometimes go "bump in the night" as they browse along their well-worn paths through the nearby alder groves. I was startled by footsteps on the decking across from the Tree House and then recalled the presence of a woman visitor who was staying in the small guest room just down the walkway. It was Erica Fielder, a naturalist and artist, who would be taking my place as a resident writer in about ten days. Earlier, as I had watched her arrival through my studio window, and noted how her incredibly long legs made short work of the distance between her car and the administrative offices, I experienced a surge of resentment.

She had come to check out territory that would soon be hers. "Reconnaissance," Dad would have called it. I did the same thing, in fact, some months ago, receiving a rather chilly greeting from the novelist I would soon replace. The worm has turned. A book worm, probably.

Tonight, Erica is on her way back home to California and I really am alone up here. Fortunately, before she left his afternoon, I managed to get over my pique and invited her for tea. As I saw Erica glancing around the Tree House—"my" Tree House, I was about to write—I knew she was looking at things from the vantage point of a prospective tenant.

She turned out to be very likeable; I loved her paintings of sea mammals, her lively manner and passionate talk about the natural world. But the best part of our visit, which turned out to last an hour or more, was that Erica gave me a gift that will keep me company tonight—perhaps the most wonderful gift that any one person can give to another: a good story. Writing down this story, about Erica and her cat, is the task I have set for myself for the rest of this evening. I am hoping that there is not another power failure that will leave me all alone in the January dark, writing with my automatic pencil by the meager light of my death's head candelabrum.

Erica's cat, Franceria, was gray, exactly the color of a Pacific coastal plant known as beach silverweed (*Franceria chamisonis*; lately revised to *Ambrosia chamisonis* by botanists). That Erica should name her beloved cat after a plant is perhaps not surprising. Erica's parents, devoted to horticulture, botany, and bird-watching, bestowed on Erica a name inspired by *Ericaceae*, the classification for plants in the hardy heath family.

Franceria's name was never shortened for convenience except when Erica and the cat communed. The name "Franceroo" might be cooed.

Russian Blue formed part of the cat's genetic heritage, but really Franceria was a farm cat that never weighed more than seven or eight pounds.

"Not cat show material," Erica laughed.

Further, like all cats of my own acquaintance, Franceria had some unlovable characteristics. Still, the fact that Erica's cat was a dandy mouser made her indispensable since Erica lives in a rural setting bordering the Mendocino coastline, where field mice are plentiful.

Erica was grateful that the mouse population was decreasing, but as a naturalist and environmentalist she worried about Franceria's impact upon relatively uncommon marsh birds, such as rails and snipes. When danger was near, depending upon their camouflage to protect them, these birds stayed put rather than fly away. They were "sitting ducks" for the likes of Franceria, who was also fleet enough to catch hummingbirds and song sparrows, usually leaving only the wings as evidence of her bloodlust.

Franceria seemed undaunted by the size of her prey. Once, Erica discovered a pair of bunny ears, a fluffy tail, and two hind legs left over from a small bush rabbit that, when alive, had been about the same size as Franceria. Usually slender, and even slightly dainty in appearance, Franceria was lounging nearby, her stomach bulging like a post-meal python's. Weasels, too, diversified Franceria's diet.

Erica was upset when she noticed that Franceria's weight was dropping. A veterinarian diagnosed the condition as a kidney disease. Erica took her back and forth to the vet's for weeks, where Franceria received medications through saline injections that she obviously hated. Erica eventually learned to administer the injections herself to avoid long trips by car on the winding California Highway 1. For a while, the injections seemed to improve things. Eventually, however, Franceria's moments of seeming like her former self became less frequent.

Formerly, Franceria had been able to leap nimbly to a favorite "perch" inside the house: a windowsill where Erica grew starts for her vegetable garden, sometimes warming them artificially by placing an electrical heating strip under the seed pots. Erica kept attempting to grow tomatoes but she was no match for her cat, who quickly knocked the pots of seedlings on the floor each time she sprang up on the sill to warm herself.

Despite the vet's and Erica's loving ministrations, Franceria soon lost the ability to leap; rather pathetically she climbed to her spot by terraces of furniture. To give her cat comfort, Erica removed all her seed pots and placed the heating strip on the sill. Erica felt it was just the thing "to warm old bones." After all, Franceria was sixteen years old.

Erica had known Franceria since her kittenhood. She was a strictly outdoor cat at Jug Handle Farm, where Erica had her first job as a naturalist and interpreter. There, Franceria was adopted by a handful of staff members. But in the end, Franceria became Erica's cat—although, as everyone knows, cats really "belong" only to themselves.

Erica was grateful for the financial contributions she sometimes received from Franceria's many friends as Franceria's treatments became increasingly expensive. After months of visible decline, and given Franceria's long and active life, Erica talked to her cat. "Okay. Franceroo, it's your call. You're in charge. I'm no longer going to try to change what seems to be the natural course of things."

Because the cat could no longer groom herself, Erica began combing Franceria's hair, lifting her up and down from the windowsill. When Erica went to work in her vegetable garden she gently carried Franceria with her. Franceria seemed not to eat or drink but somehow kept on living, insisting on dragging herself outside on her tummy.

Once, Franceria disappeared from where she'd been sunning and resting. "She's gone off to die," Erica thought, knowing this was the way of some cats. Later that morning, on a trip to her compost pile, Erica heard pathetic mewing. She followed the sound, found Franceria, and carried her back home.

"On her last day," Erica said, "the two of us spent hours together in the garden. I'd pick her up carefully and move her as I went from the chard bed to the zucchini bed. When I finished gardening that day, I called old friends from Jug Handle Farm to tell them Franceria was on her last legs. Several of them drove a considerable distance so they could say good-bye."

Next morning, Erica found her cat on the floor in front of the sill, utterly stiff, devoid of that mysterious life force we mostly take for granted. It was a gray, drizzling coastal day.

Erica called her friends, who drove down again. All who came knew Franceria's essential wildness. They talked about Franceria, trying to guess how many birds she'd eaten over the years.

After a discussion about what to do with Franceria's body, Erica finally said, "You know, I think we should put her up on the hillside, have a little ceremony and leave her there. The birds and mice can nibble on her. After all, she's partly made out of birds and mice and the other things she's eaten, and she can re-enter the cycle of life."

Franceria was carried up to a beautiful chaparral-covered headland overlooking the Pacific. Erica tenderly placed Franceria on the ground, as the group of friends formed a reverent circle around the small body.

"After that," Erica said, "I went back up the hill to see the progress and, yes, I thought of it as *progress* and not deterioration." Erica noted how the grass grew higher around Franceria each time she visited. Not that Franceria was just a living thing gone dead—something to merely observe.

I think suddenly of Leonardo da Vinci as I write this, and his passion for sketching dying old people, and even cadavers, when the opportunity presented itself. When I heard about da Vinci's visits to hospitals and morgues, I was a young woman attending art school and thought such dispassion was reprehensible. How could he have been so cold and unfeeling? How could da Vinci just sit and concentrate on his drawing as the person lying there died before his eyes?

Now I look at this a little differently. It's possible that Leonardo, like Erica, observed with a compassion that lived beside his curiosity. Yes, he drew the gnarled, vein-roped contours of old men on their narrow cots. But all the while, perhaps, da Vinci was reflecting upon how this one must have been a textile worker, hands still stained purple from the vats; and how that one—who had one leg shorter than the other—must have lurched home, making his way down narrow, winding streets. Who knew, perhaps at one time, the old man lying there, his mouth bubbling, had once had a plump wife and six or seven children who loved him? Surely Leonardo did more than simply mildly gaze at Death's approach as his expert fingers slid colored chalk over vellum.

Who's to say that he did not lift a cup of water to old parched lips in those waning moments of life, or hear some last confession because the priest was late and Death was on time?

For about ten days, Erica watched the grass growing taller around Franceria who appeared largely unchanged. The rising ruffle of grass, Erica said, made it appear as though her cat were sinking into the earth despite the fact that she was not buried. One morning when Erica arrived it was obvious that some creature had found Franceria but hadn't moved her. Ravens, probably, Erica thought, remembering how she had heard that Tibetan Buddhists deliberately placed cadavers on hillsides so that raptors could clean the bones.

Despite Erica's training as a naturalist and artist, she had never watched the process of decomposition at such close range. "I was fascinated," she confessed. "As the flesh disappeared, I could see all the mechanisms of animation; the pulleys and levers that were bones, muscles, and sinew. Franceria, we used to say, owned the sharpest claws in the West. We felt them every time when she climbed up on our laps, kneading them into our knees."

The same claws were there, the same teeth. Erica would touch the changing body. Finally, the spine and tail, strung like white beads were all that remained, along with the delicate skull. Once or twice, as days became months, Erica held the skull up, turning it in her hands and then lifting it. "I wanted to see through Franceria's eyes. I looked through her empty sockets, following the steep descent of the headland clear to the rocks and crashing surf. I sat there and thought, 'In death, a mystery, is revealed to me.' "

She continued, "I'd even talk to the skull, thinking, of course, of the lines from *Hamlet*: 'Alas, poor Yorick.' " Erica laughed, "But the only response I got from Franceria's skull was a grin. She just grinned and grinned. An endless grin, I guess you could say. It was quite a sensation to feel those sharp little teeth under my fingertips—the same little teeth that bit me, once. And of course, bit into all those birds."

Erica quietly sipped her tea and looked for a moment as

though she might cry. "I became . . . well . . . quite at home with Franceria's skull. I have a personal relationship with it, now. This is not macabre to me and is in no way disrespectful. Yet, when I've occasionally talked about Franceria, and the fact that she is still up there on the hillside, some people seem repelled, particularly those with bona fide house cats. 'How could you leave that poor cat out in the cold!' they chide me, as though burying a cat in a shoebox in the backyard were a better fate."

Erica last saw Franceria on the day of solstice, in the weather-beaten December that has just passed when storm systems brought snow even to the California coast. A skiff of white briefly covered already pale beaches—a sight to see, Erica said. When she and her partner, David, took a long, cold hike, the snow was melting but the temperature was dropping again, freezing long grasses into shining lines and covering crests of higher headlands with intricately patterned "frost heaves." Even the leaves of the Franciscan chaparral glittered with ice as though decorated for the season.

Until this walk, Erica's partner had been a bit squeamish when she spoke of her "visits" to Franceria. Perhaps, like many people, he felt he would rather recall those he loved as living and breathing rather than still and dead. But on this solstice hike, surprising Erica, David suggested that they call upon Franceria, which they did.

"He talked to her," Erica recalled. "*We* talked about her—*tenderly.*"

To Erica, Franceria is still a "thing of beauty," as well as a stimulus to inquiry and a source of fascination.

She added, in a thoughtful tone, "You see, I try to live a conscious and artful life. My relationship with Franceria in all her stages of living and dying seems consistent with my philosophy."

I tried to imagine stalks of glittering grass arching over a small white skeleton. I know that part of the California coast, the sweeping views, the cold veils of mist descending and ascending, revealing and concealing. I saw myself on the headland standing over those little bones. Only the cat was named Cybelle: my old cat.

Erica looked as if she were puzzling over something as she finished her tea and rose to take her empty mug to the sink. The wind was the only thing talking, or perhaps singing.

That was the moment, I remember, when suddenly I glimpsed what the Tree House might soon feel like without me. Surely, Erica would move things around to suit herself. The place would look less cheery without my brightly colored throws from home. Would I take or leave the collection of spruce cones, and the black-and-white stones I'd placed in the blue ceramic bowl found in the cupboard? Who would help me carry the heavy sleeping couch back to where it had been when I arrived?

I was already moving out in my mind. It was an unpleasant, disengaged feeling. I called myself back, just as I am doing now, so I can finish writing down Erica's story. No question about it: I am better off up on the Mendocino headlands, standing over cat bones. I will make myself hear the steady murmur of breaking surf under winter wind.

When Erica made her way from the sink back to the chair, she moved with remarkable grace for a woman of her height. I was about to write that she walked like a cat, but her legs are far too long for that.

She folded her arms and looked out the window that is over the sleeping couch, out past the deck—useless in this blustering chill season, and mounded with dead alder leaves. I watched her lift her head slightly. She was surely admiring the shadowed semi-circle of big spruce—the sentinels that guard this place.

But when she finally spoke, it became clear Erica was far from spruce; much closer to cat and composting. "You know," she began, "I find myself questioning certain burial practices after all this. Why are people buried several feet under the earth when almost all the microorganisms which promote decay live in the top six inches of the soil?"

"Ever the naturalist," I said. We both smiled.

The modern European idea of death holds that one moment we are alive, and the next we are dead—a matter of breath or brain, a severing, a complete break measurable on the dully glowing screen of a hospital monitor.

"He's gone," someone said in the San Diego hospital. But when I went into the room, Dad was still there. Just an hour or so earlier, while he was lying there I had been massaging his shoulder and talking to him. I told him I loved him one more time and, although he was unconscious, I felt that he heard me. Later, when he apparently had fled his body, according to the medical definition "had died," I could still see his feet, bare upon the bed sheet, and the long rest of him reaching out from under the hospital gown before they pulled the covers up. Soon, he was wheeled away. And somehow, lifted stranger to stranger, laid out in a boxcar or refrigerated van, he made his silent way home to Oregon.

It is strange to think this but somehow comforting: I like knowing he is really under there. Up in the cemetery. He is still a fact. Whether I can see it or not, an active physical process is taking place. Dad must have wanted it that way since he wanted to be buried, not cremated.

In some parts of the world, the physical undoing of us, the final stripping down to essentials is acknowledged and made visible.

I would not want to go so far as the Torajan people of Indonesia that I've just read about, however, who, when visited by an anthropologist, introduced him to a dead grandmother who had been seated in her grandson's living room for three years, wrapped in layers of cloth that were supposed to absorb the odiferous liquids of decay. One is reminded of Anthony Perkins and his desiccated old mother in her rocking chair in the movie *Psycho*. Of course, there was no Smell-O-Vision, thus the impact—fierce in my case as I clutched my boyfriend Jeff Nilson's arm—was merely psychological and visual.

Curiously, according to anthropologist Nigel Barley, the smell emitting from the Torajan grandmother seemed endurable to her family who treated her as though she were not really dead at all. To them, death was far from abrupt and extended for years marked with rituals linked to various stages of the body's decomposition. Other groups, whose mortuary customs include keeping the corpse in the house for a time before cremation or burial, seem similarly inured to the smell of death or find ways to offset it.

Makah people, for example, whose territory clings to the westernmost edge of today's Washington state, sometimes threw their dead into the breakers to let the saltwater work on all those odiferous bodily fluids. A nineteenth-century diarist named James Gilchrist Swan wrote of the corpse of a headman named "Swell" who was pitched into the surf after being shot to death. After this treatment, even eighteen days later, no one complained of the smell of Chief Swell when he was finally "rolled up tight in two new blankets and put into a new box nailed shut." Since white customs had already replaced many Native customs by 1860, canoe burials, practiced by many other Northwest peoples, may have fallen out of favor with the Makah.

The same Pacific waters that cleansed Chief Swell, so many years ago, have also cleansed me. The other day, crying salt, high on my rock, I suddenly stopped. I heard a roar in my ears: The waves making thunder. I could breathe again; I could watch the waves, one after the other, after the other. I felt incredibly alive, glad that grief had not swept me away after all.

For a long time, I just sat there waiting for the transcendent moment in the life of each wave. Just as a wave reared—opaque and swollen in satin tautness—it received a fleeting instant of stunning translucency. Water's real nature was revealed for what it really is—nothing more than liquid light whose utter blue-green color comes not only from the sky's reflection but from incandescent depths, as well.

As a child, aquamarine was my favorite colored crayon. I applied it vigorously to everything—even to girls on swings, baby lambs, and elephants. Aquamarine: Greek and Etruscan artists believed it was a sacred color that resembled more than just the vivid shade of waves on the Mediterranean Sea. Reserving it for frescoed depictions of the skin color of their death gods, Greek artists applied aquamarine until it glowed. The color within waves was also the color of putrescence.

I have read about many customs relating to the decomposition of bodies, but I most appreciate the straightforward and symmetrical viewpoint of the Merina people of Madagascar. Maurice Bloch explains that to the Merina, death is merely a stage in a much longer process that begins at the moment of birth. Every human and animal changes gradually throughout life, from being wet and soft, with malleable infant bones, to an adult who is a mixture "of hard dry elements, principally the bones, and soft elements, principally the flesh." Gradually, after death, the corpse becomes mainly dry, the wet stuff sloughing away, completing the process from wet to dry, from soft to hard. The transformation of the body is complete. The spirit has moved on. Those left alive keep on living.

Many people, including numerous tribes of historic North America believed in secondary burials. That is, immediately after death and appropriate ceremony, an individual's body would be buried in a relatively shallow grave. But such a grave was understood to be temporary. Burial for a ritualistically specific period of time was necessary to complete the decay of flesh. Once the "wet" parts of the body had drained away, usually within two years, the "dry" parts, in the form of bones were exhumed for reburial.

The second funeral, and final farewell, occurred when decomposition was complete, marking a change that was both real and culturally symbolic. Most peoples perceive all bones as looking alike (although any forensic scientist would say that bones range from "highly, to minutely individual"). Secondary burials acknowledged that "the one" had finally reached the state where he or she is merely part of the "many." The corpus has become incorporated into the clan or group. The group is the "one" made out of the many.

In the secondary burial then, the corpse found itself no longer alone; it joined others in a mass grave—a term that makes many of us shudder because we may not fully understand its symbolic function in various world cultures. Even in Europe of the present day, the practice of reburying the dead is still taking place, although it is not understood in the same context as say, the secondary burials of the Merina people of Madagascar, or of the ancient Klamath peoples of Oregon. In crowded parts of the Western World some cemeteries decree that a grave may be occupied by an individual corpse only a few years; after that period it is time to make the space available for more newly dead, thus, human remains are exhumed and transferred either to a "charnel house" or mass grave.

But what I like about the idea of secondary burials in non-European cultures is that they provide an interval in which to get used to the idea of death. Enough time has passed for things to simmer down, for shock to be replaced by acceptance, for battles over inheritance to be resolved, for old resentments to fade, and for some of the overwhelming sense of loss of a loved one to reach more endurable levels. In two years or so, life has resumed for those "left behind" simply because it must.

This is quite different from what Louis-Vincent Thomas observed when he commented upon the failure of modern funeral customs, or the lack of them, when he wrote, "The signs of mourning have fallen into disuse—we have passed from mourning clothes in twenty-four hours to twenty-four hours of mourning."

When we are not permitted to even glimpse the dead, or, as in open coffin "viewings" when we see a corpse cosmeticized by some funeral home makeup artist, it is difficult to absorb the fact of death. In this culture, the corpse of anything is reviled. In our sanitized world, even the word "decay" makes us cringe. Perhaps seeing the bones of our dead after two years or more of mourning would not be such a bad thing.

We could say good-bye at a second funeral that could be much more meaningful than the first. Many people describe a funeral as an ordeal that it impossible to absorb because it comes on the heels of death. Funerals are frequently experienced as surreal and insubstantial. They are to be "got through"; disorientation, detachment, and perhaps a drug from the doctor leave only the sensation of guilt and a feeling of lack of closure when the event is over.

In fairness, ours is not the only culture that wards off the fearful spectacle of the corpse. It has been ever thus, almost everywhere on the globe, even among people who practice secondary burials. Corpses have always been perceived as inimical to the living. All recently dead—to use a term employed by cultural anthropologists—are "liminal."

The root for "liminal"—"lim" or "limn"—once referred to the word for "threshold," as in the threshold of a door that must be stepped over in order to pass through to the other side. The dead are especially feared during this liminal period when they might, in their confusion, before passing over the threshold of living into whatever comes after dying, decide to come back to the world and do harm instead.

Corpses that have not yet found their way back to bones are seen as dangerous—a source of pollution that is not necessarily connected to hygienic concerns. Death carries a threat of contagion, even if it is merely psychological. As I think of my early experiences as a sexton when I felt that I was somehow "attracting" the death of people I cared about because of my connection with the cemetery, I now realize that, in a sense, I was unconsciously making death "contagious." I had brushed up against it.

By being in the proximity of the dead there is a fear that it might be catching. People have felt this fear for millennia, long before the communication of diseases through direct or indirect contact was scientifically understood.

In rural China, women, such as married daughters and daughters-in-law—"but not the sexually inactive unmarried daughters," according to an anthropologist named Watson— were supposed to rub their unbound hair against the coffin and thereby symbolically absorb the pollution of their dead so it could not contaminate others. This is an extraordinary image: family women, robed in white—the Chinese color for death. Did they sway in unison, as they took their place in the incense-clouded procession? Did their dark, unbound, curtains of hair swish against the lacquered surface of the coffin?

Corpses in most societies are considered unlucky when they have no family members to clean and prepare them as custom dictates. Without relatives to care for them, the dead may be left to the un-tender ministrations of others whose job it is to handle corpses and who are often despised. Corpse-handlers are often restricted to the fringes of the general population. Among Hindus, for example, only the "untouchables" have contact with the dead; within Judaism, the priestly class is forbidden contact with a corpse. In some cultures, "death handlers" are ostracized by other members of their community.

All over the world, even today, some feel there is a certain taint to the business of "undertaking." I wonder, does a modern "fear of contagion" extend to those who manage cemeteries? Cemeteries, after all, are places where both the recent and long dead are known to congregate. Some people know me only as a cemetery sexton; someone with whom they are forced to interact during one of the most upsetting times of their lives.

Just before I left for my writer's residency I was surprised when an associate funeral director that I was talking to on the telephone called me a fellow member of The Industry, by which, I suppose, he meant the death industry.

And I have my father to thank for it. Before I left for Sitka, as Daniel and I sat making sure all the cemetery records had been properly updated, cross-checking the two ring binders with the card file, I gathered copies of death certificates received over the past year and placed them, according to date of death, in a green binder. "Well, it's all yours now," Daniel said.

I snapped a copy of Dad's death certificate and "authorization of transportation" sent from California into the binder, and promptly burst into tears.

Tomorrow, I will leave Sitka. But I still have one more lovely coastal morning, illuminated by the oblique light of winter. Today, I will not take the road to the beach but, instead, choose the path that leads toward pale alder trees. I feel the wind bite as I walk with my head up, as I watch the alders changing into white candles glowing in the forest ahead. Sometimes you have to go away to get home.

Feasting the Dead

We come only to dream
We come only to sleep
It is not true that we
Come to live on Earth
        —Aztec King of Texcoco, 1459

"The worst part was not being able to tell my brother good-bye," I think as I look out the scratched, double-paned window of the aircraft. Beneath me the brown *montañas de México* are crinkled like brains; roads are gold snakes; fields are animal pelts. When will the volcanoes appear in the distance?

"Look for the caca-colored cloud of pollution," Lisha said a few days ago when we last spoke on the telephone. "That's how you will know you are getting close." According to the stewardess, the plane is still about forty-five minutes outside of

Mexico City. Tomorrow or the day after, Lisha and I will make our way through the vast city to Panteon de Español where we will place the other half of our brother's ashes in a family crypt.

The man sitting next to me continues to cough and cough; explosive, helpless coughing that has been going on since we lifted from the runway at Dallas/Fort Worth. At first, I thought he was suffering from a severe cold and I wanted to protect myself— as though one could in this enclosed coffin-like metal lozenge.

When he first arrived at this row of seats, I looked up. He was placing a snappy looking leather carry-on in the overhead bin. I noticed his neatly creased trousers, the pinstriped shirt, and silk Italian tie under a well-cut sport coat.

Like many of my brother's friends whom I met last year in Houston at the funeral, the cougher seemed less Texan and more *Gentlemen's Quarterly*. When he sat down I judged him to be around the same age as Rexito's buddies: in his late thirties or early forties. Before the serious coughing started, I would have pegged him as just another variant of the prime-of-life, upwardly mobile business or professional type one sees around urban centers and on airplanes. I did notice, fleetingly, that like some other men his age, he was beginning to experience a little thinning in the hair department, and a slight thickening in the belt department.

It was only after I stood up, in order to make my way to the restroom, that my impression of him changed. Glancing down, I took in the oddly placed dark tufts of hair on the perspiring, ashen crown of his head. Then I experienced an awful recognition. This was not just another anonymous stranger on an airplane but someone going through chemotherapy. The hair and terrible cough were—are—dead giveaways.

Except for smiling and saying "Hello" not a single word has been exchanged. I sense he wants it that way, that he is mortified by his terrible coughing spasms yet cannot prevent them from exploding out of his lungs. Perhaps, he can't even speak without coughing.

Occasionally, he has sipped carefully from a bottle of water but when lunch was served an hour ago, he declined by shaking his head. Of course, I didn't blame him. It was the blandest "gringo" lunch I have ever seen, even allowing for the quality of most airplane food. I just picked at it then decided to save myself for better things. We are, after all, winging our way to a country that boasts an outstanding national cuisine—the cuisine of my childhood.

But surely, this fellow next to me, now wracked by another bout of coughing, doesn't care about cuisine. All he wants to do is to be able to breathe. And he is heading for one of the most polluted cities on earth.

I close my eyes and tilt back the seat, trying to make myself relax. A little tremor goes through my body in response to each cough. Do I actually smell tobacco on the fellow's jacket, or am I imagining this? I even think it might be emitting from his lungs but dismiss this as unreasonable.

Since I stopped smoking years ago, I have become hypersensitive when it comes to the odor of cigarette smoke. Last year, after my brother's funeral, at the gathering that I have come to think of as The Texas Wake, I was astonished by the numbers of smokers in the crowd. The rooms were hazed with smoke—not only from Salems, Camels, and Marlboros but from a Cajun-style barbeque cooker, brought in for the occasion. At one point, I remember the host of the gathering say, "My God, it is amazing how much people are eating! The caterer is running out of stuff."

Amidst occasional bursts of hilarity, and the sounds of popping beer tabs, my brother seemed to be silently reigning over his own wake, grinning from ear to ear, in the form a life-sized color photograph. He held a drink in one hand, and a cigarette in the

other; it was the same enlarged photo his fiancée had made for his fortieth birthday party, the previous year. At the time, the Rex of flesh and blood, was faraway in a wintry Bosnian landscape ridden with land mines—unable to attend his own birthday except by proxy.

When I saw the same life-sized photo at Rex's wake in Houston, it occurred to me that it was a modern version of the effigies once fashioned in medieval Europe from beeswax or stuffed kid leather so that an image of the dead person would be present in the funeral procession and later at the wake. Sometimes the deceased was actually present. There are stories about old-time Irish and Welsh wakes where the dead man's corpse was propped up in a corner or lashed into a chair so that it seemed to participate in the festivities while people around it ate copiously, made toasts, and passed clay pipes. Each turn of the pipe was punctuated by the act of blowing smoke into the corpse's face as a kind of blessing. It is clear that American Indians aren't the only ones who consider tobacco smoking ceremonial.

But the smoking in Houston wasn't ceremonial but habitual.

I know—Salem addict that I was for twenty-five years and the fact is, I wish I could light up right now.

The man seated next to me tries unsuccessfully to sip his water again but breaks out in his cough. It is too painful. I deliberately turn my gaze to the window where there is nothing to look at save dense congealed cloud cover thick as forest fire smoke.

I remember my father sitting in that smoke-filled room. Still, as Buddha. In the middle of that Houston townhouse living room, he sat in a wing-backed chair surrounded by a haze of tobacco manufactured by his dead son's friends who came to him singly, or in pairs, all evening long, paying homage and telling stories about Rex.

Dad was an asthmatic who never smoked in his life. For years, he begged his son to stop smoking. Now my father continues to sit in my mind. Managing to smile slightly, his thinning hair slicked back, his head up, both hands resting on the top of his cane. I know now as I knew then: He was not there at all. Not even as he nodded and laughed briefly at some reminiscence about his son. Not even when some attractive young woman in a low-cut blouse smiled coyly as she leaned down to offer The Colonel a plate loaded with aromatic Texas barbeque. "No, thanks," Dad said without a flicker of interest. "No, really . . . no."

Eating, drinking, and smoking: Perhaps we do these things with such zest in the wake of someone's death to remind ourselves that we, the lucky ones, are still alive. Stories about the deceased, even hilarity and debauchery, have always been part of the aftermath of death. What went on in Texas has gone on in Africa, Asia, and South America, too. In the Western World, gatherings held for the express purpose of "waking" and "watching" the dead have flourished since pre-Christian times. They have persisted despite prohibitions enacted by both church and state. No institution has ever succeeded in curbing the impulse of people to comfort each other as they simultaneously mourn and celebrate in the light, or more aptly, the dark of death.

At the gathering of Rex's friends, I heard one of them say—as he stood in the midst of a Cajun style feast, drinking libations spiked with sadness—"You know, I think this may be a *wake* up call." There is yet another new spin on an ancient tradition.

The rhythmically fitful wheeze next to me tells me that my fellow passenger is sleeping. I steal a look but resist giving him a maternal pat. Unlike him, I have heard the clicking sound of the speaker overhead and know his rest is about to be broken as we are all advised to stash our trays and place our seats in the upright position.

It is staggering to realize that in a matter of minutes all of us passengers will be adding our bodies to the throngs of one of this planet's most densely inhabited regions. The District Federal (sometimes referred to by Mexicans simply as "D. F."—pronounced "dee effay") is now estimated to contain twenty-one million souls and is outnumbered only by Tokyo and the megapolis that begins in New York City and ends in Philadelphia.

When the moment finally arrives to begin slowly filing out of the plane, I catch a last glimpse of my pale seatmate who has stayed behind, surely hoping to avoid the jostle and crush; the aisles filled with fretful people juggling carry-on luggage and small children.

I feel a surge of excitement. It has been nearly fifty years since I have been in this beloved city of my childhood where I lived for the first six years of my life—a truly "impressionable" time that is still remarkably vivid to me. I feel a sense of returning to something important.

But anxiety soon overcomes excitement as I am carried along by a querulous stream of strangers, calling mostly in Spanish to other strangers. How will I find Lisha in all this mayhem? Maybe she isn't even here?

She supposedly landed in Guadalajara yesterday. Lisha hoped going through customs at a smaller airport might be easier than here in D.F. She has always considered herself culturally Mexicana; Spanish is her first language and she can speak it faster, and more emphatically that anyone I have ever heard. I can only hope she has already talked herself out of the lack of some official documents.

Earlier in the week, my sister was very worried about difficulties that might well arise surrounding the two containers of cremated remains she was bringing into Guadalajara as carry-on luggage. She had obtained the requisite papers for her maternal grandmother's container of ashes. "Ya Ya" (her grandmother's nickname) died in her Arizona home just a few months after Rexito's death. Since she had been a Mexican citizen, it was a fairly simple matter to get permission for the return of her cremains to Mexico.

Rexito's cremains were another matter. He had been born in Texas and Lisha had not been able to connect with the Mexican consul prior to leaving to make the case for the return of his cremains to Mexico. She was also concerned because she and her mother Adela had been unable to locate the deed, thought to be in Ya Ya's personal effects, for the Mexico City crypt. But that is a problem Lisha hopes to surmount here with the help of her well-connected Mexican cousins.

I am feeling trapped inside this aisle of cyclone fencing as I make my way in this long serpentine line to my own potential problems going through customs. I have no illusions about just how pathetic my Spanish really is despite the fact that I was bilingual as a child.

When I last spoke to Lisha, after warning me about how dangerous life was becoming in Mexico City and telling me that travel advisories had been issued, she added, "In D.F., they are only too happy to put gringos through the same experience gringos put Mexicans through in U.S. airports. Be careful what you say. Don't stand out!"

I'm trying to remember all the different last names of Lisha's cousins, one or another of whom would pick me up at the airport if Lisha could not. I know I have at least one of their phone numbers in my wallet, or did I transfer it to my pocket? How well do they speak English? I can't remember what Lisha told me. I'm not thinking clearly. I'm feeling that lightheadedness and mild disorientation I always have when I am too hungry. I should have eaten my gringo lunch on the plane.

Lisha made me promise that in no circumstance would I take one of the taxicabs in front of the airport, even if, by some fluke, no one appeared to pick me up. "Just be patient and keep telephoning. You'll reach someone."

Moments later, I am finally through customs—caught in the pulse of the crowd. As people push against me and call out excitedly as we surge toward the greeting area, I feel a sense of rising panic. The gate slides open as people are yelling happily to one another. The din is remarkable—tinny and echoing. Everything is elbows and arms; shoulders are grazing shoulders. Whistling. Names shouted. Suddenly, a familiar and unmistakable voice rises above the rest. "Channon!" it is calling. "Sister! Over here!"

It is my first morning in Mexico City, and I am comfortably seated at the breakfast table of Juan and Suzi Gonzales, Lisha's cousins, who say they will "adopt" me, since they remember my father fondly, and were the official witnesses at the civil ceremony when Dad married his second wife and their cousin—the statuesque and charming Adela.

I am so happy to be adopted by Suzi who is perhaps ten or fifteen year older than I; so happy to be hungrily holding this wonderfully fresh, glistening with lusciousness, mango from Vera Cruz that is presently impaled on one of her silver forks, designed especially for this purpose. And then there is the tantalizing array of Mexican pastries on the oval platter, the smell of chorizos cooking in the air, and the fact that, without my saying a word, a young Mexican maid brings me *Nescafé con leche.*

Looking into her mocha-colored face and warm brown eyes, it all comes back to me: The best thing about my childhood in Mexico was Nati—short for "Navidad"—the young maid who was my special caregiver, confidante, and sweet defender. I feel at once both welcomed and at home.

Suzi is beautiful and truly *elegante*—in that maddening way of señoras and señoritas in Mexico City, who are surely among the most well-groomed women in the world. She is speaking slowly, in good English, although I am sure I am missing some nuances, particularly when she and Lisha lapse into flurries of Spanish. She is explaining the plight of the dead in her city, the crosscurrents between the Catholic doctrines that she believes in, and the realities of living in an overcrowded environment.

Earlier, I learned that on top of the population pressures in D.F. caused by the living, there were also population pressures caused by the dead. It seems that annually, thousands of Mexicans who die in the United States are flown home for burial. Even among people who have become U.S. citizens or have struggled in life to achieve legal residency in *Estados Unidos*, most still want to be buried in their place of origin.

From the standpoint of undocumented immigrant families in the U.S., returning family members to home soil is not only expensive but is fraught with nearly insurmountable legalities. From the standpoint of Mexican cemetery officials and other bureaucrats, the difficulties surrounding the sheer number of returning corpses is boggling.

Now, Lisha explains the sharp contrast between typical U.S. funerary customs and those of Mexico. At the root of the recent overcrowding in Mexico City cemeteries that were overcrowded to begin with is the Mexican perception that mourning the dead is a privilege, as well as family duty. The dead should not be far away from their roots. Even when several generations have intervened, Mexican families still remember their ancestors in special ways during one of their most important holidays *Día de los Muertos* (Day of the Dead, which actually, takes place over three days: October 31, November 1 and 2.)

In many parts of Mexico, the local cemetery is viewed as a kind of "second home," especially during *Día de los Muertos*. Unlike most cemeteries in the rest of North America, Mexican cemeteries are places that represent warm and ongoing family connections.

In general, this Mexican connection to cemeteries and to the subject of death is not without humor. Lisha gave an example of the fun loving and slightly irreverent views held by many citizens of D.F. Several years ago, when Lisha worked in Mexico City, she was amused to learn the names of several *cantinas* (bars) located in the vicinity of cemeteries: "My Last Will and Testament," "The Second to the Last Stop," and "The Afterlife." She promises to explain more about *Día de los Muertos* traditions later—a subject she has researched extensively.

"It is like a party—granted, a sacred party—held both in local homes and at cemeteries. It is also a feast where special foods are served for both the living and the dead. Sometimes, mariachi bands play right at the graves," Lisha says, adding that it is a shame it is only April. If we had come here for *Día de los Muertos* we might have visited a place called Mixquic located on an old Aztec farming island not too far from here.

"No, Lisha," Suzi says, shaking her head. "You don't know

how things have changed. You would not want to be here in D.F. for *Día de los Muertos* anymore." She notes that many long-standing and beloved celebrations are changing. It is yet another aspect of the pressures of overcrowding and poverty she thinks.

"But," Suzi adds, "this is not only the nature of our time—our modernization, although it is certainly true many young people just want to forget old traditions." She gives an exaggerated shudder. "Go into a cemetery on *Día de los Muertos* in D.F.? No. We are growing more afraid all the time of going into cemeteries. There is little protection, even when you go just to visit a grave. These days, every place has its dangers, especially cemeteries."

Suzi, who, unlike me, has managed to not sully herself with telltale signs of breakfast, says that in any case, tourism has become such a major aspect of *Día de los Muertos* that as many as one hundred thousand people attend various festivals. In Mexico City, where liquor flows freely and celebrations some-times get out of hand, extra police are hired just to handle the crowds. Cemetery officials have come to dread the holiday. In D.F., she adds, most revellers congregate in a mere half-dozen of the district's one hundred or more cemeteries. Whether Panteon de Español is one of these (where we will soon place Rexito's and Ya Ya's ashes) Suzi doesn't know.

"Lisha, you should be glad you are conducting cemetery busi-ness now, during relative calm," Suzi shrugs. "But, I suppose you could say that these days there is no 'good time' to do busi-ness in a cemetery. The officials are always irritable and hard to deal with. They are overworked."

According to Suzi, cemetery officials have their hands full for a variety of reasons. For one thing, they are forced to deal with the "returning dead," so-to-speak. The dead that are shipped back to Mexico, especially from the U.S., arrive as cargo at the Mexico City airport in a perpetual stream. Corpses must be quickly routed to various municipal and private cemeteries. But the real problem facing the cemetery officials of Mexico City is where to bury such bodies once they arrive.

Arrangements for interment must be made long in advance. There are no new burial plots available any place in Mexico City unless someone else is dug up to make room, or a family gives its approval to share an existing plot.

If I understand Suzi—who is using more and more Spanish as she tries to explain—Mexico City's cemeteries could benefit from "crowd control." They need the expertise of someone like Dad, whom, I discovered recently, actually served as a crowd-control consultant to the Mexican government in the 1960s, during the worst of the student riots.

In the face of Mexico's City's extreme cemetery overcrowding, cremation has become an alternative, although not one that many traditional Mexicans prefer. Suzi explains that some people are opting for the modern *hornos verticals* (upright burials) similar to those being considered by overcrowded metro cemeteries in the Philippines, Malaysia, and other parts of the world in order to conserve precious space.

Actually, overcrowded cemeteries have been a problem for decades. She remembers the controversies when the Mexican government attempted to address cemetery overcrowding in the 1970s when one of the most stringent burial laws of which I have ever heard was enacted.

"Muy complicado," she sighs when I ask for details. The gist is that anyone buried in Mexico City after 1975 is only entitled to a cemetery plot for seven years. After that time, the body must be exhumed and cremated to make room for more recently departed. There are a few provisions for "extensions," Suzi adds, so that people can put off exhuming their dead for a while, but the price for such extensions is deliberately set high.

As it stands, only families that paid for a grave "in perpetuity" before 1975 may bury the body of a loved one, provided it is stacked on top of another family member. Still, there is gossip: In extreme cases, as many as ten bodies have been buried, one atop the other; at least, that is what Suzi has heard about the city's largest cemetery, the Panteon Civil de Dólores—the biggest cemetery in all of Latin America.

As a result, there is a fantastic demand for exhumation and cremation services. These days cemeteries are busy places in the capitol. There is continual digging up and burying going on simultaneously.

"I can't stand to go," Suzi says, grimacing. "You see coffins on wheels, everywhere. Some are old and leaking under plastic. And noisy workmen are everywhere."

Suzi pauses, taking a dainty bite of the *chorizo* next to her small portion of eggs. For our part, Lisha and I have not stinted ourselves. Our plates are heaped high. Suzi goes on describing the frustration she has experienced as she has dealt with beleaguered cemetery officials and their underlings. "I try to do as much as possible by *teléfono* to avoid driving in the city traffic that is worse than ever."

She outlines all the steps she has undertaken and details the various negotiations and changes in plan. It seems almost miraculous, she says, that on top of arranging for exhumations and convincing cemetery officials at Panteon Español that she had the authority to enter the Allen (Ya Ya's married name) family mausoleum, she also succeeded in arranging for the cleaning, re-plastering, and painting of the *capilla* (little chapel) and its *cripta* (crypt) underneath where we will place Ya Ya and Rexito.

The exhumations she speaks of are those of two of her children who died in infancy, along with those of her mother and Aunt Queti (Ya Ya's sisters.) Lisha explains this to me quietly in English as Suzi pauses to confer with the young housemaid about some domestic matter.

"She's arranged for a special Mass to be said on everybody's behalf." Lisha continues, "And for the priest, the floral offerings . . . everything!" It seems that when Suzi found out why we were coming to Mexico City she decided to try to do everything pertaining to burials all at once. She said she had been avoiding it, so it is sort of a blessing we came to push the process forward.

I always thought that cremation was frowned upon, or even forbidden, by the Catholic Church. When Suzi rejoined the conversation I asked about this. She told me that the ban was lifted during Vatican II (1964.) Still, she admits that it has been difficult to change a Catholic culture that once strongly rejected cremation. But Suzi has accepted the fact that cremations are necessary. Tears well in her lovely eyes and she looks down, "Perhaps, even as we speak, my babies are being cremated." She looks up. "But now, all will be well," she says. "No more cemeteries for Juan and me."

She likes the protection afforded within the sanctuary of her church where cremains will rest in family niches located in the shining wall of black granite that has been newly installed for the use of church members.

"When the time comes, that is where Juan and I will be also. Beside the babies. *Descansen en paz*," Suzi says, crossing herself. "May they rest in peace."

I am amazed. There must have been a terrible emotional drain as Suzi dealt with the reality of all these matters all at once. I say with sincere admiration, "I just don't know how you managed to accomplish so much!" I add, *"Muy difícil!"* for emphasis.

I find myself reaching for another tortilla as Suzi sips thoughtfully from her cup of Nescafé and smiles. Her cup chimes lightly as it is set upon its porcelain saucer. She smiles as she raises her hand and then rubs her fingers three times against her thumb: a universal gesture meaning, "Money, money, money." Throughout the week,

I gather, she has been paying a little here, a little there. This is on top of the "official" fees. In Mexico, this type of financial exchange is known as the "bite." It is the part of Mexican culture that American's perceive of as bribery.

Suzi says she thinks of it more as tipping—as in tipping the young housemaid for ironing my suitcase-crumpled dress that I intend to wear at the mass at the Church of Madre de Dios de Czestochowa.

The phone, which seems to have been ringing continually since we arrived, rings again. This time I am surprised: The call is for me. Ione, my wandering daughter, is telephoning from Queretaro—a Spanish colonial period city located about one hundred miles north of here, noted for its historical preservation. She tells me that she is able to come to Mexico City after all. She has a bus ticket and has made arrangements to miss some classes at the college that she has been attending for several months—an institution that accepts special students from the University of Oregon.

She can't get here in time for the Mass tonight, she says. It will have to be tomorrow. I promise to take her with us to the Basilica of the Virgin of Guadalupe where we intend to look for statues to leave in the *capilla* in Rexito and Ya Ya's honor.

Ione, who shines with the new minted gold of Ethnic and Women's Studies says, "You know, Mom, the Spanish put all their churches and stuff right over the sites the Aztec's dedicated to their ancient Mother Goddess. I have so much to tell you!" That's my girl.

On the way back from Panteon Español I realize that we have succeeded in "encrypting" our brother. Now, no one will ever be able to figure him out.

I share my dark joke with my sister who usually rises to the

occasion with a rejoinder. We love our pun-fests. Lisha, a gifted poet, is an obscure punster, however. "The plot thickens," she says halfheartedly. She looks tired.

Descending down the iron ladder into the crypt was no fun. It was surely even more difficult for Lisha since her losses are double. She had to leave both Rexito's and her grandmother's urns down there as iron doors clanged shut in noisy finality.

The sprawling, ragged, cement-bordered grounds of Panteon de Español filled with crumbling marble monuments is as distant from our green little cemetery in Yoncalla as Tierra del Fuego is from the Bering Straits. Interesting that I think in terms of such chilling waters. The crypt felt moist and cold, not cool.

The Allen family *capilla,* less showy than its Gothic pointy-roofed neighbors, was clean inside, thanks to the workmen Suzi hired. The new plaster shown icy white. Our statues were inexpensive. In the days when family mausoleums weren't quite so likely to be robbed, people left objects of better quality. These statues are just mementos. Still, I felt sad to leave the little Virgin of Guadalupe on the bare alter by the single, small, barred window. At least she had St. Francis for company—a rather primitive wooden carving that Lisha, Ione and I bought at one of the stalls near the Basilica two days ago. There was a little bird upon St. Francis's shoulder and one resting upon his extended bony hand. But it was the pair of lambs at his feet that really sold us on him. When Rexito visited Oregon in his late teens he used to help mend the pasture fences. He always said how much he loved the look of the sheep dotting the hillsides.

The morning, really afternoon by now, finds us both listless. It seems that all I can think of is eating. Lisha says she is hungry, too, though neither of us has a right to be.

"I think we may be literally stuffing our feelings," Lisha opines. It's true: I feel flat. Empty. Visiting Panteon de Español was in no way soul-satisfying. It was anti-climatic, in fact. Food stimulates the senses, brings feelings of fullness and I'm ready again.

Thus far, we sisters have had quite a gustatorial romp through Mexico City and it is far from over. Tonight, *por ejemplo*, we have reservations at Lisha's favorite restaurant, Refugio del Fonda in Zona Rosa. She is already talking about what we should order there.

Oddly, while I feel hungry, I also feel queasy. Fortunately, I am very fond of the hibiscus-flower, ruby-colored beverage called *jamaica* served throughout the day in many Mexican households that Juan Gonzales swears is *excelente* for the digestion. It certainly helped last night after too many *gotanas* (appetizers) and a huge Argentine-style flank steak.

It seems natural, given all this, that we have just spent some time discussing Day of the Dead cuisine, a subject I find fascinating. The glistening sugar skulls and coffins I remember from my childhood were evidently part of *Día de los Muertos*. They are the only things I remember about the holiday, along with a vivid recollection of being hustled off to a cathedral by Nati and being impressed with the lovely visage of the blue-robed "lady" wearing a starry crown. But perhaps this recollection emanates from some occasion other than *Día de los Muertos*.

In many parts of Mexico, bakeries prepare bread and sweet rolls, *panes de muerto* (breads of the dead) that come in different varieties—some are dark and unadorned loaves shaped in human or animal forms and called *animas*; others are made of chocolate, or amaranth-seeded dough with decorative scraps shaped like bones stuck atop each loaf.

The exquisite celebration of the individual and his or her tastes when alive is manifested in the preparation of family *ofrendas* (offerings.) Food forms an essential part of the offerings decorating the makeshift home alters that often include traditional dishes such as various *mole* sauces poured over different meats.

Tamales which, like many Mexican foods, are Aztec or Toltec in origin, are *Día de los Muertos* favorites and are prepared according to the tastes of the deceased, made with fillings of chicken, or red chile and pork, shrimp, or even sweetened bean. Other main dishes which might be served in the course of the holiday include special *tingas* (stews) such as *tinga poblano de pollo*—a chicken stew with poblano chiles.

Mexicans indulge in their national sweet tooth during holidays, especially during Christmas and the *Día de los Muertos*. Desserts of many varieties are prepared such as *calabaza en tacha* (sweetened pumpkin), *sopapillas* (deep-fried pastries), flans, and crème brûlées made with Mexican chocolate—the beloved international treat many consider the Aztec culture's ultimate culinary gift to the world.

Interestingly, no food is left as an offering on the graves, although people sometimes eat their lunches in cemeteries while visiting or bring the "bread of the dead" or other food as a token. Each loaf of bread supposedly represents a soul.

As exotic as these practices may sound, I am struck by their connection to customs in parts of the U.S. A couple from Arkansas, for example, met in my travels, described what they call "dinner on the ground." Annually, they visit the local cemetery, bringing a single flower to leave at each grave, a tablecloth, and a hardy picnic lunch, usually including fried chicken. They then eat next to the grave on the ground and reminisce about the dead. It is a tradition in their part on the country that extends many generations back.

I doubt whether the sandwiches and beverages people in Yoncalla sometimes bring on a cemetery cleanup day can be counted as a feast for the dead. Still, we come to clean graves and, thereby, honor the dead. Inevitably, thoughts stray toward those we sometimes refer to as "the departed." We feel their absence, remember their personalities and past deeds. After we put down our rakes, eat our bag lunches, and swig our soft drinks and before we leave the cemetery, we often leave floral offerings and say "good-bye." We may be closer to *Día de los Muertos* than we know.

Farther away are the traditions of medieval times. The "soul cakes," passed around during All Souls' and All Saints' Days celebrated on November 1 and 2 (holy days still observed in many Catholic countries) are very close to the *panes de muerto* of the Mexican people.

Halloween—on the eve of All Souls' Day—with its special edible "treats" is also part of the cycle of holy days, but its largely secular traditions lead many to consider it more closely connected to the pre-Christian Celtic feast of the dead, Samhain.

But feasting the dead predates even the Celts. In an ancient Egyptian festival, honoring Osiris in his aspect as God of Death, followers prepared and then ate wheat cakes that represented his flesh and his eventual resurrection in an incorruptible physical body.

Lisha tells me that during *Día de los Muertos* in Mexico, the *angelitos* (little children who have died) are often honored on their own day; their *ofrendas* include miniature pottery, tiny candleholders, small clay replicas of fruits and vegetables, and toys and treats decorated with death symbols. Except for smoking and drinking alcoholic beverages, children always participate in most aspects of Mexican festivals.

By contrast, in the U.S., many people believe that children should be protected from the fact of human mortality. *Día de los Muertos* seems morbid—a far cry from the reserved rituals of Memorial Day in which American children rarely play a part. In Mexico, death is an event with which almost any child is intimately familiar and that is congruent with ancient Indian beliefs as well as church doctrine. This is not only because Mexican children cannot help but be aware of depressingly high mortality rates, but because death, like birth, takes place in Mexico's "first culture"—that of home and family. As Mexico increasingly absorbs a commercial world culture, as Suzi pointed out when we first arrived, many traditions are changing and even disappearing.

The Day of the Dead embodies Mexico's inherent duality: the distinct but intertwined influences from ancient Mesoamericans as well as Spanish "conquerors." Aspects of this duality continually replay themselves, even today Lisha insists, and are manifest in virtually every aspect of Mexican art, music, and other cultural expressions. Seen in this perspective, I feel better about dividing our brother's ashes and honoring both sides of his heritage.

Today, our last full day in Mexico, we have convinced Suzi, who has circles under her eyes, to relax and go with us to the Aztec pyramids at Teotihuacán. Jorge, the driver Suzi engaged for us earlier in the week at a taxicab company she trusts, is again delivering us from evil. At least, we hope so, even though he probably drives as recklessly as everyone else in this country. The rosary that Lisha bought for him on our trip to the Basilica dangles from his mirror and swings back and forth as we make sharp turns. I now understand why many Mexicans make the sign of the cross each time they settle behind the steering wheel.

The drive is more than an hour long and the hazy vistas we are passing are uniformly brown and bathed in grit. I'm reading from a book about the Aztecs I got at the *Museo Anthropologica* where Jorge drove me yesterday afternoon while Lisha visited friends.

Aztecs, apparently, did not believe in an infinite afterlife. The manner in which a person died was "a call" by the gods. Only a few were privileged to go to the dwelling place of the Sun deity, e.g., those women who died in childbirth, those who died in battle, or anyone who was lucky enough to have his/her beating heart cut out on the top of one of the pyramids we are heading toward. Later, these dead were wrapped in mortuary bundles with their knees drawn up and buried with appropriate grave goods. Most Aztecs, however, who experienced natural or undistinguished deaths were cremated.

Festival foods honoring the dead in Aztec society included a kind of amaranth-seeded bread that was fashioned into the shapes of clouds and human figures—reminiscent of the *panes de muerto* still eaten almost one thousand years later during the Day of the Dead. *Tamales*, also an Aztec invention, were stuffed with meat from tiny indigenous dogs and eaten as the main dish.

The same type of little pooch used in *tamales* was often a pet whose fate it was to be cremated with its Aztec master. Owner and dog then made an arduous after-death journey through eight deserts and eight hills, where they faced wild animals and endured obsidian-bladed winds. What did they attain after four years of this wandering? *Nada.* They just passed into Aztec oblivion, according to the historian, Sahagun.

I look up and see that luminous long views are now possible through the taxicab windows. In the distance, the pyramids appear blue and mysterious, mounting the smooth swell of the plain. When Aztecs first approached this site, a principal city of the ancient Teotihuacanos, the vast complex of temples and other buildings was already in ruins. Before repairing the city to suit themselves, the Aztecs mistakenly believed that the mounds they saw were tombs instead of temple bases. Hence, the large street, more than a mile long at the center of the city we are heading toward became known as the Avenue of the Dead.

As soon as Jorge has parked the car in a vast lot surprisingly empty of other tourists, I am struck by feelings of déjà vu. Surely I have visited this place before, perhaps with my mother. Touching the cool stuccoed surface of the stone as I pass the magnificent carving of the feathered serpent, *Quetzacoatl*, the cool shadow of the long portal covers me.

Before Jorge leaves us, promising to return in an hour or so, he reminds us that two thousand years ago when the city was built, it glowed with color. Brilliant colors, he tells Suzi and Lisha in Spanish: *rojo y amarillo* (red and yellow). All the stone construction was covered with limestone stucco stained crimson from the carpaces of million upon millions of dead beetles. The yellow came from the *piril* tree.

We walk and walk with the April sun beating down, the plaza nearly empty so that we are the focus of groups of vendors who follow us from place to place, hawking their handmade goods, trilling in Spanish. When we step into a magnificent exhibit area where there is a model of the vast Aztec marketplace and temple complex, a dignified man named Emilio approaches us, explaining that as a former student of anthropology he would serve as an ideal guide. Suzi nods. It is implicitly understood she has agreed to pay for his services later.

He leads us into the "citadel"—an enormous structure surrounded by slanting walls and vertical panels. I am looking at the head of enormous carved *Quetzacoatl* when Emilio claps his hands twice in rapid succession. What returns is a startling series of echoes that Emilio assures us is the exact sound of the *Quetzal*—a bird venerated by many Mesoamerican tribes. Some attribute this auditory phenomenon to a "picket-fence" effect and believe that Aztec and Mayan temple architects deliberately designed the placement of buildings, angles of steps and ramps, etc. so that an echo could be produced designed to impress the multitudes, especially during sacrificial ceremonies.

We are growing tired, but Emilio stops at the base of the pyramid of the Sun and asks if we would like to climb to the top. Lisha rolls her eyes. "I can't do it," she tells Suzi and me. "I just can't climb all those steps." Given all the eating I have been doing since visiting Mexico, I'm not sure I can make the climb either. Suzi also shakes her head.

But Emilio is soothing the three lazy señoras. He tells us that on the spring equinox of the previous year more than a million people from all over the world converged upon this vast plaza. Dressed in white to represent world peace many climbed the nearly three hundred steps of the pyramid. Throngs of others supposedly "felt the energy" of the plumed serpent by just standing inside the plaza.

"Señoras, you can feel this energy which some believe to be

magnetic and healing anywhere in the temple complex," Emilio assures us. "I will take you to that platform in front of the pyramid where the ancient Aztec priests incanted before the minions. That will be high enough. Just right," he says, smiling.

We are winded by the time we reach the platform's top. The sun breathes fire on our foolishly hatless heads as Emilio demonstrates how to extend both arms to best receive the "energy." We must do this, he advises, if we are going to benefit fully from the vibrations here in one of the most powerful places on earth. Then, he disappears, leaving us to our private ceremony on the Avenue of the Dead.

The three of us extend our arms. I confess I feel nothing in particular. As Suzi heads for the shade, we two sisters are suddenly gripped by the same impulse: This is surely the appropriate place to say a final farewell to our brother and father. "We've done the best we can," I announce aloud.

"We don't know what else to do now, Rexito and Daddy!" Lisha adds, as we hold hands and raise our arms in a kind of salute. "Good-bye!"

We sigh and then stand apart. I am looking at the panorama before us, and turn ever so slightly. I feel such great calm, but as I inhale deeply I feel a sudden, unwelcome sensation. I am pushed downward by an invisible agency, how else to put it? I fall hard upon the stones, and find myself splayed upon the ancient pavement, like a supplicant or perhaps an offering.

Truly, I am stunned, but after the first moment of surprise, I begin to laugh. Lisha helps me stand, just as Suzi and Emilio appear, clucking concern and brushing me off. "Are you hurt?" they inquire with worried looks. "You fell so suddenly, so hard."

But I am not hurt in the least. As amazing as it seems, I feel fine. I rise, loving the way everything looks in the clear, uncompromising light of Teotihuacán.

"What do you think, Lisha?" I ask her as we all walk back to the parking lot. "I don't know," she confesses. "Maybe Dad and Rex are laughing their asses off. It's a joke." She stops and squints at me. "You're sure you aren't hurt?" she asks. "Not even a little?"

"I'm fine," I say. "Finer than a frog's hair."

"What?" she asks, unfamiliar with the sayings of rural Oregonians.

"Nothing," I say. We walk on in silence for a moment with Suzi in the vanguard warding off vendors with a queenly wave of her hand.

At last, Lisha says, "Well, you know, Sis, it may not mean a thing. Sometimes 'a cigar is just a cigar!' " Then we both laugh. Laugh and laugh and laugh.

And later, at a little outdoors restaurant near the pyramids, I pick at the not very tasty *enchiladas verde*. I make the same dish at home, only better, I decide. Now, I'm wondering, how many times do I need to say good-bye?

> *Where are we to go from here?*
> *We came here only to be born.*
> *As our home is beyond*
> *Where the fleshless abide.*
> —Nezahualcoyotl, King of Texcoco, 1459

A Finger Pointing Upward

*They shall die grievous deaths; neither shall they be
lamented; neither shall they be buried.*

—Jeremiah XVI: 4

I used to be a proponent of cremation, along with the forty percent plus of people in my part of the country. Cremation
seemed sensible, and relatively uncomplicated. Now, as I get
back into the car, and pat Mr. Boyle, I realize that cremation is
laden with its own dark possibilities, or perhaps, "in-the-dark"
possibilities, given the windowless upper room in the mortuary
with its shut door, that I now know about.

As I buckle up and prepare to leave the Chapel of the Flowers'
parking lot, I see a half dozen cheerful, hefty looking mourners
exiting cars, wearing World War II campaign hats—set at a
whimsical angle—and blue Veteran of Foreign Wars vests,

embroidered with initials and numerals stitched in sunny yellow thread. Evidently, these folks are on their way into the memorial chapel to say good-bye to a former member of the armed services.

Mr. Boyle was a veteran, too, I think glancing at the cardboard cylinder on the seat beside me. I know he did not have a funeral, given his presence in my car, and thus, no graveside service either.

"Don't worry. In about forty minutes we'll be in Yoncalla, where you can rest in peace," I say as I pull out of the parking lot, almost grazing a very wide female member of the local VFW auxiliary with my rear fender. Pay attention, I tell myself, feeling very tired. I certainly didn't expect to spend the end of my week "springing" anyone out of funeral home jail, yet here I am.

Or should I say here *we* are. "Mr. B."—as I am coming to think of him—was not someone I ever met in the flesh. I didn't even know he existed until a year ago. To date, the relationship has been quite complicated, full of shadowy figures, disappearances, and perhaps just a pinch of larceny.

It all began on a rainy afternoon when I received a phone call from a local woman who said she and her sister were friends of an old man who lived in a Yoncalla trailer park. He was too enfeebled to come to the cemetery to pick out an appropriate plot for himself and they had agreed to help.

I had the impression from the woman's voice that either the old man's death was imminent or that he was trying to set his affairs in order while he still could make decisions. She insisted upon meeting in the cemetery as soon as possible. I changed my plans so she, her sister, and I could rendezvous before her shift started at the plywood mill that same afternoon.

At the appointed time, I drove to the cemetery and waited in my car in the parking lot for fifteen minutes or more. At last, an older model Ford pulled in, and two thick-set women of middle age waved perfunctorily in my direction. The three of us spent at least a half hour walking around the cemetery. It was still cold and still spitting rain when a plot "with a view" was selected— something the old man wanted.

They told me that as far as they knew the old man was all alone in the world, that he wasn't originally from around here, but that in the last few years he had developed an affection for the "country feeling" of our cemetery. He especially liked our big trees; not that *they* would want to be anyplace so shady, they added; *they* had bought plots for themselves at the Masonic where it was cheaper; where there weren't blackberries. As we passed among headstones, they also found fault with many of the people buried under them.

The wind picked up, and there was nothing for it except to

retire to my car, where we all sat as I took care of the paperwork. I was instructed to make out the receipt to Robert Boyle, and they watched to make sure I filled in the pertinent facts, including the price, which they twice commented upon. Explaining that we were using money raised by selling plots for insurance, gravel, and other maintenance, and that everyone, including me, was a volunteer, didn't seem to make a whit of difference to them. They acted as if two hundred dollars were highway robbery.

They watched me add the site location to my permanent file; they even asked directions to the county clerk's office in Roseburg, the hours it was open, room number and so forth. I had the impression they were going to officially register the plot sale as soon as possible.

Then I waited for one of them to hand me some sort of payment. Only then did the older sister let me know that the plot couldn't be paid for until "the old man's check comes"—presumably, a Social Security check. The older sister murmured something to the other, then. "It could be longer than that," she admitted. In any case, she told me severely, practically shaking her finger at me, I was to be certain to save "his" plot for him and not sell it to anyone else.

I do understand that many elderly people live on limited incomes. I've occasionally made payment arrangements with this in mind; sometimes the cemetery has even donated plots to people in need. But what most irritated me about the situation was the women's attitude. There was something indirect and even shifty about how they handled things. The words "thankyou" didn't cross their lips. They were entitled, and I was a dirty dog if I didn't do what they wanted.

Later, I was doubly annoyed when I discovered that these sisters were relatives of the Obscene Telephone Screamer who scared me so badly when I first took on responsibility for the cemetery. The acorns, apparently, didn't fall very far from the Kelly family tree.

Several months passed. While I was away at my writer's residency, a check paying for Mr. Boyle's plot finally arrived. Daniel deposited it in the cemetery account and neither of us really gave the old man another thought. Just a few days ago, however, Mr. Boyle—or what is left of him—became a source of speculation and then concern.

I learned of Mr. Boyle's death from the newest teller at the small branch bank where I do cemetery business. A bottle blonde in her early thirties with a self-important air, she made a point of mentioning the fact that she knew that Mr. Boyle had purchased a plot at our cemetery. "Didn't you read that he died?" she asked, as though I, if anyone, should be keeping up with the obituary pages. "It's been several weeks now."

I wondered how she knew that he had a plot at our cemetery. She just went on chatting, her pale blue denim-colored eyes widening as she recounted details, such as the fact that Mr. Boyle died in a Roseburg rest home, where his "condition" had worsened, etc.

Then, despite the fact that the other teller was away at lunch and that I was the only customer in the bank so that there was no one to overhear, she lowered her voice and said in a confiding tone, "You know, the old man still has quite a little bit of money in his account, here. A pension check from the Union of Railway Workers just came for direct deposit. I don't think they know he's gone."

When she said, with an air of pride, that she had been able to access a surprising amount of information about Mr. Boyle on the bank's computer, I understood suddenly that she was a watery woman; a seeking, sliding kind of woman, trolling the fathomless blue of her computer screen so she could cast her net in places where she had no business. She was the wrong kind of woman to be working at a bank.

"But I couldn't find out if he had any next of kin. I couldn't get into those files," she said in a disappointed tone. "If the old man has relatives, though, I bet they would give a lot to know that he left some money behind." She smiled. "Really, I bet they would."

I said that I had no idea whether Mr. Boyle had a family or not. What I wondered was how she accessed information about the cemetery via computer? Was she nosing around into other people's accounts besides Mr. Boyle's? It gave me a chill. I was somewhat relieved when she explained that she heard about Mr. Boyle's plot purchase because she was related to the two women who came to the cemetery. "By marriage," she emphasized, as if being related by blood was distasteful to her.

I should have called the bank manager, I thought later, but I didn't. Perhaps the bank teller meant well, or it was a one-time occurrence. But my instincts are usually right, and it was certainly interesting that I was dealing with yet another member of the Screamer's extended family. What is it with these people? I can't bring myself to like any of them.

The bank teller also told me that when Mr. Boyle had been taken to a rest home several months before, she and her relatives had helped him by cleaning out his trailer. Then they kind of lost touch until they heard he died. Actually, they read about it in the local paper. As to where he was buried, she guessed that the people at the rest home directed his body to a V.A. cemetery— probably the one in Roseburg. The old man had sometimes talked about being in the infantry during World War II.

I remember how she lowered her pale eyes, and then looked up at me, smiling in what she must have thought was an engaging manner. She then asked a question that literally left me speechless; in fact, I wasn't sure I heard her properly and asked her to repeat it. Since the old man wasn't "using it," she said again, what would I think about transferring his burial plot over to her? After all, she and her relatives had befriended him.

I must have frowned when I shook my head. Just as I was about to give her a piece of my mind she shrugged and said, "Well, it was worth a try." Then she turned and gazed into the depths of her computer screen.

She gave me a deposit slip that I found myself looking over with uncharacteristic thoroughness. The last thing she said to me were words to the effect that it was just such a shame to have everything going to waste; after all, *he* didn't need it. You can't take it with you, can you?

The film version of Charles Dickens's *A Christmas Carol* came to mind, I remember. They were kindred spirits: the bank teller and Scrooge's charwoman who, when her employer's corpse was barely cold, returned with her friends to rip down his velvet bed curtains and anything else not nailed to the floor.

"Mr. B., I hope you choose your friends more carefully, wherever you are now." Of course, right now, he's sitting in the passenger seat of my car. I guess I am his friend, a pretty good friend, in fact. The Chinese claim that there is no more righteous act than that of burying stray bones and covering up exposed coffins.

But after leaving the bank that day, I knew I had to find out what had happened to Mr. B. That night I dreamed that I had been looking down into the red dirt of a deep and a quite empty grave. First thing next morning, I began my detective work about Mr. B.'s whereabouts and made several phone calls. Hours and many phone calls later I discovered that no one named Robert Boyle was interred in the Veteran's Cemetery in Roseburg, or, for that matter, in any national cemetery located in the state.

I was finally able to get a clerk at the Veterans Administration to tell me that a Robert T. Boyle was listed in the V.A. database; a notation there was made concerning his recent death in Roseburg, Oregon, without any additional information. No one had evidently ordered a grave marker from the Veteran's Administration.

After I explained the reasons for my inquiry, the same clerk clucked sympathetically and suggested, "You should start calling the commercial cemeteries in your region. Some of them have what they call a veteran's area, but of course it's nothing official. When you call, if it sounds like they don't want to tell you anything, just say you're a distant relative—that will get their attention if they haven't received reimbursement for their services."

I always assumed that all veterans could receive some type of burial benefit. The clerk explained to me that since Mr. Boyle hadn't made a career of the military and hadn't died in a veteran's facility, he was ineligible for any burial benefit outside of a V.A. cemetery. He, like any veteran, was entitled to a grave marker, which could be placed in any cemetery, and a flag. A relative or legally designated person could apply for the flag and marker on behalf of the deceased.

Next, I decided to call the Social Security Administration, wondering whether they had been notified of Mr. B.'s death. I kept thinking about the money the teller said was accruing in the bank account; some of it, perhaps, taxpayer's money. Anything about Mr. Boyle was confidential, they said, even if he were dead. Did they know he had died? They wouldn't tell me that, either.

I did discover just how little Social Security contributes toward anyone's burial costs. Only a surviving spouse can apply for a two hundred and fifty dollar Social Security burial benefit. Given the escalating costs associated with burial, this is truly a pittance. Since Mr. Boyle was apparently unmarried, his Social

Security benefit for burial was as out of reach to the funeral home as his bank account.

It was daunting to think about calling all the cemeteries, large and small, in our region. Before beginning the process I decided to try to get some help from a professional—Laverne, my Deep Throat in the local funeral industry. Laverne hates the Texas-based corporation that took over the mortuary where she worked formerly. It is the same corporate entity that owns the Houston mortuary that was responsible for my brother Rex's funeral and cremation. Many mortuaries and larger cemeteries in our region have been bought by this corporate entity during the early 1990s.

Instead of working for a corporation, Laverne chooses to make a hundred mile round-trip, three times a week, to help out at a mortuary that is still small and family owned. Despite this, she still has many viable contacts with employees in corporate-owned funeral homes, etc.

Laverne was willing to make some calls. It didn't take long. She told me that I had been asking the wrong question. It wasn't *where* Mr. Boyle was buried, but *whether*. "Cremation changes everything, you know. An old guy like that who hasn't done any planning is apt to find himself cremated whether he intended to be or not. You can't just have a corpse sitting around while people make up their minds," she explained in her matter-of-fact way.

State law requires that a cremation result in "unrecognizable" bone fragments; it mandates the necessity for a "decent" container but does not specify its nature other than to make obligatory its appropriate identification tag. "No one wants anyone to get mixed up with anyone else," she went on to say. "We all look pretty much alike at the cremation stage. Someone told me you can't even get any DNA info from cremains. You need bones and other stuff to do that."

Laverne said that if I wanted to go get Mr. Boyle, I would find him at the Chapel of the Flowers mortuary, but I would have to be willing to sign some papers releasing his "cremains" by virtue of my status as cemetery sexton.

She chuckled when she told me that she had connected with a secretary who was only too happy to gossip for a few minutes about corporate shenanigans. "The gal took a little peek at Mr. Boyle's records for me. And she even let me talk to the receptionist who had originally spoken with the folks at the rest home where Mr. Boyle died. This will surprise you," Laverne said, adding that it didn't surprise her much since she was used to seeing people behave badly in The Industry.

She was right. I was stunned to learn that Mr. B. had a half-brother living in Roseburg, not more than a mile from the rest home. The brother had a different last name, had never come to visit Mr. B. and, according to a nurse, and adamantly refused to become the "responsible party" when they initially contacted him lest he become entangled in Mr. B.'s financial obligations. Mr. B. had listed his brother's name on one of the forms upon entering the rest home.

Further, after being called several times, when the brother grudgingly came forward to sign the paper releasing Mr. Boyle's body to the crematorium, he had stated that he had "long ago washed his hands" of "Bobby." He told the staff that Mr. Boyle had two adult children "somewhere." He assumed they used "the mother's" name although he couldn't—or wouldn't—remember what the name was.

Despite the fact that the mortuary realized there might not be anyone to pay for the cremation, they accepted the corpse. Most mortuaries handle "indigents" in this way, Laverne told me. And, over my protestations that Mr. B. was no "indigent," she pointed out that, for all intents and purposes, he died a pauper. No one could access his money except his supposed heirs who were probably unaware of their father's death. If the half-brother had stayed in touch with Mr. B., he might have changed his tune; he would have known there was some money available and, even though he despised "Bobby," he might have been happy to spend some of Bobby's money.

Or maybe not, Laverne added. We both agreed that the family seemed angry and estranged. Whatever had torn all those relationships asunder was information Mr. B. had taken to his grave—or, more accurately, would be taking to his grave, if I managed to snatch him from the funeral home.

When I spoke with Laverne, I began to have some sympathy for the position morticians were placed in when they accepted bodies of people with no next of kin. There must be many indigents whose cremation costs they are forced to absorb. Laverne explained that while that was true, and that some funeral homes lost money, there was recourse, at least in this state. The crematorium could apply to the state's indigent fund. Depending upon the availability of funds, they might recoup up to four hundred and fifty dollars of the roughly seven hundred dollars typically charged for a "direct cremation," no frills. "The other three hundred dollars is paid by raising the costs for everyone else," Laverne said, finishing another of the lessons on The Industry she has been giving me for the past year or so.

What is it about mortuaries, regardless of their architectural style, that gives them away, I wonder, as Mr. B. and I head to the freeway bound for Yoncalla. I decide it is the portico entrance that always extends well beyond the double front doors, and the clipped lawn, the curving drive, and the back "service area" with ramp. Who needs a sign to read the signs?

"We're almost out of here," I tell him as we reach the edge of town and are driving past the largest lawn cemetery in our area— one visible from the highway, where a larger than life-sized concrete

Jesus extends his arms over a flock of five frisky concrete lambs that are equally dazzlingly white against swards of eternally green lawn. I think of what Daniel used to tell the kids when they were younger. He would point out the window at whatever we were passing and say, "See? If you lived there, you'd be home by now." I repeat this to Mr. B.

I'm making light of serious things, because I'm uptight, I realize. Really, there is nothing humorous about this homely cardboard cylinder with its aluminum lid beside me on the gray faux velvet of the car seat, looking, for all the world, like something originally designed to hold a few gallons of ice cream. Nine pounds of ice cream, to be exact—the approximate weight of a grown man's remains. It is hard to imagine anything that could possibly look more anonymous, and less consequential, than this container beside me. I really can't absorb the fact that what is left of Mr. Boyle is in there. It is a *virtual* corpse, unreal, once removed—the difference between seeing a cow and a steak, or, as Mark Twain put it, the difference between lightning and a lightning bug.

In this form, the dead are portable; we can move them around to suit ourselves. I understand that necessity requires this when people die far from home, when it will be weeks or months until a family can gather together to respectfully say good-bye, or when serious shortages of grave space for full burials, such as in Mexico City or Manila, make cremation the only solution for disposal of the dead.

Still, when someone is cremated and handed a cardboard cylinder or polished urn, the perception of Death is altered. That death has really happened—a fact difficult to absorb for some people even when they see a corpse—becomes even harder to comprehend.

There is an illusion that death can be manipulated in some

sense, literally held in the hands, its enormity reduced to the size of a container like this one beside me. I hear poignant stories all the time: I cannot part with him or her yet. He or she sits on a shelf in my study; is cradled in my arms in a rocking chair when my grief assails me; is under the bed out of sight; is sitting on the piano in plain sight.

Waiting. The living wait to be ready to let go of the dead. While they wait, they feel guilty that the urn, the box, the cardboard cylinder is still there, has in some sense become part of the quotidian, to be overlooked, at times, even forgotten, at times, despite best intentions, despite love, despite grief that still slices at unexpected moments and will never, in truth, completely go away, no matter what is done, or when.

But in this diminished form, weighing what one hand can hold, it is undeniable that the urn or box is easy to care for and store. I bears little resemblance to the stuff of life *corpus sacrum*— the sacred body of any man, any woman. The *remains*—all that lingers. But can it linger too long? At what point does respect for *it* become more important than the feelings of the living? One would not leave a loved one's corpse lying atop the piano. Not for long, anyway. What kind of music would that make?

Forget spiritual significance, sentiment, even grief. Stick to the dollar signs: Cremation is touted as economically viable, within reach of those who either cannot afford or abhor, on principle, the expensive rituals associated with modern death. Laverne once gave me a sheet of "low-average" charges associated with cremation—not counting the basic crematory cost of six hundred and fifty dollars or so.

If Mr. B. had wanted to have his "cremains" buried in a cemetery like the one we have just passed, it would cost six hundred dollars for cemetery space. Even with his free Vets marker, and his crematory-issue cylinder, there would be additional charges of two hundred dollars to dig the hole and cover it up again. The installation of the marker would cost another two hundred and fifty dollars. Of course, there would also be "processing fees" for paperwork.

In this country, how does a person with a limited income— much less *no* income—afford the cost of dying, even when a no-frills cremation, without a funeral, is all that is wanted or needed?

Some people choose to dispose of cremated remains outside of what they consider the constrictive boundaries of a cemetery. Many of them think that Nature contains a special kind of sanctity not found in most of the traditional places where the dead are placed. Instead, they go out in a rowboat, a canoe, or a surf-worthy catamaran and release "ashes" by the handfuls, usually with the assistance of friends. Or perhaps the same thing occurs on a moun-taintop, or by a waterfall. Let the four winds do their work, they say, thus taking care of the disposal problem and providing a meaningful ceremonial send-off. These options, are, of course, less costly than the costs indicated on the sheet Laverne passed on to me. But it is not necessarily economic considerations that inspire people to explore alternatives more consonant with their values.

In Oregon and other states, it is illegal to scatter human cre-mains at sea unless the three-mile limit has been passed. And in some national parks, where many wish to be scattered in places of stunning beauty and sacred significance, the rules say take the ashes of your dead somewhere else. Many Native Americans, for example, are offended by the use of public spaces as cemeteries.

In lieu of public space, would outer space be a good final des-tination? The company I read about recently, however, is not offering to shuttle cremains for peanuts. Their prices are literally out of this world.

I sometimes think my generation's predisposition toward "scat-tering" others or wanting to have themselves scattered is a sign of how things have come apart; of how little rootedness remains for many of us. In a time of such high mobility, maintaining a connection with a specific spot on earth, such as an old cemetery in some rural setting, or a newer lawn cemetery, is very difficult to do. And the fact is that places undergo changes; now you see it, now you don't. Places get paved over. They are sometimes washed away or bulldozed into oblivion. Over time, they may become difficult or impossible to access because of changes of ownership.

In one sense, being scattered everywhere is like being nowhere. The phrase "nowhere to be seen," comes to mind. And what about coming generations who may want to know where someone is? I think of the plaintive letter I received last year from two sisters, each in her eighties. They asked, "Is our baby sister in your cemetery? We want to know where she *is!*"

Still, it is easy to understand the urge of many of us to pull away from the modern cemetery and from funeral home package deals, full of fiddle-dee-dee and folderol. A mountaintop, a waterfall, a garden, some place beloved by a person who has died may be a better fate.

The majority of folks choose cemeteries like the one that Mr. B. and I have just sped past; cemeteries that are more and more frequently owned by the corporate entities.

At corporately owned Chapel of the Flowers it was obvious that business was brisk, though conducted with quiet efficiency. Less than a half hour ago, when I made it a point to take a peek into the "chapel's" interior on my way to the administrator's office, I got the feeling that I would rather die than have my own funeral, or one for someone I loved, in such a setting.

The funeral home lobby was intended to impress—its décor rather like some higher end franchise restaurant, somberly accented in moribund shades of burgundy. By contrast, the offices were generic and sterile.

A secretary answered my questions courteously. Perhaps she was the one Laverne spoke with earlier. I was evidently something of a novelty. An older woman at a larger desk commented, "It's unusual for a cemetery sexton to go to such trouble."

I signed a document pertaining to the receipt of cremated remains that released the mortuary of liability. "By the way," I said, holding Mr. B. in my arms and pausing at the doorway, "what would have happened to Mr. Boyle if I or someone else hadn't come?"

"Oh," she answered with her mild serene smile, "he would have probably ended up there." As she pointed toward the ceiling I knew she was not indicating Heaven. No indeed. She went on to explain there was a special place, a little room, where unclaimed cremated remains were kept.

"We have *lots* of them," she continued. Her expression changed faintly. What was it? Disapproval? "Some of them have been up there for thirty to forty years, I'm told. No one will take responsibility for burying them, you see." Translation: "No one will pay us to bury these remains."

A man I took to be one of the funeral directors, who had been eavesdropping on parts of our conversation, interrupted in a lets-get-the-record-straight kind of voice, saying, "The fact is, state regulation only says we've got to store remains for one hundred and eighty days, and then thirty more days after public notification. Then we can do as we see fit. We inherited a bunch of the canisters upstairs from the previous owners." He, too, pointed upward.

I must have frowned. He said, "Hey, we're not the only ones. I'm betting there are rooms filled with unclaimed cremains, just like this, all over America. It gets to be quite a storage problem. You bet."

"What do you think should happen?" I asked.

"It's time we adopted The Industry standard," he said. "Put

them all together like they do in the 'ossuary' sections of the big cremation gardens. Even that costs money, of course, if you put a name on a plaque. We're not obliged to do that, mind you."

"That fellow," he nods toward Mr. B., "is one of the lucky ones."

And I think of this as I lift my eyes unto the hills once covered with tall native grasses and oaks, not houses. Something is rushing through me. It is all I can do not to turn off at the first gas station exit where there is bound to be a phone booth. I want to call the half-brother, only I didn't get his name. I want to call the bank teller. Obscene Telephone Screamer? I'll show you a screamer! "What's the matter with everybody?!" I want to yell into the receiver. "Can't we forgive and forget? Can't we be decent? Take your un-love and choke on it!"

Good-bye! Good-bye World!

IN LOVING
MEMORY

Everyone has a skeleton in his closet but the person who kills
himself leaves a skeleton in someone else's closet.
                                    —Stephen Levine, *Who Dies?*

The two boys enter from the shadowy western verge of woods
that borders the cemetery. The owner of these woods, a local
developer, has recently thinned larger trees and removed
undergrowth. Still, there is enough cover for two boys to disappear from view for a moment. Now I see them again, negotiating
a low point in the fence. They are heading in our general direction
where the three of us, Katherine, Obadiah, and I are working on a
headstone rubbing. Do they see us?

"Here comes trouble," I mutter as I drape another piece of
plastic sheeting over the slick sides of a marble headstone to protect it. A mist is congealing into a light rain and the tape isn't

adhering on account of the motion of the thick lumber crayon Katherine is rubbing rhythmically across a thin webbed fabric used for garment lining. The fabric is stretched over the face of the obelisk as tautly as possible, but when it moves even slightly it is enough to spoil the crisp outline we are after.

Katherine, who is on her knees so she can apply even pressure to the crayon, is coaxing the lovely contours of a dove from the stone. Now, she looks up at me. "Trouble? What trouble?" she asks.

"Two teenagers," I answer. "I'm not sure what they are up to."

"Shannon, didn't you tell me awhile ago that you were a teenager when you really got interested in cemeteries?" Her tone is mildly scolding. "Here comes trouble," she repeats, shaking her head. "Shame on you."

This beloved twenty-year-old stepdaughter, the youngest of the six children in our family, speaks with a certainty denied to most people. When she was a little girl we nicknamed her Katherine the Great—Kate the Great for short. She generally speaks truth and has been setting me straight since she was three years old. Attending college has not diminished her self-assurance.

But I can't help the up-to-no-good feeling I am having about the two boys who cast not so much as a glance in our direction as they pass. What are teenagers doing up here in the cemetery in middle of the day? Smoking pot?

Obadiah straightens up. He has been trying to keep the fabric from slipping by standing behind the headstone and anchoring the rubbing with his hands. "Here I am hugging a headstone," he jibes. "Human tape."

Katherine calls him "O.B." for short, although he is remark-ably long and tall—the effect literally heightened by the fedora hat he wears even indoors. He has a good view of the two boys and reports in a low voice, "They're stopping. They seem to be looking at one of the graves. No, they're moving on."

I want to ask if they are touching anything but restrain myself. The boys are in a section of the cemetery where there are just a few older headstones. I can't help it, I worry about vandalism— it has happened before. During one night in the 1980s, two thirteen-year-old boys damaged more than forty stones.

Sounding puzzled, O.B. says, "They have stopped again and now they both seem to be bowing."

Katherine has no compunction about standing up and looking directly at the visitors, who are perhaps thirty yards away. After surveying the situation, she squats down again and gets back to work. "Yep. That's what they are doing. They're bowing. And one of them just gave the cross sign. You know, the way the Catholics do."

I ponder this, watching the top of Katherine's head: the silky magenta bangs, the rest of her stylish bob black as a crow's back except for the half inch or so at the line of her part that reveals the light reddish brown of her natural color.

Suddenly I remember: There is one relatively recent burial in the midst of older graves in that portion of the cemetery.

"Oh!" I say. "I bet those boys are here to visit the grave of the kid who killed himself last winter." I want to add the dead boy's first name but I have forgotten it momentarily.

Katherine doesn't need to scold me now since I'm scolding myself. Why shouldn't these kids come here? After all, what's a cemetery for? Maybe they knew the dead boy. And I remember the name. His name is, or was, Luke. From the Latin word meaning "light bringing."

"To allow beings to enter your heart," says Buddhist teacher Stephen Levine, "you can eliminate no part of them." I wonder if this truth applies to communities as well as individual beings?

Sometimes the little town of Yoncalla is hard for me to love.

Over several decades, it is as if scissors have been taken to it snipping away much that was picturesque, shredding its sweet oldness, so that the town, settled in the 1850s—once boasting a handsome academy on a hilltop, brick schools, and several spired churches—now has little to connect it to the past. It has become patternless, faded, and frayed.

Maybe too many of us moved away, and if we returned, came back too late. Our branch of the family, like the barred owl, has always been an edge-dwelling species. Just outside the city limits and a mile or so away, we occupy our own domain. Historic properties on an 1850 donation land claim the other side of the old highway.

Even so, I think of Yoncalla as my town, and it tugs at me every time I drive up the hill to the cemetery, which is in the city limits. I find myself noticing the motorcycles in the front yards of battered turn-of-the-century Queen Anne cottages, the trailer houses at odd angles in the midst of vintage apple orchards. There are still a few brick storefronts on the north side of Main Street. One, at least, is in danger of collapse and looks abandoned.

But I try to appreciate the beauty that is still here, however ragged, and make myself notice the signs of improvement. Someone is taking very good care of Mrs. MacDonald's rows of roses, for example. Several older houses are getting new foundations and careful remodeling is underway. Some streets are resurfaced and maple tree saplings are planted along Main Street. The new library will be built soon. The city is sponsoring cleanup days when old cars are hauled away and front and side yards are cleared of debris. Some of the people, at least some of the time, are trying to stitch things together again.

Not an easy task in a city that is eligible for virtually every federal grant because of its status as a "timber dependent" community that is under extreme economic stress. Sixty-seven percent of its population is in the category of low income. Drug abuse is rampant among the young and not so young. Typically, the class of drugs is amphetamines, the side effects of which include paranoid belligerence that may manifest itself in domestic violence, sexual abuse, theft, destruction of property, and occasional homicide. Suicide should also be added to the list of "what ails us."

A counselor in a nearby city recently opined that little towns like Yoncalla, with their lower rents, attract families that are in a perpetual state of transition and crisis. The abusive, the addicted, and the spiritually and morally rootless need a place to hide—for a while, anyway.

All over the U.S., small rural communities like Yoncalla are filling up with people who live in the country but who are not, in any sense, country people. Many such newcomers bring urban values with them.

If I were to characterize Yoncalla's most prevalent emotional state it would be anger, with despair close on its heels. Local schoolteachers, including my cousins Susan and Marie, tell me that a high percentage of their students are utterly unable to control their impulses. Sometimes whole classrooms, especially at the elementary school level, seem affected by attention disorders.

The boy who committed suicide this winter, Luke, came from a family that was just barely getting by, that had fractured and then splintered into several related households where he took turns living. Whether any of these places felt like home to him, I have no way of knowing. Given what happened, I doubt it.

I learned that a Yoncalla youth had committed suicide from a brief account in a local newspaper but did not hear the details until a clergyman called me. He told me that Luke hadn't attended his church for years but, despite this, his church wanted to assist the family. Luke was just sixteen, suspended from high school, and not living with his mother when he died. His mother had no means of paying for funeral expenses. She was trying to hold down two minimum-wage jobs, and the going was tough indeed. Luke had been staying with an older brother, who returned from working on the graveyard shift at a local mill to find him hanging in the front room of her trailer. In view of the circumstances, would the Applegate Pioneer Cemetery be willing to discount the cost of a burial plot?

I told the clergyman I needed to look at my cemetery plot maps before assigning a specific location but that he could count on the fact that a plot would be donated for the boy. I promised to call him back with more information.

If I hadn't learned details about Luke's death from the clergyman I would have heard plenty from any number of local people: The woman who runs the video store, for example, or one of the tired looking mothers I walked past later that day, who was sitting at a card table in front of the Yoncalla Food Center selling brownies and sponge cake on behalf of the junior class trip. Bad news still travels fast on the talk telegraph. Does good news move so quickly, I wonder? But then there hasn't been much in the way of good news for the town lately.

The talk about Luke was not merely gossip. The community was terribly concerned. Its already existing anxiety was heightened by the death of this lonely, troubled boy whom many people knew, or at least saw, walking the streets, or talking to the skinny bearded man suspected of dealing drugs—a fact that especially infuriated people because the county sheriff's department couldn't seem do anything about it. More than a decade ago, the town lost its local policemen— one cop and his deputy known to everyone and everyone's kid. Some people said that the lack of local law enforcement was at the root of the whole drug problem because all the kids and the "bad" element knew that they could set their watches by the regular cycle of arrivals and departures of "county mounties" with too much territory to cover.

Other people thought the school was to blame. What had the superintendent been thinking of when he refused to let Luke back in school? Couldn't Luke's teachers see that he needed help? They claimed that way back in elementary school the signs that Luke needed help were there.

Susan was one of the teachers who watched Luke limp through his middle-school years when he briefly attended her art class. One day she was horrified to discover that he was carving his arm with a linoleum block tool in the back of the classroom.

Didn't they try to take the kid to a counselor of some kind, people were asking each other? Not that counselors necessarily do a lot of good, someone always added. The rumor was that someone at school had tried to get Luke set up with mental health, but the mother had objected. Or was it the father? But it couldn't have been the father the story went, since the old man hadn't bothered to see his kid since he was four or five.

Other people pointed out that in a Godless society and with all the heavy metal, soulless music kids were listening to, what could you expect? It was a wonder there weren't more deaths due to punctured eardrums. And those lyrics: all the sex and violence and sick devil talk. Kids just didn't realize what they were messing with, the God-fearing averred, or what Satan would do to their everlasting souls somewhere down the line.

But on one point churchgoers and non-churchgoers agreed: Someone better do something before another fool kid decided to do himself in. What was it called? They'd better watch for the "copycat syndrome."

At home, reading a magazine to relax I find something unsettling instead: In the U.S., teen suicide occurs every two hours. Suicide is the leading cause of death in young people between fifteen and twenty-four. These days, even ten-year-olds are killing themselves, contributing to the total of thirty thousand or more people who commit suicide annually.

And boys kill themselves five times more often than girls, perhaps because they often express and experience their depression differently by exhibiting somewhat more aggression, anger, irritability, and impulsiveness, than their female counterparts. All danger signs are magnified in importance if the patient is depressed, often expressed as a loss of pleasure or withdrawal from activities. In any case, victims are not trying to end their lives but their pain.

Later, when I returned the clergyman's call, I asked him if he knew whether a gravedigger had been contacted. Typically, this is the job of whatever funeral home the family selects, but it was clear there were already irregularities in this situation. He gave me the phone number of the funeral home handling the rest of the arrangements.

The funeral home chosen by someone in Luke's family, located in a community south of Yoncalla, is one of the thousands of formerly "mom-and-pop" operations across the U.S. now part of a vast multinational corporation. When I finally spoke with a human voice at the funeral home, there seemed to be confusion: The funeral home's time for a graveside service did not coincide with what the clergyman told me.

I had the sense that the needs of Luke's family were not a particular priority, especially when the funeral director said to me in a confidential and slightly irritated tone, "You know, these people may not be able to pay for any of this."

He meant the funeral service, burial, etc., since he was aware that our cemetery was donating a plot. He went on to say that the boy's mother was having difficulty believing that the plot was being donated. He wanted me to call her. He assured me that the funeral home was offering the woman significant discounts. My sense was that he wanted the woman to know that whatever funds she did have available should come to the funeral home's coffers since she didn't have to pay for a plot.

It was not the first time I've had to speak with bereaved family members before a funeral. "Bereaved" is a word I never used in my life until recently. It means "desolate through loss." The attempt to comprehend this loss, this ruthless deprivation of hope, joy, etc. results in grief, and grieving, I've come to know, makes inarticulate people even more inarticulate.

When I finally reached someone connected to Luke's family it was a very elderly man who apparently had forgotten to put in his teeth. I finally gathered that he lived with part of the family. He told me that everyone called him "grandpa" which made me think he might not actually be a relative. When I explained that I was calling to assure Luke's mother that there would be no charge for the burial plot his only response was to grunt something and abruptly hang up.

It was time for me to go up to the cemetery and stake out the gravesite for the gravediggers. The wind was howling, the rain falling in sheets but I had to go. As I was leaving the house, the phone rang. It was the funeral director again who seemed to be in a chatty frame of mind.

After telling me that the gravedigger would be up to the cemetery to do his business later that afternoon, he began complaining about the boy's family. "We can just do so much for people. We are a business, after all."

I didn't ask him why the boy was being buried and not cremated. I assume that the funeral director's generosity did not extend to discounting a cremation, or perhaps he couldn't get the corporation-owned crematorium to extend one. Whatever the reason, it was obvious things were being hurried along. The funeral was planned for the following day. If the boy were cremated, his family would have had more time to gather its wits. Relations who lived far away might have had the opportunity to attend the funeral—a reason many people today choose cremation rather than burial.

Sometime later, I was told that Luke's mother wanted him to be buried next to one of his few friends—a boy who had been crushed to death in an accident on a tree farm that had taken place exactly one year to the day of Luke's suicide. The other boy was buried in the Masonic Cemetery across the road from ours. When we donated a burial plot for Luke, the family decided to go ahead and to get the whole ordeal over and done with.

"I think it's awfully nice of your cemetery to donate a plot," the funeral director said in a tone of voice that made me wonder whether he really thought so. Then he added, releasing a little laugh, "Of course, you're probably not worried about a profit margin out there in Yoncalla." He went on to say he had everything under control. "Just get that grave marked for us, will you? Is it as nasty your way as it is here?" he asked. But before I could answer he gave me some friendly advice, "If I was you I wouldn't be giving away a really prime location. Just find him a spot, oh . . . in some corner up there. Know what I mean?"

Not so long ago, even in cemeteries that did not adjoin churches, the stigma of suicide was so prevalent that those who killed themselves were restricted to "suicide corners." Some sextons imposed a more severe exile: Suicides could be buried only on the other side of fences or walls bounding the cemetery.

Throughout history, and in different parts of the world, the right to be buried next to one's kin was frequently denied to people. Any adult or child who was born out of wedlock, for example, or who had never been baptized could be excluded from church, and even secular burying grounds. A broken-hearted husband, trying to bury his baptized wife and stillborn child (unbaptized because there had been no "quickening") was faced with the reality that mother and baby could not be buried together in the same grave and, perhaps, not even in the same cemetery.

In addition to suicides, murderers and the unbaptized, "lunatics"—presumed to be under the Devil's power—were also denied churchyard burials. Historically, and in our own time, some cemetery officials have also denied burial to individuals of the "wrong" ethnic, racial, or religious background. Black Academy Award-winner Hattie McDaniel (*Gone With the Wind*), was denied burial in the Hollywood cemetery of her choice when she died in the 1950s. Only recently has her body been relocated in an effort to rectify decades of discrimination.

Family members have always suffered when they have been prevented from burying the remains of their dead, whatever the basis for exclusion. Still, those who were faced with trying to arrange a decent burial of a loved one who had committed suicide suffered most.

Occasionally, monuments were designed to overreach the strictures of bigotry that placed architectural barriers between loved ones. Devotion, even in death, refused to be denied. So it was that memorials were designed to overcome divisions. Sometimes a living vine was planted to connect two graves, or an extension of ironwork resembling ivy or a rose vine reached over walls or across fencing. I have seen photographs of a pair of south Holland tombstones where an ingenuous stone carver sculpted two outstretched arms—each emerging from one of a pair of headstones—so that beautifully articulated stone fingers could meet and clasp above the wall dividing the graves of a husband and wife.

But there have been eras in which more than a wall or a chilly north-facing corner isolated suicides from the world they rejected. The British, from whom the majority of our North American burial customs derive, once buried suicides at crossroads, the more remote the better; perhaps reasoning that crossroads, with their several directions, might disorient the ghosts when they rose from their graves to track down those who had once harmed them.

Some would say that fear of the "haunt" is the root of most funerary practices all over the world. Extreme fear surrounded suicides. In parts of Europe, the right hand of the corpse of someone who had committed suicide had to be amputated and a stake was driven through the heart for good measure. These crimes against corpses were intended to protect people from the disembodied since it was commonly held that anyone who resorted to suicide had an especially vengeful spirit.

As late as 1823, these crossroad burials were still being practiced in parts of Britain until they were made unlawful. Britain was not the worst at "punishing" suicides. Being buried at a quiet English crossroads, between nine and midnight, seems somewhat more appealing than being dragged by a team of horses, head to the cobbles, past crowds of people lining the narrow, sewage-slimed streets of medieval France.

Suicide, or "self-murder" as it was generally termed, was once said to occur only in advanced civilizations, although "civilized" is not a word that springs to mind, given the historically cruel treatment of suicide victims and their families. The fact is that suicide exists in virtually every culture. According to an entry in the *Encyclopedia of Death*, suicide is unknown only among the Yaghans of Terra del Fuego, the islanders of the Adaman, and a handful of Australian Aboriginal tribes. Even this may have changed.

The harsh Old Testament nature of the term "self-murder" resonates with the absolutism of the Seventh Commandment. Greg Palmer, a writer who is an expert on death customs, points out what the commandment does not say, "Thou shalt not kill except thou."

If the New Testament does not explicitly condemn suicide, as some scholars insist, it certainly inveighs against it by extension. According to some biblical sources, Judas's most heinous sin was not to betray Jesus but to hang himself.

The term "suicide" was not used in English until about 1850. In the British Isles, as well as in as on the European continent, suicide was regarded as a crime and most often known as *felo de se* (felony of self.) Until new acts were passed in 1879 and 1882, during Queen Victoria's reign, the realm could still confiscate the property and lands of someone who had killed himself.

But why was suicide considered a crime, not just a moral or spiritual lapse? Why should families be victimized?

The punishment of the suicide's family emerges out of a peculiar institution of English law known as "deodand," which itself is a vestige of much earlier Hebraic law. Many ancient societies considered that the person who killed himself was committing a crime against the state. After all, anyone who enjoyed the civil and political body's support and protection from infancy to adulthood and then elected to murder himself was shirking responsibilities to the commonwealth. Deodand meant that property of the deceased could be confiscated and returned to the commonwealth for so-called pious use.

It is easy to imagine the devastating impact such legalized retribution must have had upon a suicide's widow and children who were not merely robbed of their inheritance but also shamed by the church's refusal to bury their loved one in consecrated ground.

Further, family members lived with the knowledge that the corpses of self-murderers were likely to be ill-treated. Graveyards that accepted the bodies of criminals, suicides included, were notorious traffickers in corpses destined for dissecting tables in medical schools.

Throughout history there have always been people, such as clergy and attending physicians, who, when aware that death is self-inflicted, have been willing to lie or disguise the truth for the official record.

Once, in so-called simpler times, death certificates in many parts of the United States, gave an attending physician an "out." Under "cause of death," for example, the word "asphyxiation" might have hidden the fact that someone hanged himself.

Ours is a more thorough age. I file green copies of death certificates, which I am legally obligated to keep by virtue of my official status as sexton, in a three-ring binder. These copies are sent to me by the funeral homes in charge of the disposition of the corpse or its cremated remains.

A more complete record is registered at the office of the county registrar, which describes the immediate cause of death and underlying causes. For example: a) liver failure b) previous alcoholism c) renal failure. My copy of Luke's death certificate states merely "found at 8:40 A.M." The word suicide does not appear, though it may on the certificate given to his family.

Two thousand and more years after Judas reportedly hanged himself, the roles of officials and functionaries still echo those of ancient counterparts. Similar duties are still performed: A healer or doctor pronounces that life is snuffed out and a member of the clergy or selected spokesperson conducts the funeral or simple memorial. There are still gravediggers, and there are still cemetery sextons, like me, who decide where to place the body. And, in the case of many deaths, especially suicides, there are still family members and friends who ask themselves why and agonize over what they might have done differently.

In the United States, where historically suicides were not considered felonies, those who assisted suicide were considered felons. At least sixteen states, Oregon among them, had mid-nineteenth-century statutes based upon those of the State of New York, stating that anyone "who deliberately assisted another in the commitment of self-murder shall be guilty of manslaughter."

Now, nearly one hundred and fifty years later, when Oregonians have twice voted for assisted suicide in the form of the controversial Death with Dignity Act, many Oregonians feel closer in spirit to like-minded people in the Netherlands than they do to their neighbors in other states. Oregon stands alone in the United States on this issue.

As far as I know, no one has ever been denied burial in our cemetery. The three Applegate family members who committed suicide were not conscribed to north corners but were buried next to their respective kinsmen and kinswomen. There are others, too, buried in the cemetery who died "by their own hand." Some of their stories are lost or, perhaps, deliberately obscured.

One of the members of the Applegate family who "took his own life," the accepted way of referring to suicide in our own family, was a great-great-uncle—a man whose many descendants still live in Oregon and might not appreciate my mentioning him by his name. The stigma against suicide is still very much with us.

Uncle X was said to have been my great-great-grandmother Melinda's favorite. The story goes that even after Uncle X married a lovely woman, the daughter of a successful local merchant, and had several children by her, he still depended on his mamma. Utterly heartbroken when his mother died in 1888, Uncle X's alcoholism and periods of depression deepened until he shot himself the year following Melinda's death.

Like Luke's, Uncle X's difficulties, began when he was a teenager. Most of the Applegate men imbibed. Today we might describe Uncle X as an alcoholic even during his teenage years.

As he matured, his inability to stop drinking overwhelmed and shamed him. For years when he went on one of his periodic drunks he would stay away from his wife and children, and avoid his other family members, claiming he did not wish them so see him in a condition "so debilitated." At the end of the binge his horse would lead him to his parents' home—the same house of one hundred and fifty years that we Applegates cherish today and call the Old Place. He would hammer on one of the stout fir doors, whatever the hour, imploring my great-great-grandmother to let him in. She would take him in her arms, let him sob, then nurse him back from the "pathetic and sodden state" that controlled his life. When he was fit to return to his wife and children he always left promising he would not drink again.

Did Melinda believe him? I'm certain she wanted to. But experience may have trained her not to expect too much. For more than forty years she was married to another drinker, who kept a little whisky barrel equipped with a spigot on the porch. Charley Applegate, born in Kentucky, and no doubt comforted as an infant with a Kentucky sugar teat (a bourbon and sugar-soaked sock used as a pacifier) as were many nineteenth-century children, developed an early affection for alcohol. In 1879, Charles Applegate died from, as his brother Jesse put it, a life-long affair with "John Barleycorn." There are many ways to commit suicide.

Mark Twain ended his unfinished burlesque on funeral etiquette, published fifty years after his death, with a single and succinct sentence: "Do not bring your dog."

The dog was the first thing I noticed on the day of Luke's

burial as people proceeded on foot, passing through the cemetery gate. A dog on a rope.

I generally do not attend every graveside service, but I try to visit the cemetery a few hours before to check on things. On the drizzling early afternoon when Luke was to be buried, I was frustrated because my car battery was dead. I was already running late. I called Esther, begging her to give me a ride to the cemetery.

Esther, with her abhorrence of cemeteries, even Native American ones holding her relatives, was not enthusiastic. She said that each of the family cars were in use—kids and grandkids were staying with her again—and all she had available was what she calls the "rez" truck, a battered Chevy pickup. Her whole family jokes about this pickup, which has seen too many trips to Indian Camp and powwows to any longer be reliable. The Chevy only sputters forth in cases of emergency or desperation.

"Okay," she finally said. "I'll come to the rescue of my little pioneer friend one more time if I can get the truck started."

"I'll stay here," she said once we arrived at the cemetery parking lot. "At least the heater works."

That was the moment we both saw the dog. A skinny young woman with bleached hair, wearing blue jeans, was tugging at its rope, trying to get it to follow her. The unsteady stream of teenaged mourners walking toward Luke's grave had Esther shaking her head. Several boys were wearing their ball caps backwards, and their unzipped denim or Oakland Raider jackets revealed metal band logos on baggy tee shirts.

Esther commented, "My God, you white people know how to dress up for a funeral!"

I was feeling quite harried by then. Events seemed to be starting earlier than the funeral director had indicated. I threaded my way through several groups of young people, and when I finally arrived at the site I was relieved to see that the grave was dug in the correct spot: immediately west of old Mr. Wamsley's headstone and at the appropriate distance from the other plots. It was in visual alignment with other graves on the other side of the strip that is called the alleyway.

But the gravedigger had not supplied any amenities—or had it been the funeral director's bow to economy? Kids were standing by the edge of the grave, peering into what I heard one of them call the "Pit." There were snickers and whispers.

Typically, an open grave is covered with a bright green plastic carpet intended to resemble grass. A portable simulated brass railing outlines the grave. The rest of the green carpet defines the area where family and friends may gather during the ceremony. The gape of a human grave upsets some people, funeral directors claim. Hence the covering.

But apparently no one minded that people attending Luke's graveside gathering might feel upset as they stood exposed to the drizzle. There was no protective canopy provided and nary a folding chair in sight.

Nor could I see the gravedigger standing by, nor his backhoe in the shadows, waiting to assist, when it came time to lower the coffin and bury it. Two or three shovels were plunged into the mound of dark red earth at the foot of the grave. The gravedigger had shoved one of my marking stakes that I initial with a permanent marker and tie with a strip of white cloth into the dirt pile, giving the appearance of a flag of surrender. Was it Luke's surrender, I wondered? Or maybe it was more a metaphor about his life as a battlefield.

It also struck me that poor William Wamsley (1826–1910), who, for more than ninety years, was the solitary occupant in his six-person family plot was about to have a next-door neighbor. The play *Our Town* came to mind. I could imagine old man

Wamsley, whose pinched face and flowing beard I remembered from his photograph, saying something to Luke to comfort him or at least get him used to the idea that he was dead. Maybe Mr. Wamsley would tell him that it was better not to try coming back—a reprise of the funeral scene in Act III.

Mr. Wamsley probably believed that one day his wife would be beside him in the cemetery, eventually followed by all their children, and maybe even a few grandchildren. Most people seem comforted by the idea of family plots. When making burial arrangements they tell me things like, "Well, at least Dad will be next to John, his favorite brother," or "Mamma will be beside that little baby she lost."

Still, it is tricky to predict the future in this day and age. Modern-day Wamsleys, geographically scattered, have been busy filling plots next to their immediate families for quite some time now in cemeteries far from Yoncalla. I mentally thanked the Wamsley descendant who thoughtfully conveyed five plots back to the cemetery. "Maybe you can give some of these spaces to folks who can't afford to pay for their own," he said.

I have no idea how long I lingered by Luke's open grave. Suddenly, I was aware of cars splashing through the puddles and realized his family members were arriving. On my way back to the parking lot, I saw one or two teenagers who looked familiar. Perhaps they had attended a production of *Our Town* that a visiting actors' guild had given at the community center last year. Or maybe they were students in one of the high-school English classes where I was invited to discuss the play and make comparisons between cemeteries in Yoncalla and the one in Thornton Wilder's mythical Grover's Corners.

Esther smiled at me as I climbed up into the truck cab. The rez truck, she sits high. I was relieved that Esther seemed in good humor since I was feeling guilty about being gone for what seemed a long time. She said, "You know I've never been up here. Yep. This is the closest I've been." As she started up the truck it made a gruff, old man sound as though clearing its throat. The wheels spat water. She continued, "It's not too bad. On a nice day say, I can see how a person might want to take a walk up here, or bring a picnic and look at the view. It's pretty, even when it's raining."

I knew there was bound to be a punch line.

"But then you people had to go and spoil everything." We saw a red tail hawk flying over the fields as we came down the hill, and she flicked the little brass hawk bell hanging from the mirror. Her face was deadpan as she said, "You just had to go and put a cemetery up here."

Later, in the internal twilight just before sleep, I remember thinking about *Our Town* again. The sounds the stage directions call for all came back to me: chickens, thunder, church chimes, a town clock that rings in the hours, and the thud of wrapped newspapers scudding across porches played to the tune of screen doors humming open and banging shut.

Living in the heart of Yoncalla, the sounds would be different: the not-so-distant roar of freeway bruising the night, cars squealing out of parking lots, televisions pitching shrill inanities, and pickup trucks grinding gears and heading out of town from the tavern. And maybe there would be parents shrieking at kids, like Luke, who shut off their lights and turn their music up.

"I'll be back in a minute," I tell Katherine and Obadiah as I set off in the direction of the two boys and Luke's grave.

I like teenagers, I realize, as I'm striding across the thirty yards or so separating us. It is when I think of them in abstract terms that I fail to do them justice—when I resort to making generalizations about them and the planet they come from.

"Hi," I say, brightly enough, extending my hand. "I'm the cemetery sexton—but forget about the 'sex' part—I just take care of things around here."

They look wary. Then the blonde boy with a bad complexion grins. He gets it. He knows a good joke when he hears one. I warm to him.

At this closer range, I now realize I've taught the other boy. Poetry, I think, when I did my artist-in-residence stint at the local alternative school a few years ago. He is dark, and seems shy. He doesn't want to look at me directly. This Jake, who softly gives his name, is smaller of build. He is probably younger than the blonde boy who actually introduces himself. Darren is taking my hand and shaking it firmly, as if someone has actually taught him the rudiments of polite social contact. He must be from out of town, I think. And, it turns out, he is.

"But I used to live here," he tells me. "And maybe we're going to move back next summer."

How old are they anyway? Fourteen? Fifteen? I know enough not to ask.

I explain that I am up in the cemetery with my daughter and her friend making a headstone rubbing. I don't say so but I'm hoping they have already noticed the magenta of Katherine's hair on their way over here. After all, how bad can I be? I have a daughter who has her full, lovely lips pierced and studded in two places. I want them to relax enough to talk with me a bit. I decide it would be better to get them closer to the headstone rubbers.

I catch myself before saying anything. Perhaps I am interfering with their privacy. Maybe they are not finished being here with the boy who committed suicide, who may have been their friend.

Did they know Luke? I ask quietly. They exchange glances. "Yeah," says Darren. "We know him." The present tense says it all.

We stand silently looking down at the grave for a moment. Instead of being slightly mounded, the rectangle of earth is depressed—some eight or ten inches deeper than ground level. An excavated grave will sink as soil settles back into place over a period of time. Luke's grave, only six months old, is literally in a depression.

Ever since the graveside service, I've been wondering just what I should do about the way this grave looks. Should dirt be hauled to the site and then smoothed over? How much will that cost? Who will do the work? When I came to see the grave a short time after the funeral, I thought, at first, there simply hadn't been enough earth to refill it properly, which hadn't made any sense. Then I learned from a woman in town that the kids attending the graveside service had been put to work burying the casket and filling the grave back up. "Yep," she told me, "and I think they did some of the digging of the grave, too. It wasn't quite the way it should have been."

This shallow trench over Luke's resting place is now brimming with silk and plastic flowers that are starting to look a little worse for wear. But there is no question that the flowers and the few small stuffed animals here and there, along with other inexpensive mementos, is an improvement to the condition I found it in when I was last here.

As I scan the various decorations, I am startled by what I see. I'm sure it hasn't been here long. It's leaning against the small metal marker with Luke's name that the funeral home supplied. I feel my chest tightening. I can't believe my eyes but it is unmistakable: It is the white figurine that belongs on my granddaughter's grave, located clear across the cemetery—a small little mounded grave, dug by a grandfather and a young uncle, and covered now with forget-me-nots.

My mind presents the image: I am at the florist shop. It's like swimming or sinking to see this picture rise. It's the dead of winter. I'm telling the florist, "Please, you've got to find some daffodils—bright and yellow—and baby's breath, too."

That's the precise moment when I spot the little white ceramic cherub holding a tiny violin on the top shelf. There are four or five of them and I want one. It's for Grace. Her name is Grace, I tell the florist and tears surprise me and close my throat.

The boys look up. Maybe, I've given a little gasp. It takes all I have not to lean down and pluck up the little figurine. My heart is accusing these two boys, but my brain is reminding me that they weren't over in that part of the cemetery. Or were they?

I want to ask them, but I refrain, and I'm not sure why, except that I can see that Jake and Darren are looking at it too. "Hey, is that angel holding a fiddle?" Darren says, "That's cool." And Jake's face is so soft and sad, suddenly. He looks like a little boy. Five? No. He's a two-year-old.

I breathe deeply. "Just let the boy have it," says an inside voice. It means Luke. Luke ought to have it. And the fact is the cheap toys, the artificial flowers, little Grace's cherub, all are better, light

years better, than the goddamned Zima bottles and beer cans and dozens of stubbed out cigarettes that were here in such unholy profusion the morning after the funeral.

Darren says, "This looks pretty good. Yeah, Luke would think this was okay."

I can't restrain myself. "At least the beer cans and bottles are gone."

Darren says, "Huh?"

"You weren't here," Jake tells him and then looks at me with a question in his brown eyes.

"No, I didn't clean them off. They were right on top of the grave, I noticed, and not scattered in the grass like someone had just been partying."

Jake nodded.

I added, "It didn't seem very respectful when I first saw all that stuff, but then I decided someone, or ones, meant it to be there. I thought it might be a statement of some kind."

The boys look blank.

"Maybe, an honor?" I add.

Now Jake nods vigorously as he starts talking in a way that makes me think he needs to despite the fact I'm only the "Whatchamacallit?"

"Sexton," I say again.

"First wise," he begins, "everybody knows Luke liked to get stoned and drunk. It was always that way. Even when he was little." He said he ought to know, since Luke's sister had been his babysitter, way back when Jake himself had been a kid.

"And those bottles and stuff? One of them was full?" he has the speaking style of so many teens I know: Statements become questions. "He would have thought it was cool . . . way cool, that people were up here doin' that for him when he couldn't."

It's clear Jake thinks it's pretty cool, too. He's very animated now. His eyes are shining. With what? Admiration? Is Luke some type of hero to these kids who pay homage by crossing themselves, bowing, and taking things from other people's graves? Luke may be many things but a hero, surely, he is not.

According to Jake, Luke liked "messing around" with knives and guns.

"The louder the better. That was Luke's kind of music," he says. "And the morning they found Luke," he continues, "and he was just hanging there?"

Jake assures me he was one of the first to know about it. "We live really close to Luke. Yeah, really close." He repeats this as though to confirm something for himself.

I try to get a word in. Darren, too, has something he would like to say by the look of him. I win. "What do you think about getting Luke a real monument of some kind? Maybe something that would last, with his name and dates on it. A bunch of people could go in on it, if it's too expensive for just his family. And then maybe the grave could be filled in a little, so that it's level with the grass and real flowers could be planted. All the things on his grave now," I gesture, "won't last very long, you know. The weather will ruin them."

Jake points at Mr. Wamsley's headstone—a rather small, not very impressive tablet made of granite that is almost flush to the grass. "You mean like that?" He's looking doubtful.

"Well, it could have some picture, or a saying on it. Maybe an expression that Luke always used."

Jake grins at Darren. "Man, oh, man. You don't know what you're saying here." They whisper something to one another and laugh. "Yeah, that's the one."

Darren pipes up. "No, you wouldn't want that on a sign or whatever."

Jake is still laughing but he sputters to assure me, "We're not laughing at you. Really. We just can't say it."

"It wouldn't be right, know what I mean? It might shock you," adds Darren the Polite, or, perhaps, just more polite.

I'm thinking how far away I am from the life these boys are living as I lead them toward the headstone rubbers.

Darren is the talker now. He likes Katherine. He tells us, really Katherine, that since it is against the rules to hold a fight on the school grounds, kids meet up here at the cemetery to duke it out. They come from all directions, he says, and fight right in the center. He points to the crossroads, near the two family plots that are surrounded by fine wrought iron fences with classic Victorian gates.

He loves the big trees, he says. When he comes back to town to visit, he comes here first. It's the best place. The big trees are perfect to play hide-and-seek around. He did that kind of stuff when he was little, of course, and not now.

"Once I was up here and some older guys decided this would be a good place to do paintball. You know, kind a chasing around and throwing balloons filled with paint so you could keep score." I am rolling my eyes.

"But, hey, they didn't do it. I guess it was because some of them had relatives buried up here and didn't want the grave stones trashed."

He really likes that dove on the "picture" Katherine's made, he tells her now, as though her beau, Obadiah-in-his-fedora, were invisible.

Darren goes on. The cemetery is the place where they break in the new kids. They have to camp up here. Sometimes older kids—he says his sister once did this—dress up, "you know, dripping with fake blood," then, around midnight, creep up the hill to freak everyone out.

Jake interrupts now, describing how he used to love waiting for the deer and elk. When he was a *little* boy he is quick to qualify.

He would watch a long time, but he didn't hunt them—not back then—he just liked to sneak up on them and then get them to run.

Darren says, taking the conversational bull by the horns again, that one of his uncles told him a story about a ghost up here. Darren claims his grandfather told his uncle the story and who knows before that: A Civil War soldier who hated children because he died before he could have any of his own, would rise, giving a rebel yell, whenever a kid came near his grave. According to Darren, everyone was afraid to go by that part of the cemetery until they got older, when they began making up scary stories of their own to pass on to their brothers and sisters.

It's colder now and wetter. The rain is falling steadily. Katherine is rolling up the rubbing, and Obadiah is putting our supplies in the covered plastic box I keep in the trunk of my Honda. They are going to head for the car, they say.

But I am hating the idea of leaving just yet. I'm so struck by what these boys are saying. I've known, or course, that some kids in town come up here to smoke pot, and maybe worse. And yes, I've cursed the lot of them every time I've picked up their Gatorade bottles and candy wrappers. But the truth is, as I think about it, there hasn't been a headstone broken lately, not for a few years, in fact. Now they have a friend to visit. There's so much more to all of this, and to all of them, in this homely little town so long on loneliness but so short on solitude.

I have an urge to return to the grave. I walk in that direction. I suppose they are wondering why. So am I. But they are following, falling in beside me, step for step, and the fringed outstretched boughs of the big cedars glistening with raindrops are sheltering us. We stand close together, still some distance from where Luke is buried, but we can see the grave clearly. I ask what I've wanted to ask. But until now, it hasn't seemed right.

"Why do you think he did it?"

They know exactly what I mean. Jake answers quickly. "It was about Cody Phipps."

"The boy who was killed last year?"

"Yeah. It really broke Luke up, real bad. Cody was his best friend and he didn't have a lot of friends. Not really."

Darren says, "I was still living here. When the accident happened? Luke would just go around saying how he didn't believe it. Cody couldn't be dead. It got weird. He got really weird. He'd gone to the funeral and everything and he had to know. He did know. But he said, 'Don't talk about it. I don't believe it.' "

And I'd like to hug these boys. I'm worrying about them. I tell them so.

"We're okay. . . . Really." Jake looks as if he might cry.

"Yeah," Darren says soberly, "I'm real glad I came up here, today. I guess I need to. I'm glad I met you . . ."

I fill in the name that Darren can't remember.

We are ready to go in our separate directions.

"I'm really glad I met you guys, too."

Believe it.

"Good-bye! Good-bye world! Good-bye, Grover's Corners!
—Thornton Wilder, *Our Town,* Act III

Little Stranger

Above all, be at ease, be as natural and spacious as possible.
Slip quietly out of the noose of your habitual anxious self,
release all grasping and relax into your true nature.

—Sogyal Rinpoche, *The Tibetan Book*
of Living and Dying

"I n Oregon, fall and winter are great times to clean headstones, water and natural bristle brush only, please . . ." says an historic cemetery association's newsletter to which I have subscribed this past year. The availability of water is the key factor when it comes to cleaning, evidently lots and lots of water. How stiff should the bristle brush be? "Decide whether you would use it to wash the paint on your car."

I am up here early, although not so early as the morning train that shakes the ground subtly, from my human standpoint, but

drives our dog, May, wild. She carries on even when the loco-
motive is still two miles away and I have yet to hear the stuttering
clatter of boxcars, brakes screeching at the siding, and the har-
monica sound of the whistle. Two shorts and a long: "I . . . come
. . . throughhhhhhh."

Since Daniel's and my return from our Kentucky trip, I have
had difficulty sleeping and adjusting to the time change. We had
a rousing time this morning, the dog and I. I gave up tossing and
turning in favor of being "up and at 'em!" as Great-Uncle Vince
and probably every other Applegate man liked to say.

I'm on an odd mission considering the hour, but I am following
an impulse: I have wanted to clean my great-great-grandparents
Charles and Melinda Applegate's marble headstone for several
years. But there is always so much else that needs doing up here;
so much maintaining of the common ground in terms of mowing,
clipping, gravelling, spraying for blackberries and poison oak,
and, lately, pulling up baby Scotch broom plants. It never seems
to let up.

One article I read recently, written by someone else who is

responsible for an historic cemetery that still accepts occasional burials describes such tasks in terms of a cemetery's seasonal round with Memorial Day at the center. With so much to do at the cemetery, when it is finally time to turn my attention to the care of our own family plots my energy will stretch only as far as pulling weeds, raking, and decorating with fresh flowers. I never seem to have time to plant anything special on a family grave, much less clean a headstone with a bristle brush.

But something else pulls me toward the cemetery, I realize, as I turn on my headlights and follow fog fingers: After being away for two weeks, I want to spend some real time up here. In a way, I am calling on old friends and relatives, taking time to catch up on things since I've been gone. Of course, the conversation is bound to be a little one-sided.

I am not alone in feeling the need to say hello to the dead and pass on news. The Norwegians, in former times, placed benches surrounded by a low railing next to family graves. The idea was that several relatives would meet at the grave and discuss family affairs and matters of local interest. In many parts of the world, the belief still persists that the dead are very much interested in what is going on. It's comforting to think of my talking out loud to dead relatives in light of such traditions.

Susan was responsible for the cemetery while we were on our trip. Last year during our vacation, just a day before a funeral was scheduled, confusion arose concerning the location of a burial plot. This year, I left Susan better prepared with all records and maps. I called her from Kentucky once or twice just to check in. She laughed and said, "Don't worry, so far no one 'has up and died' on you. Enjoy yourself."

The late fall colors in Oregon are not as vivid as those in the Appalachian country, where each mountainside, hollow, and cove glows with the fiery scarlet of sumacs and other trees. Here in Oregon, river valleys are of relatively low elevation, autumn is essentially yellow and green. The leaves of ash trees and oaks are curry-colored, big-leaf maples are bronze, and so on, and all these variants of yellow intermingle, providing splendid contrast to the rich, sober greens of conifers.

November's ax and wedge are poised. One sharp blow is all that will be necessary to make these colors vanish. As I drive through fog and ragged mists, smoke feathers waver from wood-stoves. I like knowing that Daniel and I managed to fill the woodshed for both our Tumblelow and the Old Place before we left for our trip.

I found a natural bristle brush down at the Old Place among cleaning supplies that have been there on back shelves for some time. One of these days I've got to sort out all those piney-smelling bottles and dump the mystery fluids. I brought a plastic bucket, old towel, and cellulose sponge from our house. Rubber gloves to ward off the inevitable chill of cold water would have been useful, too, if I had thought to bring them. As I get out of the car and gather my supplies from the backseat, judging from the way my breath makes a fog of its own I realize that I prob-ably haven't dressed warmly enough.

I also brought a bottle of liquid dishwashing soap that was not on the recommended supply list. I figure a squirt or two can't hurt. If I can wash my underwear with it, I can't see why using it sparingly on a headstone will do harm. Why do I always think that I know better than the experts and balk at directions? I cook the same way.

But I didn't need an expert to tell me not to resort to bleach for headstone cleaning, since I already know bleach and other harsh chemicals damage porous properties of stone, especially marble. I know, too, that some harsh chemicals literally pour from the air in the form of acid rain. The result is that in many parts of the world, buildings of marble and other materials have suffered disfigurement and destruction. Cemetery monuments, statuary, and other architectural treasures are literally dissolving from other forms of pollution.

What is the chemical that makes marble so vulnerable to atmospheric acids? It comes to me: calcium carbonate.

"See?" I say out loud. "You know a little something." Damn little. I see that I have forgotten to turn off my headlights. I place the load of cleaning supplies in my arms on the ground for a moment while I open the car door again.

From the east, light is streaming through fog banks and rolling toward the cemetery's evergreen heart. In a sudden siege of pale brightness, the whole length of the road before me is illuminated.

Unfortunately, my task will take me to the still shady family lots on the south side of the road.

Charles and Melinda Applegate have the largest grave marker in the whole of the cemetery's five-acre expanse. I suppose I could go as far as calling it a monument, albeit a modest one. I tend to think of monuments as much larger and more impressive: equestrian statues or twenty-foot-high obelisks. Still, at roughly eight feet high, my great-great-grandparents' monument is tall enough, considering I am five feet two with short arms.

I am examining the monument's familiar contours a bit more critically this morning so I can gauge what it will take to get it clean. For the first time, I note how it was made to appear far more imposing than it actually is. Rectangular sandstone blocks placed in three tiers of diminishing size form a base that adds almost three feet to the overall height.

The monument's most notable feature is its double marble columns that stand close together, suggesting a pair of human legs. Sitting like shoulders, an arch joins the two columns, and a miniature urn, connected at the arch's midpoint, rises like a tiny head with a hat on. After having anthropomorphized it like this, I have trouble seeing it any other way.

This monument style, with its twin pillars, typically marks the graves of a husband and wife, and can be seen in many other cemeteries that have nineteenth-century stones. Still, whenever I see one, whether in Georgia, California, or Kentucky, I immediately think of the twin pillars of our branch of the Applegate family, my great-great-grandparents'.

Each pillar rests upon a small square platform, or plinth, to be more precise. Each plinth bears dates and names: "(Left side) Melinda—Wife of Chas. Applegate—Died Jan 29 1888—Aged 75 ys. 9 ms. 29 ds.; (Right side) Chas. Applegate—Died—Aug 9 1879—Aged—73 ys. 8 ms. 4 ds.—."

As a left-handed woman, I have always suspected that there is something symbolic and slightly sinister (Latin for "left") in the old Christian graveyard tradition wherein a wife is always placed on her husband's left side—supposedly because it is "his heart side."

An alternate meaning of "sinister" is "unlucky side." He, then, occupies the dexter (right) or correct place, while the woman beside him occupies the wrong place, because she lacks his dexterity.

The nineteenth-century society of which Melinda Applegate was a part considered that she was an appendage. She was part of him, as in "made from his rib." She was only "Melinda, wife of . . ." It was literally written in stone.

There are many nineteenth-century marble headstones in our cemetery but I didn't realize this until recently when a friend, botanist Martha Sherwood, who specializes in fungi and lichen, pointed them out as we walked much of the cemetery one rainy afternoon.

Because of the uniform grayness of many older headstones, I assumed they were carved from local sandstone or some type of granite. Even though I realized our particular region was relatively unpolluted and free of acid rain, I thought that the ubiquitous sooty color of many of our stones was caused by atmospheric conditions, especially wet weather. (They had been "slimed," to borrow an expression from the movie *Ghostbusters*.)

What I was seeing that afternoon with Martha, and now recognize upon the marble surface before me, is not weathering but a living film of crustos lichen that, over time, has covered most of the surface of Charlie's and Melinda's monument. Lichens develop slowly. For example, an area as large as my palm can be as much as one hundred years old.

Older cemeteries that are largely undisturbed are often great places to find lichen, including rare varieties. The British Lichen Society, I'm told, counts old churchyard cemeteries as some of the best places to discover species of endangered lichens that are seldom found elsewhere these days. In places where pollution is heavy and acid raid occurs, lichens become degraded and may eventually disappear.

"Since lichens are here in abundance," I said to Martha who was down on her knees that day with her hand lens, despite the wet and a chilling wind, "our cemetery must be a happy place. I could use that in an ad, and maybe sell more plots." She looked up at me and didn't crack a smile.

She estimated there were at perhaps fifty or more species of lichen throughout our cemetery living on trees, soil, concrete, and grave markers. Evidently, lichen is quite choosy about habitat; for example, a member of one species likes a granite headstone while another prefers marble.

I can't recall scientific names for lichen, but I am familiar with a few picturesque common ones such as pixie cups, red-capped British soldiers, tar spots, and beaded bones. Lungwort, a lichen species that Esther and I dry to include in our holiday potpourri is common in many Northwest forests and grows in the cemetery.

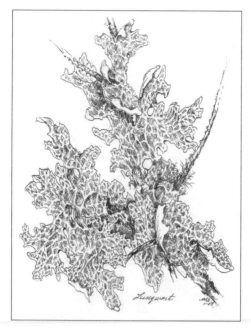

Lungwort

It turns out to be a gift to the environment in that it, and close relatives, fix nitrogen by extracting it from the air and converting it into organic nitrogen compounds. Eventually, these compounds enrich soil, making an important contribution to forest health.

For a cemetery sexton or, for that matter, an archaeologist trying to protect rock glyphs and pictographs, effects from lichen growth are not purely positive. In conservation terms, lichen encrustations sometimes pose a dilemma. As I rub my fingertip along the outside edge of the "shoulders" of Charles and Melinda's monument, I can feel pitting. Although hardly as potent as the acid in acid rain or in other types of industrial pollution, the fungus component of lichen does produce acid. (Lichen is basically a sandwich composed of layers of two distinct organisms—fungus and algae.)

Still, as Martha pointed out recently, lichen also forms a

coating over stone that may protect it from some exigencies of weather. In cemeteries, the reasons for cleaning headstones may be primarily cosmetic—allowing a visitor to read inscriptions more easily or to take better photographs or to make clearer rubbings. From the standpoint of preservation, however, it may not be a good idea to scrub lichens from headstones.

I am going ahead, but proceeding carefully, as I imagine the rewards awaiting me—the marble's pale sheen and how good it will feel, once it is cleaned, to run my hand over its cool, unblemished, surface. And there is something more, something about the act of scrubbing itself that induces a kind of meditative centering, inner silence, that I imagine is experienced by Catholic or Buddhist novitiates.

I am thinking about this as I walk toward the water faucet down the brightening corridor of road, plastic bucket in hand. I have read that the Buddha taught eighty-four thousand ways to tame and pacify the negative emotions. But then, because I have what Tibetan monks call "monkey mind," I cannot keep my thoughts on what little I understand about Buddhism. I cannot even just keep my mind on walking or just on the surge of water pouring into the bucket.

My mind is scattered, drawn to whatever is in front of it. Now, I am looking at the headstones nearest to me, noting how the curbing is cracked; seeing the rust on the Victorian fence I am passing, which leads me to the conservation conference I attended in Savannah, Georgia, last year, and to wondering whether I should try to find the company that made the fence on the Internet, if they are still in existence, and so on and so on. My anxiety begins waving like a flag. Monkey mind. It's bigger: Orangutan mind.

I am much more aware of cemetery conservation since I accepted a position on our state commission, and have begun attending workshops these past two years. There are certainly a lot of "don'ts:" Don't use a weed whacker when getting rid of unwanted plants near standing stones as nicks can result; don't use cement or any type of adhesive you haven't thoroughly researched when repairing broken stones; in fact, don't repair broken stones until you get professional advice; never set a stone in concrete; and don't use garden herbicides when old heritage plants or unusual native plants may reside within the undesirables. Is there any task in this world, anymore, that doesn't have a "correct" protocol connected to it?

But now I am caught again by the sheer beauty of this place; the gifts I receive as a result of care and attention. Not so long ago this unique little headstone I am passing was buried under an invasive patch of periwinkle ground cover. Over years, people have introduced many ground covers into the cemetery landscape, such as ivy, ground juniper, and others that end up hiding headstones and escaping into neighboring plots. I put my bucket down to take a closer look.

The design incorporates a three-dimensional tree trunk, accurate in every detail, rather like the concrete castings of tree trunks and branches found on Woodsmen of the World monuments, only this little headstone appears to be carved and may even be marble. The tree trunk represents life cut short. Because a lamb, one tiny ear up and the other down, reclines in front of the stump, when I first saw it I thought this was a child's grave. But the dates say otherwise. The girl who died was twenty years old. This is a case where the lamb may be intended to reflect purity and innocence, not age.

How lucky it is that it is still possible to read inscriptions on most of our headstones here. In Kentucky, numerals and letters, chiseled as recently as seventy years ago, were almost impossible to decipher. Coal emissions, Daniel and I decided. Back there, coal is used to generate electricity. The atmospheric carbon load must really be damaging throughout the Appalachians since even in small graveyards, far from urban centers, headstones were clearly being eaten away. It didn't help that some stone carvers made headstones from local limestone, marble's much poorer cousin, which is even more susceptible to pollutants.

Ravens and crows are caviling in the tops of the Port Orford cedars as I make my way back to the family plot, still thinking about Kentucky as the water in my bucket lifts and falls, flirting with the rim and catching light.

I remember one Kentucky cemetery in particular. We followed a sign across railroad tracks and turned down a little-used road. I expected to find the whole place wrapped in kudzu vines—the South's killer weed. How did the kudzu cross the road? It hitched a ride on a telephone wire and we have a photo to prove it. In the Northwest, we complain about blackberries, gorse, and Scotch broom. Thank God Almighty we don't have kudzu to contend with.

After a long climb up the road to the cemetery, we reached a miraculously kudzu-free, picket-fenced green sward of a graveyard. I was thrilled, grabbed the camera, and then felt dismay. Presumably because of pollution, age, and the type of stone used, there were only nubs of headstones, tilting like some old crone's teeth.

In terms of setting, however, our cemetery has a lot in common with many Kentucky graveyards that are also set on ridges. There, they would call a ridge a bench, and pronounce it "banch."

Wrentits are twittering now. They are so shy I rarely see them, only hear them. We had hoped to add Kentucky birds to our list, and do more hiking, but finding graveyards distracted us. Or me, I should say. Poor Daniel. Still, we both liked the feeling of Kentucky, and I felt a certain sense of connection as well, since the three Applegate brothers who came to Oregon were born in "the bluegrass."

Great-Great-Grandmother Melinda Miller and her sister, Betsy, married Charles and Lindsay—two of the three adventurous Applegate brothers. Along with the third brother, Jesse, who, like Charles and Lindsay, was an avid horsemen, and stock raiser—called a "grazier" back then—the three were attracted to this Yoncalla countryside on account of its rich oak savannahs. "Where the grasses were as high as the sides of their horses and just a mite bluish," our family storytellers always say. Then they add, "It must have put them in mind of Kentucky." And, now, having seen the bluegrass country myself, I am sure it did.

I have dawdled long enough for the Sun to reach the edge of the family plot, where I put down my bucket, take brush in hand, and begin my task. I am carefully working bottom to top, as the article advises, so as not to leave unsightly streaks running down the stone.

Someone who spent a year in Brittany in the early 1970s—in the portion called lower Brittany, known as *Le Pays de la Mort* (The Regions of Death)—told me that her most vivid memories were of Breton cemeteries where elderly women came each day bringing buckets and brushes. She was struck not only by the way these women made a pleasant ritual out of washing family headstones but by the central role the cemetery played in people's lives. She heard one woman call a new granite above-ground family crypt, for example, her *re'sidence secondaire* (second home). Aside from being humorous, the woman was expressing a view of the cemetery that placed it in the realm of the sacred, where her beloved dead, and eventually she herself would "come Home." She was simultaneously acknowledging it as a familiar realm; part of public and family life.

By contrast, I know there are people in this community who come up here only once a year, if at all. The contemporary cemetery no longer functions as a bridge between the living and the dead, and even an old cemetery like ours fails to comfort many moderns who are loathe to think of dying.

What if this cemetery served as a kind of public square or mall, where townspeople sat under the big trees and talked to one another instead of watching television? But maybe, by now, they are watching television in Brittany, too. Perhaps Breton customs aren't holding on any better than our own.

I stoop low, wringing my rag, rubbing the shallow carving that runs the whole length of the second sandstone tier where three-inch-high capital letters proclaim "Applegate" in vaguely Gothic style. Then I scrub each plinth and its incised inscription, using a fairly brisk circular motion that eventually travels up the outside of each pillar that, despite my efforts, as I run my fingertips over it, still feels grainy and minutely pocked. I have managed to reveal some of the stone's luminous white, but mainly the marble still has a dingy look.

I work my way clear up to the outer curve of the arch, rinsing every so often and squinting at particularly darkened places on the stone to see if I have made progress. My arm is tired; I have scraped my knuckles several times, and the joints of my fingers ache from repeated baths of cold water and gripping the brush. Gradually, I reach the arch that joins the two pillars. I try wrapping my rag around the little urn at the top, and moving it from side to side as though I were polishing a hood ornament or drying myself after a shower.

How long does this all take? I can't say, since I left my watch at home. There is something timeless and hypnotic in surrendering to this task; in the repetitive rotary motion of my arm; in trips back and forth replenishing rinse water and watching the bright liquid circle caught in the bucket; in truly breathing in the coolness of morning; in looking up into the fine penetration of light that reveals cedar branches in fringed filigrees. With the stone silent in the center, I am finding something of the inner stillness I was hoping for. What if I had not listened to myself and had stayed in bed?

Melinda's headstone: For some reason, I think of it as principally hers and not his. Not Charley's in other words. Why? These twin pillars are connected with an arch that surely represents marriage. This is a union between two people, one of whom is my great-great-grandfather. Charley, an 1843 Oregon Trail pioneer, a great reader, and tolerable blacksmith, was also expansive, assertive, and immensely practical. Despite a life of heavy drinking, he managed to hold on to his fine home and property, passing it down to his children in a long winding line of ownership that now reaches clear to his great-great-great-grandchildren.

But it is Melinda I think of most as I finish cleaning this stone, finally reaching and exploring this last place, where at this moment I am wiping my rag between pillars—between "legs," I almost wrote. On the inner side—the private place, touched by few. My rag slips along, almost skating, from the pale upper to the slightly less pale lower.

It is cool and smooth and white in here—a pleasure to the touch. I can't resist curving my hand, and moving it up and down, relishing the original smoothness that the stone carver must have felt. So smooth now, it feels as though nothing ever, not even years and years, has the power to sully this virginal and utter whiteness. Here, between great-great-grandmother's "legs," where no lichen has dared to tread. Or swim, possibly.

Yet, none of this is true. It is a conceit. For God's sake, the poor woman ached with children who were slipping between her inner thighs until she was forty-one. Fifteen children lived—almost unbelievable, in this era—not counting the baby who died in Missouri, whose body is buried who knows where, whose fate it was to be left behind, that poor, unnamed "Little Stranger."

Blue Walls

He dies. The shock possibly deprives her of life, or if not, she lives as one desolate and alone, anxiously looking forward to that world where she may meet her darling child, never to part again.

—John C. Gunn, M.D., *Gunn's New Domestic Physician: or Home Book of Health,* 1865

In 1856, Great-Great-Grandmother Melinda, was forty-three years old and just two years past having her sixteenth child, Milton. She was finished with giving birth but still had many birthings before her since she was a midwife, like her mother before her. Melinda shared the experience of many women before the modern era: She was pregnant at the same time as some of her daughters.

I know this because I have just opened Melinda's family

Bible, which weighs more than a good-sized baby. At the approximate midpoint, just before the New Testament ("Translated Out of the Original Greek"), smooth, purple-bordered, gold-lined pages record family beginnings and endings. Just as in real life, birth and death face each other on opposite pages.

Down here, in Melinda and Charley Applegate's home—the Old Place it has always been called, even by my great-grandparents—I sit comfortably in the west front room, on the women's side, also known by Melinda's daughters as "grand mammy's room." In the beginning, it was painted delft blue, a color that can still be seen by scraping off layers of lighter colors. Where they would have found this particular shade of blue in the 1850s I have no idea. Perhaps it came by schooner and they "fetched it up" by mule or wagon, traveling forty miles each way. However it came, it is a depth of blue that

I have trouble fathoming. On a day like today it would have seemed especially oppressive.

In the late 1960s, when family history first engaged me, Great-Aunt Eva—who, with her identical twin, Evea, now looks down at me from the oval frame they share above the fireplace mantle—told me that this room was where "babies were born and people died." Life and death is all still here, submerged in blue walls. I can feel it.

It has taken me nearly thirty years to learn how to build satisfactory fires in the two sandstone fireplaces that share the same chimney. The east room, or the "men's side," fireplace, is much easier to start. The fire on the women's side tends to smoke and sputter unless the one in the opposite room is lit first. I have the knack if the day is not too windy, and I have the patience, to build a tolerable fire in the women's room that warms sufficiently without lighting its counterpart next door.

The fire I have lit is finally talking back, but on this gloomy afternoon it really took coaxing, requiring more shavings from old cedar shingles, left over from re-roofing. Dry as the shingles are, they can't offset the slightly damp newspaper I used earlier. Therefore, I trekked back to the woodshed for more wrist-sized branches of madrone and fir. This wood is very well seasoned— the result of our cutting limbs from cemetery giants three years ago. Now the taciturn oak is crackling and chatting companionably. Good thing. There is a lonely feeling in here today. The rain that began to descend as I was driving home from the cemetery doesn't help.

I knew Great-Aunt Eva when I was a young woman, and she lived here with her brother Vince. She outlived her twin, Evea, by more than twenty years. I think of Evea, today—the other twin—because I am wondering what it must have felt like to live all alone in the big house, as she did when she was forced to stop working as a physical therapist in the 1940s because of the cancer that ultimately took her life. In her last years, Evea spent a great deal of time going through family materials, trying to pass the time, probably sitting in this room where I am and, for all I know, rocking in the same Mission-style chair. In her Grandmother Melinda's Bible, underneath all the family death dates, Evea made the following entry in her distinctive handwriting, concerning her father—my great-grandfather: "Geo. Applegate was the last of his family to go. He often used to say he was lonely." Then she added, "James buried in California. Fanny in Wallowa, Oregon. All the rest in Yoncalla."

Thirteen of Melinda's children are up in the cemetery; a half dozen or so buried next to her and Charley in their family plot, where I have spent the morning. Others are buried in their own nuclear family plots.

Someone whose handwriting I don't recognize and didn't spell well added to the names on the list of brothers and sisters: "One died in infantcy." By adding this infant, a baby born and buried in Missouri, the total number of children on this list becomes sixteen, not fifteen—the number that has traditionally been given in some family genealogies. If my calculations are correct, this unnamed baby could only have been born between March of 1839 and March of 1842.

That the infant was unnamed was not unusual. Many headstones, even well into the twentieth century, simply bear the word, "Baby." Naming a child connected it more closely and more painfully to the family who might well need to bear its loss. Better to call it the "baby," the "little one," or, when waiting for it to be born, the "little stranger." Historically, so potent was the act of naming that in some societies, children remained unnamed until they were more than a year old.

In the nineteenth century, when as much as forty percent of

the total death rate reflected the deaths of children between birth and the age of five, it is not surprising that some parents, especially fathers, emotionally distanced themselves from children until survival seemed fairly certain.

Healthy nineteenth-century American women seem to have spaced babies at about two-year intervals. Running my finger down the Bible's birth page column and doing a little figuring, I note that many of Melinda's infants were born from ten to twenty months apart. Apparently Charley didn't restrain himself during the period of nursing. Or perhaps Melinda believed in the number nine: Bear a baby in nine months, "lie in" for nine days (a day for each month of pregnancy), and nurse for only nine months. Women of the upper and middle classes "back east" suffered their "confinement" for longer periods—sometimes as long as four to six weeks. Nursing was extended in a more leisurely fashion, typically until "denticulation," when the baby's two upper and two lower teeth appeared. Frontier women didn't have the luxury to adhere to such customs. Great-Great-Grandmother had to get on with it.

Melinda's last child, Milton, marked the end of twenty-five years of perpetual childbearing. Is this why her new house, completed between 1852 and 1856, had a "women's side" with a separate entrance and a separate flight of stairs?

And why didn't she—she was a midwife, after all—practice some form of birth control? By the 1850s, many home medical manuals discussed various forms of contraception, including withdrawal, spermicidal douches, diaphragms, condoms, abstinence, and the rhythm method.

Yet, I am feeling frustrated as I look over Melinda's well-used copy of *Gunn's Home Book of Health* which has more than a thousand pages, and herbal illustrations. I find that the verbose Dr. Gunn says little on the subject of birth control. In my

cursory, impatient examination of the text, he does extol the virtues and responsibilities of motherhood, of course—a manipulative Victorian rant, despite a soft and flowery style. Whatever Dr. Gunn might have had to say about fending off the amorous advances of a whisky-breathed husband is still buried in this tome. In the end, Melinda may have discovered that a room of her own with a door that locked was the birth control that worked best of all.

None of the birth complications visited upon mothers was worse than the emotional anguish of watching a sick infant slide into decline despite loving ministrations.

"Taking sick" was an easy thing to do. Old cemeteries everywhere are studded with the graves of infants and children. Sometimes the mothers of these children share their graves.

Beginning with little Jerome, in our cemetery there are fifty-eight children who died before reaching age twelve. No. There are fifty-nine. How could I forget? She is linked to all the rest. She is "history" now, like them—all those others who died being born, or from accidents, or from the scourge of childhood diseases, such as diphtheria, smallpox, scarlet fever, measles, whooping cough, and a host of other infections.

When Melinda Applegate lost one of her granddaughters, she told people it was the worst thing that ever happened. Four-year-old Nellie Burt died in her arms in this room. I only got to hold baby Grace in my arms once. Just once.

Most cemeteries reveal cycles of neighborhood epidemics when children and old people were "taken." Around here, the Diphtheria, and other contagious diseases reached Yoncalla and other relatively isolated rural settings when trains began running. Soon after diphtheria, dozens of local children caught scarlet fever, for example.

Years ago, I was told how, at times, the women's side functioned as a small children's hospital. More than once, mothers brought sick babies and boys and girls "over to the Applegates" from various parts of the valley. Here, in this room, these children would lie on straw-tick pallets and be nursed by Melinda and her unmarried daughters, Lucy and Irene, who still lived with their mother.

"Fourteen pallets on the floor," my elderly cousins told me. "It was wall-to-wall with sick children."

I feel so sleepy at this moment. It steals over me. I tell myself, "Just sit here a moment or two, in front of the fire, and rock and rest." Fourteen straw-tick pallets. Some of those children must have lived to tell the tale, but others grew silent. They left without describing these swimming walls, the utter blue washing over them; their fevers sweeping them out and over, clear past their mothers' understanding.

When we complained of a sudden downpour in Kentucky a few weeks ago, a gas station attendant told Daniel and me, "If y' all don't like the weatha' now, jest hold on a minute."

I once thought only Oregonians offered such wry advice, but I have learned that people in many parts of the country, and world probably, feel this way about caprices of local weather.

Around here, at this particular time of year, weather often changes about four o'clock. A storm will suddenly rear up, whinnying with wind and darkening sky. Or the opposite may occur: After hours of bluster and oppressive cloud cover, suddenly the sky begins opening, revealing extravagant banks of cumulus in the west as the sun tints the atmosphere mother-of-pearl. I call this Old Testament sky; mighty shafts of light reach down to reveal all us sinners.

This is my favorite time of day to sit on the women's side. Tawny light bends through western windows, pushes through ripples and seed-sized bubbles, softly infusing the room, glancing across surfaces of mirrors and glass-fronted dark wood cabinets.

This room's western orientation was a boon to Great-Great-Grandmother Melinda and subsequent generations of women, all of whom, especially in winter, treasured an extra hour or so of natural light. Those who weren't preparing supper, mended and quilted as long as they could without resorting to oil lamps. Hooks that held the quilting frame are still here on rafters.

We don't use handmade family quilts; they are carefully stored upstairs. But one, a nine-patch, pieced from squares of dress fabric worn in the late 1850s and 1860s, is kept in this room to show visitors, who marvel that so many cheerful pinks and reds were worn by pioneer women, whom they imagine in more somber shades. They are also struck by the alternating squares of blue-green cotton patterned quaintly with black wavy lines that give this quilt its predominant color. "A wedding dress? It's so plain," visitors often remark.

As I pass, wearing my outside coat, turning off lights, making sure the screen is tight against the fireplace's stone opening, I can't resist patting this quilt that rests on the back of the Mission-style sofa. Soon, the quilt will be taken upstairs where it will be safely stored and Susan and I will replace it with a vintage red velvet runner in honor of the holidays. Susan's painting of Melinda, who is depicted gathering herbs with her granddaughters near a bare-branched winter apple tree, will come downstairs then, to replace the picture of family women drinking tea under the pergola in summer. I check all the doors, and enjoy the feeling that I am leaving the Old Place safe and sound.

I'm not ready to go to our house, the Tumblelow, I realize as I am walking up the hill. I think, not for the first time, how much my life is connected to my family's past. The bungalow, tumbling low until we can afford a remodel, was built for my grandparents by Great-Grandfather Buck. I'm feeling exhilarated by the burst of afternoon light. Instead of going indoors, I decide to take the car and go back to the cemetery where I can take pleasure in all the headstone scrubbing I did this morning. I imagine marble, glowing white on the headstone. I turn on the car radio, wishing for a musical exultation of some kind, like Vaughan Williams's "Lark Ascending" or Samuel Barber's "Adagio for Strings." Instead, the news is on the classical station.

"Turn it off," I command myself, and I do. Better to have quiet and take in sheep-dotted pastures, a line of Ponderosa pines, the soft rising of hills flattening into subtly colored patches of fields.

At this hour, there is a "land of counterpane" quality in these vistas. I hear Mother's voice in my mind, and the lines of a childhood poem I loved. I must have been sick when she read it to me, just like the little boy in the poem, lying in his bed.

"I was the giant great and still/That sits upon the pillow-hill/And sees before him, dale and plain/The pleasant land of counterpane."

Counterpane: a quilt top that a bedridden child transformed into countryside. But has there ever been a quilt—I think now, as I stop at the railway crossing and turn left onto Eagle Valley Road—like that one in Kentucky? I suppose from now on it will often come to mind when I visit cemeteries, especially older ones where generations of the same families are buried. It is a grave-yard quilt. The Graveyard Quilt, it is called. Indeed, it is *the*—surely, one-of-a-kind—now safe in a museum in Frankfort, Kentucky.

Quilts have always been a commemorative art form, celebrating as well as memorializing family life. Individual burial, coffin, and casket quilts have been an art form for centuries. Nowadays, quilts sometimes speak to larger societal themes, such as the devastation and grief caused by AIDS or breast cancer.

Even so, the quilt made by pioneer woman Elizabeth Mitchell, with the help of her two daughters is unique. It became the family's portable graveyard as time and miles pulled them from loved ones whose graves they were forced to leave behind when family men found an excuse to move on.

For Elizabeth Mitchell, as for other women, death was some-times learned about through "sad tidings"—scrawled hurriedly, in brown ink, on blue paper. The riverboat brought the news, or perhaps a friend on horseback who had kindly agreed to "carry it" to the door of the simple frame house or cabin. These unseen burials, where one had not been present to cry as the preacher intoned, or to pick up a handful of dirt to throw in the grave—these were the burials that were especially difficult to understand and accept.

The process took time. For Elizabeth Mitchell and her daugh-ters, time passed gently with the snip of scissors cutting blocks of floral print cotton and triangles of calico for the points of the eight-sided LeMoyne stars they chose for their quilt design. As the stitching commenced, plain and fancy, there were quiet conversations as memories of loved ones were shared aloud, their names spoken—the same names that were placed later on narrow strips of paper sewn to miniature, carefully cut-out, six-sided cloth coffins. Representing the living members of the family, most of these coffins were basted at the quilt's borders, so that, when the time came, they could be reverently moved into the center of the quilt, where a symbolic graveyard awaited them.

As I drive up the hill, turn on the cemetery road, and take my ritual glance at the Elm Street sign, I seem instead to see hands holding needles that carry brown and white thread, stitching in and out, carefully quilting the top of the counterpane. I see fingers idly stroking the fabric, touching the laboriously appliquéd rose and ivy vines fashioned from the best silk floss purchased in some Kentucky mercantile on the banks of the Ohio River.

Once in awhile, when life intervened, and quiet quilting hours were hard to come by, perhaps Elizabeth unfolded the quilt top and stole a moment to admire the work she had already done: the graceful lines of the weeping willow tree—that most funereal of trees so associated with mid-nineteenth-century cemeteries—stitched carefully into a corner of the quilt graveyard close to the rose bushes and the twining vines winding between the carefully cut "palings" that bordered the long, picketed path leading to the center.

Years earlier, Elizabeth and her daughters began another graveyard quilt in honor of a baby who died, and whose body was left behind when Shadrach Mitchell took another notion to relocate. The second quilt was better planned and unlike their initial experiment, was eventually completed.

I can't help but remember the exact year that second quilt was started. I remember standing in the museum, quite moved by the coincidence. The year was 1843.

In 1843, while Elizabeth Mitchell was planning her quilt, making the pattern, outlining the space for the family graves in her cloth cemetery, Great-Great-Grandmother Melinda was packing up to head West.

By May of that year, as the wagons were gathering at Ash Grove, Missouri, what part of the quilt was Elizabeth working on as she sat, perhaps looking out her Kentucky window? Was she ready to dye the backing with black walnut shells so she could achieve the somber soft brown she was after? Or had she finally purchased just the right fabric—yellow-sprigged pale calico. She already had scraps of some of her dead children's "school cloathes" to incorporate in her design. She was forty-four years old and had just given birth to her eleventh child. I wrote that down, as I was standing in the museum, thinking about great-great-grandmother's sixteen children.

Melinda Applegate had the comfort of having her sister Betsy with her for much of her life—until 1857, in fact, when Betsy, after burying little baby Jerome in Yoncalla, accompanied her husband, Lindsay Applegate, to southernmost Oregon where some restless gene bade him go. But in 1843, Melinda and Betsy, married to brothers, started West, knowing they would at least be close to one another, however many miles separated them from their family of origin.

Eleven years younger than quilt-maker Elizabeth Mitchell, Great-Great-Grandmother Melinda perhaps had a bit more energy. She surely needed it since she had connected her fate to that of nine hundred other people. Melinda and Betsy were about to begin on a two-thousand-mile trek that would one day be known as the Great Migration. At the time, both she and Betsy were pregnant. Melinda delivered her ninth child about a month after finally arriving in the Willamette Valley, just as winter rains were starting in earnest.

Family stories tell that Melinda and Betsy saw their elderly father, John Miller, for the last time at Ash Grove when he rode up on his big gray horse to bid farewell to two of his daughter's and their families.

As I am thinking of old John Miller, I almost hear the hooves of his horse. And strangely, in this present moment, as I arrive in the cemetery parking lot, there is another older man—this one getting into a decrepit Dodge, on the passenger side. I can't help wonder whom he was calling upon up here? What grave was he visiting? A young woman is driving, his caregiver, perhaps. The old man is rather gaunt, tall, hunch-shouldered. I wave but he looks confused and doesn't wave back.

What did John Miller look like? Supposedly, he was a "lay" Methodist minister. I imagine him wearing a broad black hat, trying to sit tall on his horse, but his big shoulders are misshapen with age just like the shoulders of the elderly fellow now leaving the parking lot without a backward glance.

I keep John Miller sitting on his horse and make Melinda ask him, as she is looking up at him, seeing her father's face under the shadow his hat, for the last time, "Please, Papa. Now and again . . ." I was about to add a name. But the baby had no name, at least none that anyone knows. In any case, a sad old man like John Miller, who had but recently lost his own wife, probably wouldn't be inclined toward grave visiting; his own was waiting for him, after all, in a future not far distant. Besides, he lived in a time when Death was on speaking terms with almost everyone, especially babies.

This western light makes it difficult to see into the cemetery as I walk west in the direction of the marble monument. Here, at Melinda and Charles Applegate's grave, the back lighting is dramatic, almost operatic. Overhead, thickly fringed branches are refracting daytime stars through a splayed tracery of fir needles.

The contours of Melinda and Charley's marble monument are edged in unbearable brightness. But the surprise, the curious and delightful revelation, is that life insists upon occupying this ancestral stone. A spider has moved into the diminutive urn on top. In this dazzling light, the web is spun gold, drifting angel hair upon the arch's shoulders.

But I find another destination is calling me. Still west, and a bit south, my eyes are fighting the light as I try to find the sheltered spot I'm searching for that is beneath a Douglas fir tree with two huge oaks nearby. The small grave is mounded. In spring, snowdrops and miniature daffodils bloom here. It is hard to believe that several years have passed and that there can be so much comfort in this gray granite heart, deeply inscribed with family connections that reach back and forward in time.

The light makes the back of this little headstone difficult to read but I remember: Daughter of Jessica F. Applegate Brown and Brooks R. Brown/Sister of Julian M. Applegate Brown/Twin of Sophie Jane Applegate Brown.

My daughter Jessica and Lisa Ponder, a friend who is an award-winning monument maker, designed this stone, patterning it after children's stones made in the early 1900s that can be found in this and other old cemeteries across the country. They wanted the upright design of the stone to fit in this particular setting—a pioneer cemetery. Expressing the chain of family connections was Jessica's idea. In years to come, she wanted Julian and Sophie Jane to come here and remember. She didn't want Grace to be left out of the family but to be part of it.

Now I can see the front of the stone and that lovely name: Grace. "Grace Applegate Brown, January 1, 2000."

Cut from the famous quarries of Barre, Vermont, the granite Lisa selected is medium gray, containing shining sparks of light-catching feldspar and quartz. This type of granite has wonderful attributes, according to Lisa. It is extremely hard, tight-grained, has a lacy look she likes, and is less porous than Georgia or California granites.

"It will stand up to Oregon weather," she told me. "The rains won't leave their mark." Judging from the smooth gleam of the surfaces before me, lichen won't be moving in soon, either.

Lisa said she has learned a great deal from fashioning Grace's stone. She is now making standing monuments that deliberately evoke the past, despite the fact that she uses today's technology. She even told me that she is closely watching the experiment of a botanist she works with who is trying, for aesthetic reasons, to hasten the growth of moss on some new park monuments Lisa designed. The botanist applies a concoction of buttermilk, bits of moss appropriate to this ecosystem, and "a bit of egg."

But I appreciate my granddaughter's stone exactly as it is at this moment. In a certain way, it feels neither old nor new. It has an is-ness. It feels as though it has grown here, will always live here; that it has not been brought thousands of miles from Vermont.

Lisa etched narrow fronds of sword fern at the bottom of the heart, and forget-me-nots at the top. Sword fern is a native plant, growing in many parts of the cemetery. The summer after Grace died, forget-me-nots and alyssum were planted on her grave.

Before a permanent headstone was even considered, there was a large garden fairy on the little mound that Jessica now has in her Portland garden, where she has made a kind of living shrine for Grace, complete with a pink climbing rose. A ceramic cherub playing a violin that I placed here is now on the other side of the cemetery on the grave of a local boy who committed suicide.

Making plans for a headstone in the difficult months following the shock of losing Grace was simply too much. The process took a year or more. I know from Lisa that this is true for many families. Sometimes the process is delayed for several years or even longer. It is not due to indifference or neglect. Instead, it is because the placement of a headstone opens the heart again to the reality of one's irredeemable loss; it is because the stone speaks someone's name within the finitude of numbers.

Though by now Lisa has designed countless monuments, she made the transition from graphic artist by designing a headstone as a favor to a friend who had lost a baby. The mother felt that the doctor, the hospital, the funeral home, and the cemetery—intent on selling her one of their standard monuments—simply did not understand the depth of her family's sense of disappointment. She wanted the headstone to acknowledge her baby's existence, however brief.

Once, Lisa designed a baby's headstone for an older woman who had silently mourned the loss of her baby for more than thirty-five years and who didn't want to die leaving only a small mortuary marker on her baby's grave. After showing Lisa the baby's ink footprints on a yellowed certificate that the hospital had supplied so many years before, the woman asked Lisa to incorporate them into the small headstone that she ordered. She was grateful to pay only for the materials and added her own gift of apple jelly.

"A gift of hands," was how Lisa put it when she told me the story. "A *real* exchange."

Today, in this soft afternoon filled with light, I stand here full of strange gratitude. Quilted upon this grandmother's heart I carry grief to this place, where I receive the gift of pausing, of breathing deeply, of placing my palm on the serene and steady coolness of this stone—a little grace, a small silence at the center.

Stories Under Stones

"The honour which you conferred upon our loved one by acting as a bearer is gratefully acknowledged and deeply appreciated," says the small card, engraved and printed on good stock.

The quaint, stilted formality of this standardized thank-you card, perhaps provided by a funeral home, is doubly peculiar by virtue of the British spelling of "honour," which would seem to connect it more to Great Britain and the Victorian era than Oregon in the mid-1960s. The card was sent by working people with strong rural ties—members of the "George Edes Family"—in January of 1966 to thank Jeep Emery, for serving as a "bearer" at a Yoncalla funeral.

I have found this bit of American death ritual in the midst of four decades' worth of obituary clippings and other community-oriented mementos that belonged to Dr. Lydia. Jeep has recently passed all this on to me. Lydia has been gone several years now and Jeep is tired of living alone in his and Lydia's Queen Anne cottage stuffed with memories. He is "lightening his load" and, hence, has passed on these half dozen or so small boxes, along with many other objects, as he prepares to sell his house and move into a care facility.

Just as Dr. Lydia, the community's favorite physician, kept track of every local birth, engagement, wedding, and commencement, she also noted the times when Death called on the neighborhood, leaving messy tracks on floorboards and carpets, visiting trailer houses and three-story farmhouses alike. Looking through this homely and poignantly revealing archive, I see many changes, both subtle and obvious, in local customs surrounding death.

This card, in and of itself, reveals some of these changes. For example, the term "bearer." Despite the fact that only forty years have passed, I feel sure no schoolchild today would understand what this word means, or what it was that was borne.

I've looked through perhaps fifty or more funeral programs that Lydia kept and note that six "casketbearers" are always named even when what is left are cremated remains. Before the 1980s, judging from these documents, most of the people in this area were buried, not cremated.

Even the term "casket" is interesting. "Casket" began to replace "coffin" in the American vocabulary during the Civil War period. (The Victorians favored "casket" because it suggested a container that held something precious—as in a jewel casket.) The century's old design of the lozenge shaped, six-sided wooden coffin fell into disuse. People in Yoncalla, when speaking of carrying a casket in a funeral service, however, still refer to themselves as "pallbearers," not casket bearers.

"Pall" extends further back than the Victorian era (the "Sentimental Era" when so many death customs were established, quickly making their way to America and even to remote mid-nineteenth-century Yoncalla). The pall was a vestige of the ceremonial pallium of Roman times—a voluminous rectangular piece of cloth, often made of heavy velvet, that was once spread over a coffin, bier, or tomb.

I've just been interrupted. The man on the telephone—a picky, I-know-I'm-right Virginian genealogist who has twice called me long distance from Roanoke inquiring about his grandparent's family lot, wanted to know the precise size of each plot, each family lot, and whether they were all alike. (They're not!) I was ready for him, since this kind of thing has happened before. With just a smidge of hauteur, I gave him measurements surely invented by the Marquis de Sade—in rods, links, and chains. He doesn't know he is dealing with the mathematical idiot of Douglas County, that I have trouble making accurate measurements of anything, that I have to call the surveyor's office to help convert rods, etc., into something I can understand.

Of course, he wants me to follow this up with something in writing. Never mind the time it takes to do so. *And* would I copy the record page listing his relatives? If my records were on a database, this would be no problem, he pointed out.

Glancing in the mirror, I see that I am the epitome of country glamour this unseasonably cool morning, as I pull my bright red winter bathrobe closer to me. I am wearing it over my clothes because it is long and keeps my legs warm, and because I refuse to start a fire in the wood stove this early in the season. Instead, I have wheeled the heater, as far as its cord will allow, toward the dining room table where I now sit trying to not immolate myself as I huddle next to the heating coils.

There is much about my job as sexton I really don't like, including dealing with certain members of the public, such as my recent caller. But there are things I like very much, about this job not paid in coin but in so much else. It is a pleasure, for instance, to be looking through Dr. Lydia's archive. By reading these clippings and thumbing through old funeral programs and letters, I get closer to the heart of things: the lives people lived before they ended up in the cemetery. I've even started a biographical file that may eventually include a thousand or more people. And when someone new comes, I ask their family members to send me an obituary, or anything they feel like sharing about the life of the deceased. "The deceased?" I'm starting to sound like a funeral director. Dead, say dead.

"There's a story under every stone," I tell schoolchildren, hoping that if they know something about the cemetery, and people buried in it, they will take out their aggression somewhere else. It seems to be working, in fact.

It occurs to me as I sit down by the heater again, happy to get back to my reading and organizing, that it might be a good idea to interview Doug Lund who is retiring as a funeral director soon. If anyone can share information about how funerals have changed, he's the man.

I have questions for him. For example, are people still sending formal little cards to "bearers" as did the Edes family? How is "honour" spelled these days? I want to put the card back into its envelope, but I'm having trouble doing so. Where is it in the pile I've made? My life is like that old joke: "How are you, Mrs. Murphy?" I, too, am suffering from "piles."

I search and think about the funeral director. He's turning his business over to his son. The father, genuinely kind and soft-spoken, goes out of his way to help people have the kind of funeral they envision. He knew and respected Dr. Lydia and made all her funeral arrangements with the help of Doris Means, Dr. Lydia's closest friend. He also arranged to bring Dad home from the hospital in San Diego.

It doesn't matter that three years have passed since my father has died or five years since Dr. Lydia has left us. In unexpected little bursts, grief switches on and off. When the circuit is on overload, the breaker clicks and suddenly there is a little stretch of dark. I really need a morning like this that is quiet and meditative, for a change.

As I slip the card into its rediscovered envelope I note how a signature is scrawled at the bottom in absolutely upright blue ballpoint by an obviously elderly hand. The signature contrasts sharply with the embossed, black elegance of the slanting typescript above. "Edes." The name is familiar and I finally make the connection, although I doubt these Edeses are actually related to the William Edes buried in our cemetery. "Billy" Edes was a runaway slave. William Edes (or Eades on some records) escaped from his owner, was befriended by soldiers that he later served with in the 1846 Mexican War, and eventually—perceiving rare freedom, given the time period—headed to the far West where he mined for gold. Swindled out of his gold dust, he ended up in Yoncalla sometime in the 1860s and was befriended by a prominent pioneer family named Wilson. He lived out his life in Yoncalla and is buried in the Wilson family plot, but that's another story.

There is a certain symmetry in the fact that Reverend Lee Whipple, white civil rights leader and 1960s activist, is buried in the same cemetery as a former slave who settled here in the 1860s. I hear myself saying this to cemetery visitors, who don't get out alive without hearing one of my "history lessons," as the high-school boys who sometimes work for me always say.

I defend myself: Do you see many black faces around here? Do you know about other cultures and the great stream of diversity in this country that barely touches Yoncalla except on television? My high-school boys give me a tolerant grin as they earn prom money clipping blackberries, pulling up Scotch broom—our latest anathema—and mowing. "We're paid to listen," they tease.

The Leo Club kids who have been a splendid help in the cemetery, lately, aren't so lucky. They volunteer and don't get paid except in hot chocolate and pizza. And I mustn't forget the Mormons who work like whirlwinds, in groups of twenty or more, and don't have to listen to me at all when they appear to commemorate their own pioneer roots by doing service work. And bless them for it. Annually, they save the rest of us countless dozens of hours.

Many types of Christians, including a few Mormons, Seventh-Day Adventists, and Catholics, along with a single Buddhist, and two or three Jews are about as diverse as we get in terms of religious denominations. Culturally speaking, our dead are extremely homogenous, with but few exceptions. Now that there are several Mexican-American families and American Indians in our area, local kids are learning a little more about different cultures. But I still hear horrible racist slurs on the part of high school kids, and if the cemetery can serve as a point of departure for a lesson on social history, all the better. "You can tell a lot about a community, and what people care about by going to the cemetery," I tell the kids. "Things have really changed over the years and you can see the evidence all around you."

Once when I said this, someone stooped down and picked up a golf ball, then another one. "It's a multiple-use cemetery," I parried.

I go on: "This is an art gallery up here. Look at that sculpture. This is a bird refuge: pileated woodpeckers, Northern flickers, wild turkeys, California quail, and Chinese pheasants . . . they were introduced, you know. Do any of you know what that means: an 'introduced' species?"

I go on and on and on in a way I swore I never would when I grew up. Pretty soon someone is going to provide the sexton with a soapbox—or perhaps a muzzle.

I have just found another note from the Edes family. This one, in its own stamped envelope, is addressed to Lydia: Mrs. Clifford Emery, not Dr. Emery. In the year 1966, when this note was written, some of us were burning our bras, but not in Yoncalla, which was still the emotional age of 1950, or even 1940.

The five-cent stamp is upside down, giving this indigo George Washington an odd and addled look. The envelope was canceled at the post office in Sandy, Oregon, on January 15 and mailed at the same time as Jeep's more formal note. In distinct blue handwriting Lydia's note reads: "Thank-you again for your lovely tribute in song. I meant to tell you that yours was the last letter she received the day before she died and how much she enjoyed it. We took it to the hospital for her and it was sent home with her things. Love M——."

Dr. Lydia must have sung at the funeral for the unnamed Edes woman. I can't remember ever hearing her sing but her voice was surely sweet and bell clear.

But, I *have* heard my cousin Doris Means play the piano at funerals, and she plays very well, indeed. I find her name on many of these funeral programs that I have been looking through. These hand-sized pamphlets—a single sheet, folded in the middle—contain a poem on the left-hand side. In my informal survey it seems that Tennyson is the almost universal secular favorite: "I hope to see my Pilot face to face when I have crossed the bar." Psalms 121 and 23 are also abundantly represented.

The right side of the program is reserved for the order of service and contains such headings as "Officiating," "Pall Bearers," "Vocalist," "Organist/Pianist." I wonder what Doris Means thought of being called a *"painist"* and not a pianist? The evidence is right here in my hands. I'll take along this particular program, with its cover picturing three pale pink roses, and words "In Loving Memory" written in celestial white, when I deliver the Applegate family portraits I've promised her. She wants to have them copied for the Yoncalla Historical Society's new book.

I think I won't take the odd, small tintype of Great-Great-Grandmother Melinda, however, who is holding a very stiff looking little four-year-old Nellie Burt on her knee. I've looked at the picture many times trying to determine whether Nellie is dead or alive; Melinda, perpetually dressed in black, especially mourned the loss of Nell, who, it is said, was named for Little Nell in *Uncle Tom's Cabin*. Melinda raised Nellie from infancy, and when the child died at age four from diphtheria, felt a loss so acute that following generations still speak of the "impenetrable darkness" of her grief.

I think we have pretty much overcome most of the Victorian funeral excesses, in our own era—we are minimalists. The fact that some Victorians went so far as to have their dead photographed because they had no other "likeness" is more understandable to me than some of their other customs; for example, the intricate wreaths woven from the hair of a dead loved one, or, worse, the pigment obtained by boiling said hair that was mixed with white paint and used to produce a doleful portrait of the deceased, often embellished by emblems of mourning such as the lugubrious weeping limbs of a willow tree.

We have developed a few of our own funereal mementos when I think about it. I met a woman who fuses cremated remains into glass pendants in jewel-like colors, clouded with a little of Mom and Dad. I've heard, too, that cremains are sometimes incorporated into glazes on pottery. Even taking into account other newly minted practices, and the reemergence of interest in death and dying that began in the 1970s, today we still don't hold a proverbial candle to the Victorians, for whom death was not only an eternal theme but an inescapable companion.

How ironic that I, of all people, am a cemetery sexton. As a child,

except for a dead parakeet—whose unparalleled turquoise lightness lay mysteriously still in my hand after I had picked it up from the birdcage floor—I was never in direct contact anything dead. Road-kill, whose inevitable twist of fur and slash of red, lay squashed upon the asphalt, was hurriedly passed by, with my mother murmuring indistinctly some variant of "Oh! Poor thing . . ."

I don't even remember seeing my beloved dead cocker spaniel, Rusty. Perhaps I was prevented from the "upset." Oregon country cousins of my own generation laugh at such admissions from one who spent most of her girlhood in pleasantly middle-class suburbs with patios and carports. Their childhoods, they tell me, were full of death. Their fathers hunted for deer and elk, whose blood-dripping carcasses they would find hanging in sheds and garages. Farm animals died, of course. The horses they loved, panting, whinnying, their eyes terrified and their handsome heads lolling, were the hardest to bear. Some of these cousins not only witnessed death but also inflicted it. They learned to chop off chicken-heads, and slit turkey-throats—sometimes the throats of the same turkeys that but recently followed them around the backyard and that they had called by name. They knew that in order to have meat or poultry on the dinner table something had to die, to, in fact, be killed.

They also carried the lifeless bodies of their own dogs and cats, and watched the birthing and burial of stillborn calves and lambs. And, unlike me, they attended funerals, probably many of the funerals that I am reading about in these little funeral programs. I didn't go to a funeral until I was twenty-six years old.

Fear of funerals began with my mother. I remember when she, the lovely, fun-loving Edie, who devoured every book she could get her hands on, read, and then saw the film *Three Faces of Eve* (released in 1957 and starring Joanne Woodward). Mother was appalled that Eve, suffering from a multiple-personality disorder—although that term had not yet come into use—apparently became mentally ill as a result of childhood traumas. One of the traumas was graphically portrayed in the film when Jo Anne Woodward's character was forced to lean over and kiss the corpse of a relative.

Funerals, especially open casket ones, were morbid affairs, my mother thought. She detested funerals, and under no circumstances would have taken me to one because, in addition to her own prejudices and, perhaps life experiences that she has yet to share with me, there was the sound advice of Dr. Benjamin Spock. He warned parents that children were "highly impressionable." Mother wanted to protect me.

Nor were there cemeteries to visit, on Memorial or any other day, within the cul-de-sac sanctuaries with elegant names like Franconia Estates and Manor Club that were beginning to devour countrysides in Virginia and Maryland, where I spent my teenaged years.

My Oregon cousins, though, attended funerals—lots of them. Unless it was the funeral of a close relative, in which case they were supposed to glumly stick close to their parents, they were permitted to wander around the cemetery, talk to their friends, and quietly amuse themselves while the graveside "preach" was going on.

But it was the potluck following the funeral that was the main event as far as they were concerned. Often mourners gathered in the multi-purpose room of the Church of Christ, or the Methodist Church but sometimes people opened up their front rooms, and visitors, along with their condolences, brought warm casseroles covered with checkered dish towels, or flavorful pies of apples and berries various that had the name of the person who owned that good Pyrex pieplate they wanted to be sure to get back written on a strip of adhesive tape underneath.

I recently learned that funeral feasts once had a special name. In medieval Britain, they were called *averils*; the word *averil* or *arvel* originally meant "heir ale"; in other words, the feasts were not only to remember the dead but to celebrate the living, the new heir. Out with the old, in with the new. The king is dead, long live the king.

I'm reminded of this because I recently sang at a local funeral with some of my friends, ate at the averil, and shook the hands of the new heirs—the grown children of the rancher who had died, and who would now, to the best of their ability, try to fill his boots. There were no toasts of ale but there was coffee served "leaded and unleaded."

I don't think that most people see themselves as carriers of culture, part of the stream of history that may be altered drastically or subtly by their own actions. For example, when did that woman that I saw at the rancher's funeral decide that it was all right to bring store-bought pie in a disposable aluminum plate and chicken fried by Colonel Sanders, instead of food she prepared herself? Probably when her husband left her and she got a full-time job to keep fast food on the table.

While it's certainly true that there are more elders present than youngers at most of the funerals I attend now, and that many people don't know the names of other people at such gatherings, it is still the case that such events are part of community life. People travel, sometimes from long distances, to renew ties as well as say good-bye.

The people of Yoncalla, with what seems in this day and age extraordinary devotion, still take it upon themselves to regularly participate in the rituals surrounding death. They still write obituaries, carry caskets, deliver eulogies, prepare floral arrangements, sing, play the piano or organ, and cook and bake for the "bereaved," not to mention the rest of the community. But these traditions may not last beyond the next decade. More and more families disperse and disband, turning the care of their dead and their memorialization over to "professionals."

It has been many years now since I have seen one of those hastily hand-printed signs hanging in the window of City Hall, the feed store, the barbershop, or local post office that says "Gone to Funeral" with, truth to tell, the word "funeral" sometimes misspelled. My funeral director friend says businesses don't give a day off anymore; most funerals are on weekends.

Out the tall Tumblelow windows I see that the sky is changing. The temperature is climbing and may soon reach the standard for mid-September that we expect around here. It's time that I disrobed—literally. Across the valley I can see the cemetery ridge rising like a shoulder to cry on.

Something has been happening to me since I entered my fifties. Surely this is more than nostalgia—that dread disease. Occasionally, a whole scene, a picture, reveals itself with the startling clarity of a pebble underwater. I *am* there.

Is this the sensation that visits many old people? Or is it a special affliction of cemetery sextons of middle age who are more aware than many people of how quickly time passes and where we all end up, or, perhaps, down?

A moment ago, I experienced what Great-Great-Aunt Irene Applegate once referred to as a "memory picture." I was standing in front of Aunt Hazel's door, on the front porch, using my right hand as a visor over my eyes. I saw glowing headlights that were the same silver-yellow color of summer sun; their oblique beams barely perceptible in the light of afternoon, motes of dust swirling in front of sleek, black fenders.

They were the headlights of a funeral procession on its way to the cemetery. This matter of using headlights in funeral entourages is based on supernatural concerns, not an urge for safety. The custom probably reflects the old practice of night-time funerals when torchbearers illumined the cemetery route and mourners followed behind, wearing black, it is said, so that they would be as nearly as possible invisible to the spirits of the dead.

I smoked like a proverbial fiend during the summer that I helped take care of Aunt Hazel. She shooed me onto the porch, I remember. I'm betting that I was out there lighting up a Salem as I watched the entourage slowly make its way up the hill, vexed by barking, car-chasing dogs, and gaped at by knots of grimy children, as the undertaker—not called a funeral director, back then, at least not by the elders in Yoncalla during the summer of 1972—led the cavalcade, creeping along in a midnight black hearse scrolled with chrome. Then, like a tail following a dark kite, came the unevenly spaced line of cars, gearing up and down: dusty Chevy coups, Ford station wagons and old Dodge pickups kidnapped from ranch duties. They carried wives and children wearing summer cottons and big-print polyesters.

It had been a summer shirtsleeve service down at the

Methodist Church, or the Church of Christ, and men with slicked down hair, unaccustomed to wearing ties, kept them on anyway, despite the heat. Each driver's bare left forearm and jutting elbow rested on the rolled-down window. Sometimes a red-eyed cigarette dangled from fingers that lightly drummed on the driver's side door when the pace grew intolerably slow.

Occasionally, I recognized one or another of these long-faced drivers as someone who had left Aunt Hazel's dining room a few days before as one more satisfied customer, and whose check for a cemetery plot, I had dutifully deposited in the drawer of the sideboard.

How is it possible? Most of these people have gone, or are so old now I don't recognize them, or they me. Except for Jeep and Doris, the majority who are listed in these programs as having served as "bearers," singers, organists, have been buried by now. How glad I am for the fact that Doris Means, my favorite "painist," still lives down the road. But I've lost my enthusiasm for this task.

And I still have all these papers strewn over the dining table, only partially organized and the morning is gone. "Am I blue?" croons the 1930s warbler in my head. "Am I blue?" It's the same rendition that is on one of the 78 records that Dad left. "Ain't these tears in my eyes, telling you . . ."

This has been a long day. The worst part was the trip to Roseburg where I left my purse in a shopping cart in a parking lot while practicing the art of inattention. Stupid, stupid, stupid.

Now it is twilight, and I am trying to concentrate on the beauty of the tiered hills rimming this place we call home, that are presently hazed peach, and smoky blue. Having seen the Great Smokies on our trip East, I feel qualified in identifying these particular hues.

Following my afternoon shopping trip, I arrived home to discover not only the fact that my purse was not in the car but that I had forgotten to buy something I needed for dinner tonight. I spent several hours making calls: the store, the bank, the Department of Motor Vehicles, the Roseburg Police Department, and worst of all, the credit-card companies. Now, having raided the small drawer in my desk where I always keep a little cash, I'm off to the damn store again, but this time I'm only traveling a mile or so to Yoncalla.

A bit up from the junction of Old Applegate Road and Halo Trail, I see the silhouetted forms of a man and woman walking slowly alongside the road, both using canes with their outer hands, their inner arms linked. They lean more upon one another than they do upon their respective walking sticks. It is Lloyd and Doris Means.

I have always loved knowing that Doris and I are distant cousins related through several bloodlines: Applegates, Cowans, and McKees. Doris became even more special to me after Susan's mother, Jane Applegate, died, a few years later followed by Dr. Lydia. I've been fortunate in many respects: Even in my mid-twenties I realized the importance of women elders. Only a few are still living; my mother and two or three other women I admire and speak with, but I have felt closer and closer to Doris, who may not realize how important she is to me even though I may not see her for weeks at a time.

I slow down and open the car window. Doris is wearing one of her big sun hats. Years ago, when the older women of the neighborhood—the Halo Squaws, they called themselves, which makes Esther want to wretch—walked by, I would see them carrying baskets on their way to the hills that rear up behind the Old Place, on their annual trek "to see if the lady slippers are in bloom." All of them wore big hats; they were charming, but a little daft, I thought back then. Doris was just in training since she must have only been in her fifties, just as I am.

I think of all this today knowing that the woods where those

wild orchids grew are gone. Calypso bulbosa, deer's head orchid, locally known as lady slipper, needs the rich shady humus of conifer forests to flourish.

"How do!" I hear myself say. Dad used to greet people he knew in the same country way. Daddy, in fact, gave me lessons on how to treat elders. When I'd visit him he would take me around to all the old ladies whether I liked it or not.

"Well, Shannon!" Doris responds. I love the expressiveness of her speaking voice, the alertness in her brown eyes. "What are you up to?"

I tell her about my wallet, that I am on my way to the Yoncalla Food Center. Daniel is due home soon, and I don't much want to tell him about losing my wallet.

She commiserates, and Lloyd just smiles at me. He probably

isn't getting the whole conversation on account of his hearing. I know that Doris understands my embarrassment over needing to tell Daniel, even though I'm certain, I tell Doris, that I will only receive his sympathy, and maybe a hug. She pats Lloyd's arm. "He's like that, too. He'd just feel sorry about it, but I'd hate to tell him, anyway."

She comes closer to the car, peering in. "What you need is a big tomato to put on his plate. Mother always told us girls to give 'em a good meal, *then* say what you intend to say! Stop by on your way back."

I return in a few moments to see Lloyd and Doris walking down their driveway waiting for me. On the ground is a big box of tomatoes, including several pumpkin-yellow ones—strangely shaped, sweet-tasting old-time "ox hearts," still grown around here by longtime gardeners.

I get out to help Lloyd by opening the car. The whirlygigs that Lloyd, an ingenious craftsman, makes, are spots of bright, hand-painted color on the fence posts. It is growing dark now but the tomatoes seem to glow. On top of them is something white; on closer inspection I see that Doris has added tablet-sized sheaves of paper, held together with a big paperclip.

"These are some of the pieces—just odds and ends, really—about various people in the cemetery you wanted me to write up. Just stories: you'll see. I got to laughing about the Hollomans . . ."

"Oh, Doris, I'm so glad you've done this."

I watch Lloyd head for the house with his head down like a horse heading for the stall. Doris is lingering. She puts her hands on my shoulders and looks at me intently. "I want you to know, I'm having a bilateral mastectomy this coming week. I won't be doing much for awhile—*certainly* not hugging," she laughs. "The doctor said *when* my cancer comes back—not *if* mind you—it will be the invasive kind. We're just going to fight fire with fire, that's all, and take care of it *now*. I don't *need* these at my advanced age, anyway."

I hug her *hard* and wish her well. She is so matter-of-fact. But driving the rest of the way home I feel disturbed and anxious.

After putting things away, I turn on Aunt Hazel's small blue lamp with its old-fashioned curved glass shade. What, in my life, is not interconnected, I find myself wondering? Aunt Hazel, and Doris's mother, whom Doris resembles more each year, were old dear friends. In 1971, I made a tape recording of an interview I had with Anna Kingery and Aunt Hazel as we all sat down at the Old Place in front of the fireplace on the women's side. This table, which Daniel has repaired, was Aunt Hazel's. Anna Kingery's daughter, Doris, has written down these "stories," and I am about to read them by a light that is surely larger, and more illuminating than I know.

I do know, however, that Doris has been working on these stories all through canning season. "Scribbling things for you while waiting on the kettle," she told me a few weeks ago.

Some of her small script is blue, the rest black. She wanted to make as much use of the room on the page as possible—Doris is generous, but thrifty. She has arranged things in neat paragraphs, incorporating birth and death dates, and assigning numbers from pages of a cemetery record book that I copied for her.

Some entries are very brief:

STANLEY "GEORGE" CURTRIGHT 1941–1951
Son of Andy and Ermel. Electrocuted when he climbed
a tree in their yard and touched an electric line.

LUTHER DAUGHERTY 1888–1955
A house painter who played a slide trombone in the
town dance band.

James Huntington 1891–1946

First of thirteen children of Ben and Mary to die. Very devout Christian. Never owned a car.

William Ladd 1858–1955

Lost everything he had in the bank failure of 1929. Raised prunes.

Clifford Burns 1912–1950

Killed in a logging accident, leaving a wife with terminal cancer and three young children.

Others are longer:

Minor Applegate 1884–1956

Son of Milton Applegate. A *very* large man. Doctor tried to put him on a diet and suggested ½ grapefruit and cereal for breakfast. Minor asked if he should eat that before or after his regular meal of ham and eggs. Served many years on the District 32 School Board. Signed my diploma in 1944. Farmer. Did custom threshing in neighborhood.

Thomas Hollomon 1871–1959

Born in Arkansas. Left home at age twenty-six headed South on horseback. Traveled to Texas along Gulf Coast working occasionally. Returned home late on same horse eight years later. When asked why so long he said he wasn't in any hurry. Came to Oregon in 1906 and herded sheep. His favorite book was the dictionary.

Rena Gentry 1871–1945

Married to Elijah "Lige" Gentry 1869–1942 They were poor and she was lonely. Lige begged Dad to move them into an abandoned logging shack on our place. There was only a summer road and no electricity or telephone— still, Lige insisted and Rena had to comply. Rena was so very isolated. She told my mother once, "I married Lige for a companion and look what I got. He won't even let me wash his neck."

Doris: She has the best sense of humor of any elder I know. She is always who she is; like any really good apple, though, she has a little "bite" that offsets the sweetness. She carries this community inside her; there will never be anyone like her again. Oh dear, this is beginning to feel like an obituary. "Please," I say, addressing the darkness outside but sitting in this small circle of light, "I don't want Doris to go."

And I don't want to go, either, even though I know I will. Some day. But right now, I want to live to tell about it, and I want to tell Doris.

The phone rings in odd telepathy. What else can I think since it's Doris. She's calling to ask if I have enjoyed what she's written. "Perfect!" I say. "I want more."

She goes into the hospital on Monday, she tells me. I tell her I will be thinking about her. I add, "I hope you know how much I care about you."

She says, "Well, thank-you, Shannon. We'll do more of this. We'll have some good laughs together. You'll see."

After our good-byes I see the headlights of Daniel's pickup. I go outside, stand on the back porch, and hear the sound of falling leaves; they must be from the Big Leaf maple by the chicken shed. It's a beautiful evening despite the chill in the air.

Amen

We do not yet know how to serve man, how can we serve
the spirits? We do not yet know about life, how can we
know about death?

—Confucius, c. 551–479 B.C.

We learn what we're supposed to learn, when we are supposed to learn it. I am beginning to believe this. If we're listening. If we're paying attention to our own lives.

This morning I was at the little fitness center in Yoncalla—the Palace of Mirrors I call it—walking on one of the treadmills. Beside me, on her own treadmill, was a woman in her early thirties. We've sometimes exchanged greetings on other mornings, but have never had a real conversation. Usually, this woman comes with her sister-in-law; I know this because of eavesdropping. The two of them chatter for the duration of their forty-five minute walk to nowhere, while I, on another treadmill, try to think my own thoughts. This is not easy because of their animated discussions, the rock radio station playing in the background, and the spectacle of myself—not looking my very best by a long shot—staring back at me from a wall of mirrors.

But the treadmills have just been moved to another room, so this morning there was no music to stimulate, or, in my case, irritate. Sans sister-in-law, it was just this woman and I and maybe one or two men working out in the other room. After our usual perfunctory hello, she volunteered that her companion, "hadn't even called to cancel," adding with faint indignation, "It kind of ticked me, you know?"

We began talking back-and-forth, each on her treadmill, going at about the same speed. There is a certain kind of small talk, especially with someone I don't know, that usually is difficult for me. But there I was being Chatty Cathy. I learned she lived with her family in a doublewide in the biggest trailer park in town, that she'd got her exercise outfit on sale a few days ago at Wal-Mart—not the one in Roseburg, but the one in Cottage Grove—

and that her partner kept telling her how beefy she was getting, not that *he* had room to talk.

When I don't know what to say, I sometimes just ask questions. Most people are perfectly happy talking about themselves. But something else was going on, I realize now. I was paying attention to some inner nudge.

She was obviously warming up to me—happy to talk on the walk we were each taking to feel better, or more attractive, or more something. We were perspiring a little, and as I was adjusting the timer to cool-down speed, I asked, "Do you have people in your family buried in the cemetery up there on the hill? The one with the big trees, old one I mean . . ."

As soon as I said this, I wished I hadn't. Burials are a fairly serious topic—not something casually discussed with a near stranger in sweatpants. What was I thinking of, asking such a personal question, such an intrusive question. But it turned out that the question was at the heart of what linked us.

Her treadmill had stopped. She wiped her forehead, then, catching my gaze in the mirror as she stepped down from the machine, she said quietly, "I have a son buried up there. We just got his stone installed. *Finally.* It took us a few years to do it. It's funny you asked me. We was just up there in the cemetery."

Suddenly, I knew who this woman was. After a few more leading questions, it was clear I was indeed talking with the mother of Anthony, the baby who died, whose father is Joe John Kelly. This woman's husband is the Obscene Telephone Screamer who called me up and threatened me, when I first took over the care of the cemetery. He was the guy who was on his way up to the house to get me. That also meant that the pleasant woman next to me on her machine had relatives whom I suspected of taking advantage of an elderly man—Mr. Boyle. Immediately, the face of the bank teller rose in my mind—those pale blue eyes scanning the computer screen, looking for the bank balance in a dead man's account—and I wondered how the bank teller was related to her?

"Everyone in Yoncalla is related," the joke goes, as it probably does in small towns everywhere. "Be careful what you say!" For a few moments I mentally reviewed what I knew about her family tree but couldn't decide what to say. What really amazed me about the woman, who put her machine on pause for a moment, then bent down to retie one of her off-brand workout shoes, was that she chose a man to love who had talked to me as no one had ever talked to me—a man, in fact, who had raged at me.

She smiled as she resumed her pace. Her long auburn hair was pulled back into a ponytail that swished like a young girl's who was exerting herself on a bicycle. Her bangs were sprayed into a kind of pouf, country-singer style.

I didn't say anything about her husband. Not yet. I suppose I wanted to make the most out of this unexpected opportunity. I was being cagey. Strange expression that, but I suppose being cagey is about wanting to catch something. I was waiting for an opening.

When she commented on how nice the cemetery was looking, I played my hand. I took a swig from my water bottle. I told her I was responsible for the cemetery, that many family members and volunteers had worked hard to improve things.

"Actually," I said, warming to my topic, or perhaps agenda, "I think I remember talking to some of your family members last year after we had done a huge cemetery cleanup." Was her last name Kelly, by any chance? It wasn't.

She hadn't married the Obscene Telephone Screamer, apparently, just had kids with him.

"So," I continued in a low key conversational way, "who was the woman who first called me and said we had stolen valuable articles from the grave? She called the police, you know. Was that your mother I spoke with?" I asked. "I felt really bad about what happened and tried to explain to her we were just trying to clean up the cemetery. It didn't seem to make any difference what I said. She just kept going on and then the man called."

I'd climbed off my treadmill and stood talking to her as she, too, finished up. With our feet planted on the floor we stood eye to eye, almost the same height, I remember. "That was Joe John's mother you talked to," she said. "And then Joe John, Anthony's father . . . or would have been." She looked down.

I told her how much Joe John's phone call had scared me. The incident had been upsetting enough that it made me feel that I shouldn't be involved the cemetery's management. I really laid it on: how appalled I was by his language, etc. I meant everything I was saying, of course, it was all the truth, but even at the time I was doing it something was niggling at me concerning my behavior.

She nodded her head. "Yeah, that's Joe John all right. He goes off. His mother does too. It was all a mess. It was real hard on everybody. Losing the baby."

"No one should talk to anybody like he did," I said in a firm, parental voice.

"I know," she mumbled.

Satisfied that I had made my point, I patted her arm and we went our separate ways into the inner exercise room with machines of torture that would have delighted any inquisitor. The music throbbed.

I'm getting better. It didn't take me too long to realize what I'd just done. I experienced only about a minute or so of feeling good in a kind of awful way. I'd finally gotten to say my piece about that s.o.b. I wanted everyone in his whole family to know that I hadn't forgotten the incident, or how badly he had behaved, how wrong he'd been to lash out at me—a nice woman just trying to do her job. I'd even thrown in a mini-lecture about how bad plastic toys looked after they were exposed to the weather.

As I looked for the blue exercise mat, I remember disliking the prospect of doing my various stretches with men in the room—one man, actually, probably seventy-five, who I am sure didn't give a wing what my bottom looked like. There was another prospect I didn't much like either: I knew I was going to have to say more to the woman on the other side of the room but I wasn't ready.

Was I really so bad? The fact was that there had been quite a shift in my attitude since taking over the cemetery, as I thought about it. True, I still winced at celluloid windmills, sagging mylar balloons, and other stuff people left on graves. Then there were the mementos I found utterly repugnant, like the empty Zima and beer bottles left on top of the grave of the boy who committed suicide. Still, despite my own sense of aesthetics, when cemetery visitors shook their heads at all the "junk" people placed on graves I sometimes found myself defending the rights of the people who owned the plots.

On the floor, doing my side stretches, I thought about how I had come to believe that there was a larger principle guiding my decisions: People, for the most part, had a right to memorialize their dead as they saw fit, live and let live or more aptly, die and let die. It's a difficult position. The decision I had reached in terms of my cemetery responsibilities was to evaluate the appearance of graves one at a time. While I wanted to protect a lovely green space, filled with history, I never wanted to forget its oh-so-human purpose as a place to mourn the dead. Just as the cemetery changes over the seasons, I reasoned, so did its patterns of use. Still, there were guidelines, and I reserved the right to discard any plastic flower or other decoration past its prime.

I also reflected on the "grave goods" that I had formerly found so objectionable that, for me in their own way, had become as valid as any dead Australian aboriginal child's emu feathered apron; any fallen Nordic warrior's shield. In other words, a heart-shaped rock with "Grandma" scrawled across it, a Scooby statue with a bobbing head would stay where they were placed.

There was no question about it: The family of the woman across the room was largely responsible for a lesson I had received concerning tolerance. It had been inadvertent, very unpleasant, and delivered in anger, but it was nonetheless a lesson worth having. And it occurred to me, as I wiped away tiny pearls of sweat, that other families in Yoncalla, not very different from the Kelly clan, had also taught me things.

As I felt that satisfying tiredness after working out which would soon transform into energy that would carry me through the rest my day, I realized that I no longer felt as though I were a member of an edge-dwelling species. My family and I were part of the community. I personally, may not have loved or agreed with everyone in Yoncalla—a town, in fact, known for its disagreements—but, over time, I had definitely become a member of the community. I had learned about the community of the living, from the community of the dead.

As far as the Kellys were concerned, if it hadn't been for them I would not have learned about Mr. Boyle—about the vulnerability of those who die alone. It was true, that once I was aware of the fact that Mr. Boyle's cremains weren't likely to be buried as he wished, I had done my part. But along with doing my part, I also had done some raging of my own because I was angry that other people were not doing what I perceived to be *their* part. I felt superior. I branded a whole family and the horses that they had ridden into town. I put them on my "list." A year or so later, when the Kellys had seemingly disappeared from my life, I had two of the bank teller's little boys as students during a residency. What great kids. She must have been doing something right, I thought, as I stretched my upper body, arms lifted like some convert in a revival meeting.

Who knew? All my suspicions about the Kellys may have been warranted, but I had unloaded on the wrong person—not passionately or on the spur of the moment, but deviously, in the hope that she would deliver my poison arrows to the rest of her tribe. How long was I going to hold on to my resentment, a resentment that made me behave in a way I didn't like?

It all seemed very Confucian: My primary responsibility was my own "right conduct." If the reprehensible, average, and good were so intermixed in other human beings as to be confusing and frustrating, it was also true of myself.

Across the room, the woman who had had a child with the Obscene Telephone Screamer, whose reflection I saw in the long mirror, whose face was intent as she lifted her small set of weights, had been through a lot. I had undoubtedly experienced the thinnest edge of the man's rage. "Yeah, that's Joe John, all right." She knew about it, and she loved him, and she seemed like a nice woman, too—she really did. And what was her first name? She told me, but I didn't remember.

Now I began to see that the worst aspect of our earlier conversation was that I was so concerned with how I felt, I barely heard what she had to say about her own experience. She had a child in the grave. "Full term," she had mentioned.

"Think about that, Shannon," I told myself, aware of the fact that the woman had headed into the outer room, that I needed to stand up and face the music if I was going to. She had lost a baby and the child's father—helpless, powerless, and inarticulate—felt grief, was still feeling grief. Crazy-making-hideous-gets-you-when-you-least-expect-it-fly-off-the-handle-grief.

As I struggled with an emerging sense of compassion and the depth of my own anger, I asked myself if I were willing to forgive the Obscene Telephone Screamer. If I weren't, was I at least willing not to call him that?

I remembered something, with a *sense of shame;* the words I had written in my diary on the day that Joe John Kelly had called me up. After I had a chance to look at the copy of the death certificate in the cemetery file, I wrote, "They didn't even know the baby. It was stillborn."

"How long will it take you to get over a baby you will never know, yet lingers in your consciousness, feeling more real than many things in life," I asked myself. "What's the timetable, the proper period or method of mourning? And does everyone get to feel grief or is it just for the chosen few?" Grief happens to everyone, I realized, but in some people it just comes out sideways.

And when the dying is so close to being born, so that both must be dealt with simultaneously, grief brims with such humbling humanness. Grief is messy, spilling into everything. "Oh, how I know this. I know this now, but I didn't know it then," I told myself as I stood up. I was one of the women in the mirror and, when I turned a certain way, my reflection was everywhere.

I went to the lockers in the outer room and waited. She came through the doorway shaking out her ponytail, and when she got to her locker I watched her pulling on her sweatshirt over her Wal-Mart top. Feeling a little tongue-tied, I finally said what needed to be said. "I'm sorry. I'm really sorry someone took things from your little boy's grave."

She looked at me—a kind of glazed look. Perhaps she was embarrassed. Or maybe she was surprised. "Yeah. I've been thinking about it, too. Joe John, he shouldn't have said all that stuff to you. It wasn't right."

It seemed like it was all finished when we squeezed each

other's hand, both heading for the door. Then she paused, turned, and looked back at me: "He's trying to change, you know. He really is. He's changing."

We change. Amen.

Iconography on Headstones

Many headstone symbols have multiple meanings. This partial list of Victorian-era symbols focuses on relatively common headstone motifs found in cemeteries throughout the United States. (See the selected bibliography for more detailed sources.)

Symbol	Meaning
Anchor	symbol of seafarer or more often hope for eternal life
Angel	guardian, messenger, symbol of resurrection
Broken column	mourning
Clasped hands	(male and female) farewell, until we meet again; (males) fraternal brotherhood
Corn	ripe old age
Cross	emblem of faith Celtic—fertility and life; Catholic clergy

Dove	soul reaching peace; sitting or dead dove = prematurely shortened life
Drapes	mourning or mortality
Eagle	nationalism; fraternal orders, double-headed link with Germany, Poland, or Austria
Finger pointing	"follow me"
Floral	many individual flowers: daisy = innocence of the young; calla lily = marriage and fidelity, iris = woman's soul, etc. with stems cut or in bouquets or baskets= brief life
Garlands	victory in death
Gates	heaven's opening gates or doors
Ivy	undying affection, clinging memory
Key	mystery, opening and closing of life
Lamb	purity, innocence, associated with children and virgins
Lamp	divine inspiration, eternal light
Masonic	various symbols including the compass and set-square and architectural forms. Eastern star (women's order) has own symbols
Oak	maturity, ripe old age; acorns, trees, and leaves same
Pinecone	may be confused with pineapple = regeneration, immortality
Rope	eternal binding connection
Tree stump	popular symbol Woodsmen of World; w/ivy = head of family
Wheat	sheaf means ripe for harvest, divine harvest

Selected Bibliography

Badone, Ellen. *The Appointed Hour: Death, Worldview and Social Change in Brittany.* Berkeley: University of California Press, 1989.

Barley, Nigel. *Dancing on the Grave: Encounters with Death.* London: John Murray, Ltd., 1995.

Barnard, Alan and Jonathan Spencer, eds. *Encyclopedia of Social and Cultural Anthropology.* New York: Routledge, 1996.

Bendann, Effie. *Death Customs: An Analytical Study of Burial Rites.* New York: Albert A. Knopf, Inc., 1930.

Berg, Shary Page. *Mount Auburn Cemetery Master Plan, Vol. II.* Boston: The Halvorson Company, Inc., 1993.

Bloch, Maurice and Jonathan Perry, eds. *Death and the Regeneration of Life.* Cambridge: Cambridge University Press, 1982.

Boase, T.S.R. *Death in the Middle Ages.* London: McGraw-Hill, 1972.

Buckell, Jim. "Baby carries baggage." *The Australian.* September 10, 2003. Higher Education. http://www.theaustralian.news.com.au/common/story.

Byrd, Dean, Stanley Clarke and Janice Healy. *Oregon Burial Site Guide.* Portland: Binford & Mort Publishers, 2001.

Ciregna, Elise Madeleine. "Museum in the Garden: Mount Auburn Cemetery and American Sculpture, 1840–1860." In *Markers XXI: Journal of the Association for Gravestone Studies* (2004): 101-147.

Clegg, Francess. "Problems of Symbolism in Cemetery Monuments." In *Journal of Garden History,* Vol. 4, No. 3 (September 1984): 307-315.

Coffin, Margaret. *Death in Early America.* Nashville: Thomas Nelson, Inc. Publishers, 1976.

Coleman, Penny. *Corpses, Coffins and Crypts: A History of Burial.* New York: Henry Holt & Co., 1997.

Davis-Kimball, Jeannie. *Warrior Women: An Archaeologist's Search for History's Hidden Heroines.* New York: Warner Books, 2002.

Denson, Bryan. "Grave Injustice." *The Sunday Oregonian.* 12-28-03. *The Daily Oregonian.* 12-29-03, 12-30-03. Oregonlive.com. http://www.ore gonlive.com/printer/printer.ssf?/base/front_page.

Doig, Ivan. *Winter Brothers: A Season at the Edge of America*. New York: Harcourt Brace Jovanovich Publishers, 1980.

Downey, Roger. *Riddle of the Bones: Politics, Science, Race, and the Story of Kennewick Man*. New York: Copernicus/Springer-Verlag, 2000.

Dye, Nancy Schrom and Daniel Blake Smith. "Mother Love and Infant Death, 1750–1920." In *The Journal of American History* Vol. 73.2 (1986): 329-353.

Farber, Jessie Lie. "Recommendations for the Care of Old Gravestones." *AGS Field Guide No. 15*, Association for Gravestone Studies (2003): 1-2.

Fuller, Horace W. ed. "A Modest Defence of Suicide." In *The Green Bag: An Entertaining Magazine for Lawyers* Vol. XI (1989): 38-39.

Gabel, Laurel K. "Ritual, Regalia and Remembrance: Fraternal Symbolism and Gravestones." In *Markers XI: Journal of the Association for Gravestone Studies* (1994): 1-21.

Garcia, Lisha A. "Día de los Muertos Comes from . . ." Opinion and Analysis Pages. In *The Yuma Daily Sun*, Oct. 27–29, 1996.

Gottbrath, Paul. "Beyond Flags and Flowers," *The Cincinnati Post*. May 27, 2000. http://www.cincypost.com/news/2000/graves/052700.html.

Gunn, John C., Md. *New Family Physician*. New York: Moore, Wilstatch & Baldwin, 1865.

Habenstein, Robert and William Lamers. *The History of American Funeral Directing*. Milwaukee: Bulfin Printers, Inc., 1955.

Hacker, Debi. *Iconography of Death*. South Carolina: Chicora Foundation, Inc., 2001.

Hartzell, Hal Jr. *The Yew Tree: A Thousand Whispers*. Eugene: Hulagosi, 1991.

Hedges, Chris. *War Is a Force That Gives Us Meaning*. New York: Anchor Books, 2002.

Hobbs, June Hadden. "Say It With Flowers in the Victorian Cemetery." In *Markers XIX: Journal of the Association for Gravestone Studies* (2002): 240-269.

Hoffert, Sylvia D. "Childbearing on the Trans Mississippi Frontier, 1830–1900." In *The Western Historical Quarterly*, Vol. 22.3 (1991): 272-288.

Huntington, Richard and Peter Metcalfe, eds. *Celebrations of Death: The Anthropology of Mortuary Ritual*. Cambridge: Cambridge University Press, 1979.

Jackson, Charles O. ed. *Passing: The Vision of Death in America*. Westport, CT: Greenwood Press, Inc., 1977.

Jones, Constance. *R.I.P.: The Complete Book of Death and Dying.* New York: HarperCollins Publisher, 1997.

Kalish, Richard A. ed. *Death and Dying: Views from Many Cultures.* New York: Baywood Publishing Co., 1979.

Levine, Stephen. *Who Dies?: Meeting at the Edge.* New York: Anchor Press, 1989.

Lipsett, Linda Otto. *Elizabeth Roseberry Mitchell's Graveyard Quilt: An American Pioneer Saga.* Dayton: Halstead and Meadows Publishing, 1995.

Loong, John. "Customs of the Chinese Community Relating to Death and Dying." In *The Undiscovered Country: Customs of the Cultural and Ethnic Groups of New Zealand Concerning Death & Dying,* edited by Dept. of Health, 74-78. New Zealand: Government Printing Office, 1987.

Maas, Peter. *Love Thy Neighbor: A Story of War.* New York: Alfred A. Knopf, Inc., 1996.

Mann, Thomas C. and Janet Greene. *Sudden and Awful: American Epitaphs & The Finger of God.* Brattleboro, VT: Stephen Greene Press, 1968.

Mayer, Jane. "Contract Sport: What Did the Vice-President Do for Halliburton?" In *The New Yorker,* February, 2004, 80-91.

Merrill, Christopher. *Only the Nails Remain: Scenes from the Balkan Wars.* Lanham, MD: Rowman & Littlefield Publishers, 1999.

Meyer, Lance R. "The Care of Old Cemeteries & Gravestones." *AGS Field Guide* No. 12, Association for Gravestone Studies (2003): 1-14.

Meyer, Richard E., ed. *Cemeteries & Gravemarkers: Voices of American Culture.* Logan: Utah State University Press, 1992.

Morgan, Keith N. "The Emergence of the American Landscape Professional: John Notman and the Design of Rural Cemeteries." In *Journal of Garden History,* Vol. 4, No. 3 (1984) 269-289.

Morley, John. *Death, Heaven, and the Victorians.* Pittsburgh: University of Pittsburgh Press, 1971.

Norse, Elliott A. ed. *Ancient Forests of the Pacific Northwest.* Washington, D.C.: Island Press, 1990.

Orr, William and Elizabeth. *Handbook of Oregon Plant and Animal Fossils.* Eugene: Pan Type Setters, 1981.

O'Suilleabhain, Sean. *Irish Wake Amusements.* Dublin: Mercier, 1976.

Palfrey, Dale Hoyt. "The Day of the Dead." *Mexico Connect.* 1995, Copyright via Mexico Connect. http://www.mexiconnect.com/mex_/muertos.html.

Palmer, Greg. *Death: The Trip of a Life Time.* New York: HarperCollins, San Francisco, 1993.

Puckle, Bertrand S. *Funeral Customs: Their Origin and Development.* London: T. Werner Laurie Ltd., 1926.

Quigley, Christine. *Skulls and Skeletons: Human Bone Collections and Accumulations.* North Carolina: McFarland & Company, 2001.

Ramp, Len. *Geology and Mineral Resources of Douglas County.* Portland, OR: State of Oregon Dept. of Geology and Mineral Industries, 1972.

Rhoads, Loren, ed. *Death's Garden: Relationships with Cemeteries.* San Francisco: Automatism Press, 1995.

Ricklis, Robert A. "Points of Agreement Between Cabeza de Vaca's Narrative and the Mitchell Ridge Data." http://www.english.swt.edu/css/points cdv.html.

Riel-Salvatore and Geoffrey A. Clark. "Grave Markers: Middle and Early Upper Paleolithic Burials," *Current Anthropology,* Vol. 42, 4, (August-October, 2001): 449-466.

Rinpoche, Sogyal. *The Tibetan Book of Living and Dying.* New York: HarperCollins, San Francisco, 2002.

Roberts, Darryl J. *Profits of Death.* Chandler, AZ: Five Star Publications, Inc., 1997.

Robinson, Jean Gentry, ed. *Visitor's Guide to Oregon Historic Cemeteries.* Portland: Oregon Historic Cemeteries Association, 1999.

Rotundo, Barbara. "The Rural Cemetery Movement." Essex Institute. Vol. 109, No. 3 (1973.): 231-240.

SCAnet. "Frequently asked questions about Archaeology and the Law." http://www.scanet.org/legal.html.

Schuyler, David. "The Evolution of the Anglo-American Rural Cemetery." In *Journal of Garden History,* Vol. 4, No. 3 (Sept. 1984.): 291-304.

Schwvan, John. "Memorial Types." In *MB News,* Vol. 99, No. 6 (2002.): 36-38.

Sloane, David Charles. *The Last Great Necessity: Cemeteries in American History.* Baltimore: The John Hopkins University Press, 1991.

Sommer, Jeffery D. "The Shanidar IV 'Flower Burial': A Reevaluation of Neanderthal Burial Ritual." *Cambridge Archaeological Journal* (9:1 1999).

Strangstad, Lynette. *A Graveyard Preservation Primer.* Walnut Creek: AltaMira Press, 1995.

Storl, Wolf D. *Culture and Horticulture: A Philosophy of Gardening.* Wyoming, RI: Bio-Dynamic Literature, 1979.

Surrency, Carol. "Cemetery Chores." *OHCA Ledger,* Vol. 11, Issue 2. Oregon Historic Cemetery Association. (2003) 3-4.

Suttles, Wayne, vol. ed. *Handbook of North American Indians,* Vol. 7, Washington, D.C.: Smithsonian Institution, 1990.

Trechsel, Gale Andrews. "Mourning Quilts of America." In *Uncoverings* (1989): 139-158.

Tuscon Citizen. "Day of Dead Draws 300K to Mexico City Cemeteries." November 3, 2003. http://www.tusconcitizen.com/index.

Twain, Mark. Bernard DeVoto, ed. *Letters from the Earth.* New York: Harper & Row, 1962.

Walker, Judy. "Festival for departed souls begins with food." *The Arizona Republic.* N/D. Food *Día de los muertos* series.
http://www.azcentral.com/ent/dead/food.

Wilkins, Robert. *Death: A History of Man's Obsessions and Fears,* New York: Barnes & Noble, 1990.

Acknowledgments

During the seven-year period that I worked on this book many individuals provided invaluable assistance, knowledge and insight. Some of them are already named within the narrative, indeed, are a part of my life among headstones. I'm grateful they have permitted me to share their names, experiences and stories. Bless them all.

I could have written two books with the material uncovered. Many people were kind enough to provide information that I was unable to include in this volume. I especially want to thank Laura Jo Laird-Hoffsess, funeral director of a privately owned local mortuary and Mike Holden, former mayor of Lincoln City, Oregon.

Experts unnamed in the text also cast light on many complex questions. I appreciate the information received from Dr. Melvin Aikens, director of the University of Oregon Museum of Natural and Cultural History, Dennis Hyatt, director of the University of

Oregon Law Library, and Guy Tasa, Department of Anthropology, University of Oregon. Dr. Frederick Meli, cultural historian, University of Rhode Island was also helpful.

I especially wish to acknowledge the assistance of scholar Barbara Rotundo of the American Association for Gravestone Studies, who died in 2005. For years she mentored many a cemetery enthusiast and researcher. She reviewed portions of my manuscript and contributed important suggestions. Additionally, Janet Heywood, another leader of the AGS, and vice president of interpretive programs at Mount Auburn Cemetery in Boston, very generously provided important research materials.

Visual artists have enriched this work, especially Susan Applegate, my art partner for more than thirty years, who, in this case, has produced lovely renderings representing some of the Applegate Pioneer Cemetery's headstones. Botanist and artist Martha Sherwood executed a wonderfully detailed pen and ink of Lungwort, and bird expert and wild life artist, Elva Hamerstrom Paulson, loaned her arresting image of three western screech owls. Photographs of the cemetery and community scenes are the work of Doug Stutzman, a friend indeed.

Reference librarians have helped me throughout the years, putting up with my visits, calls, and obscure questions. I enjoyed working with Heather Ward at the Knight Library/University of Oregon, Bill Easton and David Hutchison at Umpqua Community College Library, and Louise Williamson at the Main Library/Douglas County. Jena Mitchell and Karen Briggs at the Douglas County Museum of History and Natural History were also extremely helpful. Early in my research Kate Saunders (then with the Driftwood Library at Lincoln City) came to my aid.

Historic preservationist, James Hamrick, assistant director for Heritage Conservation at Oregon State Parks, believes in the cultural importance of cemeteries. He has supported me and other members of the Oregon Commission for Historic Cemeteries as we have worked on legislation, grants-in-aid, a statewide inventory and other projects. His leadership has set a high standard that preservation officials in other states would be wise to emulate. Mirra Meyer, a friend, traveling companion to conferences and scholar in addition to her duties as the indefatigable coordinator of the O.C.H.C., has supplied me with source material and valuable perspective concerning cemetery preservation issues around the world.

My residency at Sitka Center for Art and Ecology was a highlight in my writer's life. I thank everyone involved with Sitka Center, especially its director, Randall Koch for the gift of time and space at an extremely difficult but fruitful juncture in my writing.

Constant encouragement has come from artist friends I meet with every Thursday. I can't thank them enough for their faith in me and in my approach to this difficult subject matter that is personal as well as universal.

John Oakes, publisher of Thunder's Mouth Press, saw possibilities in this book and I thank him for his initial interest and ongoing support. The ever sensitive and insightful, Kathryn Belden, my original editor, lead me over some rough spots and helped shape much of the present text. Since then, Johnny Saunders has guided me editorially. I am gratified that he understands the nature of this book. His simpatico and sure-handed guidance through a complicated production process have made staff changes easier. I also appreciate his interest in making the best use of an unusual array of images throughout the text.

Finally, there are three I thank with all my heart: Over the years my friend, Mary Martin, a consummate professional, has provided me with crucial editorial advice. She is my E.F.L. Anne Depue, my steadfast literary agent, deserves bouquets and the moon for her remarkable kindness, good judgment, and perseverance. It's been a long haul down the literary trail for this book and she has been beside me much of the way. And then there is my beloved husband and helpmeet in every sense of the word, Daniel Robertson. I can't imagine finishing this book without him. I can't imagine anything without him.

Illustrations and Captions

Map and drawings of headstones from the Applegate Pioneer Cemetery are by Susan Applegate.